Remembering the Occupation in French Film

STUDIES IN EUROPEAN CULTURE AND HISTORY

edited by
Eric D. Weitz and Jack Zipes
University of Minnesota

Since the fall of the Berlin wall and the collapse of communism, the very meaning of Europe has been opened up and is in the process of being redefined. European states and societies are wrestling with the expansion of NATO and the European Union and with new streams of immigration, while a renewed and reinvigorated cultural engagement has emerged between East and West. But the fast-paced transformations of the last fifteen years also have deeper historical roots. The reconfiguring of contemporary Europe is entwined with the cataclysmic events of the twentieth century, two world wars and the Holocaust, and with the processes of modernity that, since the eighteenth century, have shaped Europe and its engagement with the rest of the world.

Studies in European Culture and History is dedicated to publishing books that explore major issues in Europe's past and present from a wide variety of disciplinary perspectives. The works in the series are interdisciplinary; they focus on culture and society and deal with significant developments in Western and Eastern Europe from the eighteenth century to the present within a social historical context. With its broad span of topics, geography, and chronology, the series aims to publish the most interesting and innovative work on modern Europe.

Published by Palgrave Macmillan:
Fascism and Neofascism: Critical Writings on the Radical Right in Europe
by Eric Weitz
Fictive Theories: Towards a Deconstructive and Utopian Political Imagination
by Susan McManus
German-Jewish Literature in the Wake of the Holocaust: Grete Weil, Ruth Klüger, and the Politics of Address
by Pascale Bos
Turkish Turn in Contemporary German Literature: Toward a New Critical Grammar of Migration
by Leslie Adelson
Terror and the Sublime in Art and Critical Theory: From Auschwitz to Hiroshima to September 11
by Gene Ray
Transformations of the New Germany
edited by Ruth Starkman
Caught by Politics: Hitler Exiles and American Visual Culture
edited by Sabine Eckmann and Lutz Koepnick
Legacies of Modernism: Art and Politics in Northern Europe, 1890-1950
edited by Patrizia C. McBride, Richard W. McCormick, and Monika Zagar
Police Forces: A Cultural History of an Institution
edited by Klaus Mladek
Richard Wagner for the New Millennium: Essays in Music and Culture
edited by Matthew Bribitzer-Stull, Alex Lubet, and Gottfried Wagner
Representing Masculinity: Male Citizenship in Modern Western Culture
edited by Stefan Dudink, Anna Clark, and Karen Hagemann
Remembering the Occupation in French Film: National Identity in Postwar Europe
by Leah D. Hewitt
"Gypsies" in European Literature and Culture
edited by Valentina Glajar and Domnica Radulescu

REMEMBERING THE OCCUPATION
IN FRENCH FILM

NATIONAL IDENTITY IN POSTWAR EUROPE

Leah D. Hewitt

REMEMBERING THE OCCUPATION IN FRENCH FILM
Copyright © Leah D. Hewitt, 2008.

A portion of Chapter 4 of the present work appeared in a different version in the following: Hewitt, Leah D. "From War Films to Films on War: Gendered Scenarios of National Identity, The Case of *The Last Metro*," *Studies in Twentieth Century Literature* 26, no.1 (Winter 2002): 74–85.
Part of Chapter 6 appeared in a different version as "Identity Wars in 'L'Affaire (Lucie) Aubrac': History, Fiction, Film," *Contemporary French Civilization*, 22:2 (Summer/Fall 1999), 264–84.

First published in 2008 by
PALGRAVE MACMILLAN™
175 Fifth Avenue, New York, NY 10010 and
Houndmills, Basingstoke, Hampshire, England RG21 6XS.
Companies and representatives throughout the world.

PALGRAVE MACMILLAN is the global academic imprint of the Palgrave Macmillan division of St. Martin's Press, LLC and of Palgrave Macmillan Ltd. Macmillan© is a registered trademark in the United States, United Kingdom and other countries. Palgrave is a registered trademark in the European Union and other countries.

ISBN-13: 978-0-230-60130-7
ISBN-10: 0-230-60130-8

Library of Congress Cataloging-in-Publication Data

Hewitt, Leah Dianne.
Remembering the occupation in French film: national identity in postwar Europe / by Leah D. Hewitt.
    p. cm. — (Studies in European culture and history)
Includes bibliographical references and index.
ISBN 0-230-60130-8
    1. World War, 1939-1945—Motion pictures and the war. 2. France—In motion pictures. 3. Motion pictures—France—History. 4. National characteristics, French. 5. France—History—German occupation, 1940-1945. I. Title.

D743.23.H48 2008
791.43'658—dc22   2007027284

A catalogue record of the book is available from the British Library.

Design by Scribe Inc.

First edition: February 2008

10 9 8 7 6 5 4 3 2 1

Printed in the United States of America.

CONTENTS

ACKNOWLEDGMENTS

This project, originally titled "Marianne at the Movies," has taken a long time to come to fruition, and there have been many people along the way who have helped me with their encouragement and support. I am glad to have this opportunity to thank colleagues, friends, and family.

I have been fortunate to have departmental colleagues at Amherst College who have provided me with invaluable feedback and bibliographical sources, as well as their friendship. I offer my warmest thanks to Paul Rockwell, Jay Caplan, Rosalina de la Carrera, Laure Katsaros, and Ron Rosbottom. Each in his or her way made my writing more pleasurable. I wish to thank my students at Amherst College who, through their insistent questioning, have helped me formulate my ideas about French identity in postwar film. I am grateful to Margaret Groesbeck for helping me locate needed sources and to Bridget Dahill and Nicholas Dahlman for preparing film photographs. I would also like to acknowledge the Faculty Seminar at Amherst College that allowed me to share my project with colleagues. I cannot thank enough the Amherst College French Department's administrative assistants, Bobbie Helinski and Liz Eddy, for their tireless dedication, generosity, even-tempered disposition, and superb efficiency. I am also indebted to Amherst College for the financial support, fellowships, and sabbatical leaves I have been generously awarded for my research over the last several years.

There are many colleagues and friends outside Amherst who have been instrumental to the realization of this project. Special thanks go to Joe Golsan, Lynn Higgins, and Panivong Norindr for their warm encouragement, invaluable suggestions, and friendship. I am grateful to my friend Martine Guyot-Bender at Hamilton College, and the graduate students in French at Princeton University for inviting me to lecture on my topic and for sharing their ideas with me. I continue to be grateful to Marie-Hélène Huet for her gentle, yet probing questions about my work. I express my appreciation to Alan Williams, who included me many years ago in a conference on films dealing with World War II; this was perhaps the spark that got my whole project started. To Keith Reader, I owe my gratitude for reading and commenting in depth on an early version of my chapter treating *Lacombe Lucien*. I thank Geneviève Sellier for having suggested that I look at téléfilms on the Occupation.

I wish to thank my parents for their constant support. Thanks to Pickle and Tica for challenging my focus. Finally, without the daily emotional backing of Kevin Clark, this project would never have gone anywhere. To him, I offer my love and gratitude.

CHAPTER 1

FILM AS MEMORY: A BATTLEGROUND FOR SHAPING IDENTITY

> The function of cinema, even above its artistic function, is to satisfy the immutable collective psychic needs that have been repressed.
>
> —*André Bazin (October 1943)*

France's ongoing efforts at self-definition at the end of the twentieth century and into the twenty-first have involved new conceptions of citizenship and nationality, as well as what it means to be French, culturally and internationally. But the struggle to set national parameters has also entailed the search for an accurate portrayal of a past in which France could recognize itself. In a 2002 essay entitled "What is a European," A. S. Byatt noted that, in Europe, "a lot of 50- and 60-year-olds seem to become spontaneously obsessed with genealogy and memoirs."[1] Belgian born filmmaker Chantal Akerman has said that the "only thing countries in Europe have in common is their collective guilt in allowing the Nazis to slaughter Europe's Jewish population during the Second World War."[2] The fixation on the war's moral dimensions has no doubt besieged all of postwar Europe. It has been particularly acute in France, as the French have persistently and agonizingly reconsidered the war's effects on their "collective memory."[3]

To be sure, France's ethical dilemmas in evaluating its participation in the war are not without similarity to those of other Western European countries. As Tony Judt has pointed out, "for most Europeans World War II was experienced not as war of movement and battle but as a daily degradation, in the course of which men and women were betrayed and humiliated, forced into daily acts of petty crime and self-abasement, in which everyone lost something and many lost everything."[4] Like Belgium and Norway, France had had a government in exile that meted out punishment and praise upon its return in the early postwar years. Akin to previously occupied countries such as Belgium, Holland, the Netherlands, and Norway, or to the losers of the war (Germany and Italy), postwar France had to contend with muddled definitions of resistance and collaboration in its postwar purges of officials and companies who had had business (willingly or unwillingly) with the Nazis, or who had carried out their orders. Just as in France, local administrations in Norway, Belgium, and Holland had readily helped manage German rule.[5] Denmark was the exception, with few groups willing to collaborate with the German authorities (and with fewer Jews deported as a consequence).[6] On the whole, collaboration with the Nazis had been less widespread in Belgium, Holland, Denmark, and Norway than in France. Paradoxically, in the former, the number of individuals sent to prison for collaboration was comparatively high, as public rage fueled judicial proceedings. In France, on the other hand, where collaboration had been more extensive, the process was incomplete, as relatively few went to jail or were executed.[7] Despite these very real differences, the unfinished accounting of wartime actions plagued nearly all European countries, east or west, with the majority having reopened the issues between the mid-1960s and the mid-1990s, as new generations of citizens looked at their elders' past.

France's unique status as a resisting *and* collaborating nation in an official capacity, at war with itself in the guise of Free France (de Gaulle's government in London) and Vichy (Pétain's government in Vichy), made its situation, if not entirely distinct, at least an extreme version of what others went through in terms of internal battles. In some ways, France's attempts at postwar reckoning are closer to those of Italy, which switched from the Axis to the Allies in 1943. In both cases, "after decades of resistance-dominated memory, a process of demystification-desecration of antifascist mythology began . . . and continues today."[8] Tony Judt has generalized France's memory crisis in claiming that "every occupied country in Europe developed its own 'Vichy syndrome,'"[9] that is to say, like France, they all repressed their complicity with the Nazi occupation, a memory that resurfaced years later.

The French battle over memories of World War II has raged in the media and the arts for the past thirty years, most ostensibly starting with the reactions to Marcel Ophüls's documentary *The Sorrow and the Pity* (released in 1972), about the German occupation in France, as well as to Robert Paxton's historical eye-opener *Vichy France*, about French collaboration with the Nazis.[10] In both, the myth of generalized French Resistance was solidly put into question. The ensuing political and artistic fights over the meaning of the war, and France's ethical responsibility as a nation, have remained current. When historian Henry Rousso published his ground-breaking book, *Le Syndrome de Vichy* (*The Vichy Syndrome*), in 1987, one might have expected that this detailed account of World War II's intrusions in postwar French culture and politics would be one of the last works to emphasize the importance of wartime representations in contemporary French identity.[11] Would the syndrome's final phase of obsession and guilt (focusing on the Holocaust) soon die out, due to a diminishing interest on the part of the general public and professional historians (for whom the ground had been covered), or because there were fewer and fewer survivors (henchmen, victims, or witnesses) left? Such has not been the case. The legacy of the battles never gelled, as historians, artists, survivors, and teachers have continued to retell these stories to new generations. Richard J. Golsan has even suggested that the very success of Rousso's "syndrome," as a "medico-psychoanalytical metaphor," may have helped perpetuate the obsession.[12] With so many competing versions of wartime representations continuing to circulate, what is still lacking is a sense of a past held in common.[13]

Whether we consider the war era in terms of its contemporary manipulations, that is, as "uses and abuses of history," or as an "indigestible past" that returns to haunt the French in the present, the period of 1940–1945 continues to inflect contemporary France's thinking about itself.[14] Even (or especially?) for historians, the sense of a topic out of control—manipulated and falsified in the media, fiction, and film—has coincided with a profound malaise about what and how history should be understood. An "explosion of history" is evidenced in the 1980s and 1990s by an almost feverish proliferation of history books and school manuals for children.[15] Pierre Nora's hefty three-volume edition *Lieux de mémoire* (*Realms of Memory*) is no doubt the cornerstone for the study of France's "commemoration, patrimonialization [and] production of memory."[16] Expanding on Annette Wievorka's description of our time as the "era of the witness," Susan Suleiman has described it more generally as "the era of memory."[17] Professional researchers experiencing the malaise have come to *actively* intervene as the bearers and arbiters of truth. This new twist has itself, in turn, been rendered fictively. Pierre Assouline's 1998 novel, *La Cliente*, portrays a contemporary historian who insists on tracking down the person who turned in a Jewish family during the war—a hidden truth that nobody else wants to dig up. Assouline offers a particularly harrowing version of the difficult negotiations among historians, survivors, and witnesses. In *La Hantise du passé: Entretien avec Philippe Petit* (*The Haunting Past: History, Memory, and Justice in Contemporary France*), Henry Rousso bemoans the fallout for historians, like himself, who unwittingly become embroiled in the political effects of bearing testimony.[18] As Pascal Ory has aptly pointed out, "the principle problem of Vichy as specter is less the availability of information about the history of Vichy than the ways in which it has been filtered. It is an ethical issue bound up with the shifting gaze of public opinion."[19] There is no past in and of itself—it is woven through our discourses, our images, our ideological constructions, and changes according to the concerns of the era when it is remembered.

For better or for worse, in the contemporary period, the media have frequently taken on the task of transmitting and/or creating collective memories that confirm (but sometimes challenge) national identities. Iain Chambers has noted "the interdependency of citizenship and the media. For language—as representation, configuration, and communication, as a potential ethics and aesthetics—secures and propagates such a relation. And the media—as photograph, film, printed archive, daily newspaper, and computer recall—have become the collectors and custodians of individual and collective memory . . . If citizenship depends on individual and collective recollection to be articulated, then the media, in becoming memory, are central to the performance of an imagined collectivity, whether it is local, ethnic, or national."[20] Chambers's use of the term "performance" to describe the media's shaping of collective identity seems particularly apt: it suggests that the public airing of memory is not bound to an unalterable truth, but is rather a chronologically defined enactment subject to change. The media's "performances" of World War II memories in France have very much been pressure points where the fabric of social cohesion is tested. When the very idea of collective memory is a source of national debate, the public representation of history quickly becomes the locus of controversy and ideological struggle in the present.

The highly publicized trial of Vichy government official and collaborator Maurice Papon confirmed in the late nineties how murky the past can become. Historian Michel Bergès, for example, seemed unable to make up his mind about who was responsible for deporting Jews in France, as he alternately attacked and defended the accused Papon in the media. Historian Henry Rousso was placed in the awkward position of being summoned by Papon's defense to testify about historical facts. In some instances, trial lawyers rifled through historical archives, leaving files in permanent disarray.

Papon's eventual conviction left many on both sides unsatisfied with the outcome. For some, he was a sick, old man, who—as a civil servant—was being made a scapegoat for France's responsibility in the deportations; for many Jewish survivors, whose friends and family members had been deported through Papon's supervision, he was a killer who had escaped punishment for too long, and who received an insufficient sentence. The judicial settling of accounts did not bring a sense of finality or resolution. Clearly, the intelligibility of French national identity via its history can only be posed as a series of questions, rather than as a given or even as an individual's legal sentence.[21]

In 2002, disputes about *how* and *whose* truth is represented in films on the war still provoked dissension and debate. Bertrand Tavernier's 2000 film *Laissez Passer* (*Safe Passage*)—about the lives of assistant director Jean Devaivre and scriptwriter Jean Aurenche during the war—attests to the (auto)biographical interest of the period for many filmmakers who base their artistic conceptions and sensibilities on their wartime experiences. The sensitivity of the material, that is, its ability to touch nerves (whose story is it?), is equally apparent in the fact that the ninety-year-old Devaivre sued Tavernier for insufficiently crediting his memoirs as a source of inspiration.[22] Costa-Gavras's 2002 film *Amen*, whose notorious poster combined a Christian cross and a swastika, fueled the flames of controversy concerning the Vatican's role in the Holocaust.

Because of film's accessibility and popularity, it is perhaps the most forceful of art forms in articulating a public sense of the historical and political stakes of the war. It is an effective way to create public (national) identity via a shared story, a communal fiction that can organize recognizable elements of a past—whether as myth or as critical re-evaluation—as totalizing narrative or deconstructive multiplicity. Seeing film as one of the arms for reinventing France after the war, filmmaker Jean-Benoit Lévy declared categorically in 1944 in *Les Grandes Missions du cinéma* ("The Great Missions of Cinema"): "Cinematography is certainly the most powerful means of disseminating human thought that has been invented since the discovery of printing in the fifteenth century."[23] In addition to its capacity to reflect and shape popular views of past events, film allows for and promotes the airing of current concerns through the lens of memory's (re)creations.

Benedict Anderson offers the well-known, and perhaps overused, portrait of the modern nation as an "imagined community." This operative fiction, which has "remarkable confidence of community in anonymity,"[24] recalls Jean-Paul Sartre's loving description of his childhood contact with the anonymous community of movie theaters and silent movies: "I had learned in the equalitarian discomfort of the neighborhood houses that this new art was mine, just as it was everyone else's."[25] It is the "art of the common man," and in its darkened theaters, social hierarchies are blotted out.[26] Although Sartre's populist characterization may be idealized, there is, on occasion, a sense of community in the movie theater, as evidenced by, for example, audience applause for a film well received when, obviously, there are no actors or participants other than the viewers themselves to acknowledge that applause.[27]

As Jean-Michel Frodon has pointed out, both the nation and the cinema are similar phenomena that exist via *images*, and their preferred form is the *story*. They both are constituted as fictions/inventions, or rather, as "the articulation of a reality and a fiction, of a factual complex and a collective, imaginary 'work,' whose projection is recognized" by its members and by others (that is, other nations).[28] This link between cinema and national identity is no doubt much more powerful in France than in the United States. France has long struggled to make its film industry thrive, as it fought the invasion of Hollywood films, and has frequently turned to the movies as a means of presenting and promoting things French. The Blum-Byrnes trade agreement of 1946, which allowed thirteen weeks of exclusively French showings before American or other imports could be distributed in France, was deemed inadequate protection by many Frenchmen as the country struggled to get back on its feet.[29] Still, the taxes imposed upon foreign films helped the French industry, so that "the success of *Gone with the Wind*, shown to a French public for the first time in May 1950, contributed to the production of films by directors such as Christian-Jaque and Jacques Tati."[30] In the cold war era, the French government developed additional means by which to defend its film industry; for example, Jill Forbes notes the 1959 creation of governmental "*avance sur recettes*, or interest-free loans, allocated on the basis of a project and which were repayable if a film made a profit . . . For all the [World War II] combatant powers, the war had brought home film's significance as a means of propaganda and as a way of promoting national cohesion."[31] With television slow to develop in France after the war, and with the creation of a cinema culture (a proliferation of film clubs or "cinemathèques," film journals, and criticism), France's public audiences and its government officials looked on French cinema as an integral part of its postwar rebuilding, and more generally of its cultural patrimony. These ties between the state and film production have remained much stronger than in the United States. What has been called the "French Cultural Exception" has included a cinema that weaves together notions of a distinctive *art*, an "interactive relation between art and politics," and a *national* trademark.[32]

This is, of course, not to say that other European countries have not produced—and watched—numerous films about the war, about occupation, and about all the complications of remembering an event that could shake or bolster national pride. In the fictional realm, Louis Malle's provocative *Lacombe Lucien*—about French collaboration with the Germans—was shown in the same period of the mid-1970s when Italian filmmakers Liliana Cavani (*Night Porter*) and Lina Wertmüller (*Seven Beauties*) were stirring up controversy about Italian complicity with Nazism. For Germany, Austria, and Poland, the showing of the 1978 American TV mini-series *Holocaust* triggered reactions and reopened the issues of generalized complicity with Nazism. In Germany, Edgar Reitz's 1984 TV series *Heimat* was a sweeping, widely popular retort that recounted, in nostalgic terms, a German family saga from 1918 to the present, a story that underplayed German guilt about wartime responsibility. In France, Claude Lanzmann's powerful nine-hour response to the American soap opera was *Shoah* (1985), which documented, in interviews, survivors' memories of the death camps. The postmodern tendencies of the French *Un Héros très discret* (*A Self-Made Hero*) by Jacques Audiard (1995) echo those in *Europa Europa* (1990) by Polish filmmaker Agnieszka Holland. Both France and Germany have recently explored their cinematic fascination with major political figures from the war. France's Philippe Pétain (*Pétain*, 1993, Jean Marboeuf) and ex-President François Mitterrand (*The Last Mitterrand*, 2004, Robert Guédiguian) find their German equivalent in Oliver Hirschbiegel's 2004 *The Downfall: Hitler and the End of the Third Reich*. In the latter two films, actors Michel Bouquet (Mitterrand) and Bruno Ganz (Hitler) offer *tour de force* portrayals of aging national leaders.

Despite many similarities with the trends in film production and viewing in other European countries, France has continued to bind together—most pervasively—wartime memories, filmmaking, and national identity. More than any other European country, it has wrapped itself in the "seventh art," with film and state relying on each other. In negotiating the troubled past of the Occupation, French films offer a highly ambiguous relationship to their "cultural exception." It is both an internal and external public reckoning, recalling Sartre's early postwar efforts in writing to explain to Great Britain and the United States how complicated and uneasy it was to have lived in an occupied country.[33]

This study of French films on World War II focuses on the connections and tensions between artistic forms (fictions, invented stories, and characters), and historical, politicized portrayals of French identity—of resisters, victims, collaborators, *attentistes* (those who waited to see what would happen), or some combination thereof. I connect *private* and *public* registers in addressing aspects of film production and reception. On the production side, as André Bazin pointed out in 1943, "cinema is an art of teamwork," a collective enterprise involving producers, production crews, script writers, actors, novelists, and a host of others "behind the scenes";[34] however, film also inscribes the individualized mark of the director. This is especially the case for New Wave directors—cinematic *auteurs*— whose works were to bear a directorial signature through their style and subject matter.[35] In postwar films about the war, directors' personal experiences and political agendas (during and after the war) play a key role in the way the war story is told, so that the works take on the allure of autobiography. Significantly enough, the persistence of *auteur* cinema as a particularly *French* phenomenon—in its origins, but also as a general postwar tradition—tightly binds national identity and autobiographical film.

On the reception side, my attention turns to the ways the shared viewing experience becomes the site of ethical (self/national) evaluation, but also of scandal and contention, as the films are read through contemporary political grids. One of my goals is to understand how individual (re)constructions fit into collective, critical apprehensions of the past. Henry Rousso's productive use of the psychoanalytical framework (pertaining to a generalized individual) to describe the *collective*, historically specific repressions and resurgences of wartime memory in French society, acknowledges a privileged role of film in its analysis. And while this model has recently been criticized, it still affords a powerful means for thinking about the intersections between individual and collective memories. But, if, as Timothy Murray has said, it is a "questionable assumption that cinematic analysis can easily distinguish politics from fantasy, force from desire, and cinema from psychoanalysis,"[36] my hope would be that the inherent confusion between the collective and singular nature of motion pictures (historically defined groups and generalized individuals) would allow us to seize upon some of the most potent—and problematic—airings of the conflicts about the past, as these representations trace the outline of a French identity at war with itself. The expression "Franco-French war" describes not only the internal battles of French against French under Vichy, but also those that followed in its wake. France has long possessed a culture of "discursive viewers," who eagerly invest themselves in their opinions, arguments, and judgments; the film object can hardly remain in a vacuum in such a tradition.

The films considered in this book are all involved in telling, either centrally or peripherally, a story of the German occupation as they navigate through the connections between memory and event, and between fictional pasts and contemporary anxieties. In contrast with the private reading of a book, the widely diffused film spectacle tells a story that takes on a *typicality*, and passes from virtual or imagined to concrete vision and sound, thus becoming an object for public scrutiny. It has often been noted that a novel's story that meets with popular and critical approval can easily turn into a scandal once it is made into a film. And when the line blurs between observer and actor, or between participant and witness, the viewer's position begins to resemble that of a judge called upon to gauge the moral force of the stories unfolding on the screen. Characters pass from the purely individual realm to the order of collective representation. Their exemplarity becomes an especially knotty issue in films about the war, for in the balance is France's sense of itself as a nation, not (just) as a function of chauvinistic bravado (nationalism), or a state trying to save and perpetuate itself (as it was for Vichy), but rather in terms of Benedict Anderson's "imagined communities," or of what Stanley Hoffmann calls an *esprit national*—a national feeling of consensus, whether explicit or not. As Allen Carey-Webb has noted: "The truly remarkable thing about the nation-state system is not its dissemination as a political form but its infusion as a deeply held consciousness, a way of feeling, thinking and acting, accepted, even cherished, by a tremendous heterogeneity of human beings."[37] For France in the postwar years, this sense of national accord was galvanized by de Gaulle's idealized, mythic vision of a France that had heroically resisted the occupant, with only a few traitors. Conforming to Ernest Renan's assertion that the nation establishes itself through forgetfulness just as much as through remembering, France "forgot" the messiness of the past in order to regroup, turn toward the future, and bolster its legitimacy.[38] What the history of postwar films pointedly unveils is the cracks in the Gaullist glossy image, and an intense awareness of unresolved contradictions that have been dramatically played out on the screen.

During the course of my initial research on political constructions and reactions to films about the war, I came across an insistent repetition that caused me to reorient my study in crucial ways. As I watched more and more films from the various postwar periods, I kept noting that one of the most powerful and constant symbols of national contradiction in these films resided in the *representations of women*. But why turn women into a duplicitous symbol of France's past? Why take women—most often associated with the particular (versus a "male universal")—to show the twists of this troubled history?

Historically, women's lives had relatively little place in the telling of Occupation history, in part because it was not always clear how the domain of private, domestic life could be told as a key part of public action. Michael Kelly has commented on the apparent opposition between "everyday life" and history: "History records processes and events of significance, and . . . the obviousness and commonness of everyday life were long taken as almost the exact antithesis of history."[39] Women's traditional ties to everyday life (described by Kelly as "daily routine, trivial, domestic, unremarkable and even unmentionable")[40] thus kept them out of the historical limelight. With an attention to matters of daily survival, however, what constitutes "action" worthy of telling becomes more complicated and leads to a rethinking of the *relationship* between public and private actions (rather than just confirming their opposition). Although the interest in women's typical activities during the war did not come until the 1980s and after, the *Annales* school of historiography, emphasizing the "history of mentalities," had already laid the groundwork for studying the dynamic between "the individual and the collective, the long term and the everyday, the unconscious and the intentional, the structural and the conjunctural, the marginal and the general."[41] With the Annales' approach to history focusing on living people over abstract theory (the latter being more the domain of old style Marxism), and with the rise of feminist studies, critical explorations of the war began to include the study of those anonymous lives overlooked by event-oriented war history (or by its "important personages" versions), including those of women. As family caretakers and heads of households during the absence of their male counterparts (imprisoned, fighting, or dead), women were increasingly perceived as the link between the private sphere of home and the public sphere of community under the Occupation.

Women's visibility in war accounts has thus increased as closer attention has been paid to the *concrete details* of daily, material, Occupation existence. Details, of which Naomi Schor wrote so eloquently, have been associated with the feminine, frequently with negative connotations.[42] In the present context, I take details to mean not just embellishment or decoration—the "local color" of the period (fashions, styles, and decors)—but rather, an actual grounding for historical understanding. Or rather, it is a matter of appreciating how such aspects of local color can (literally) point to an ingenious political response, as when women dressed in red, white, and blue—symbolically draping themselves in the flag of the French Republic—to signify their resistance to Vichy.[43] In this instance, it is women who turn themselves into "living allegories" of France.

What is so characteristic of the German occupation of France is its pervasiveness, the way war manifests itself in the exercise of routines that are, in turn, transformed through their juxtaposition to (and infiltration by) the conflict. The associations among historical detail, the portrayal of daily survival, and women's lives are so strong in this understanding of Occupation history that women's lives come to figure as examples for the French situation in general, what Dominique Veillon has described as "la guerre au quotidien" (war on a daily basis).[44] As icons of the complex inter-weavings of the personal and public spheres, women exemplify—in crucial ways—the tensions and ambiguities of the Occupation. Hannah Arendt described the modern nation as a "curiously hybrid realm where private interests assume public significance."[45] In postwar French films about the Occupation, this characteristic hybridity of the nation is enacted (for the most part unselfconsciously) through female characters, and magnified by the intensity of the national crisis. Film critics Geneviève Sellier and Noël Burch underline cinema's crucial role in the war experience, exposing social pressures and the congruities between public and private fields: "The Second World War was to establish motion pictures in France as a privileged arena for the expression of social contradictions and to reveal just how genuinely political were representations of the 'private sphere.'"[46]

In his *Everyday Life in the Modern World*, Henri Lefebvre attaches opposing values to the concept of everyday life as he views it through a philosopher's lens. The tensions in its definition(s) can help us to better understand the ambivalent views of women's wartime activities, as they come to represent the country as a whole. Appearing in 1968 at the high point of political discussions and protest, and couched in the terminology of Marxist class struggle, Lefebvre's analysis still retains a rich suggestiveness and acuity concerning women's contradictory positions in the schema of daily routine. I would like to quote his description at length because I think the tensions *within* each of the oppositional poles Lefebvre creates are indicative of the contradictions associated with the representations of "women's experience."

Attentive to the figurative nature of his analysis, Lefebvre calls his two-part description a diptych. In the "negative" panel, he identifies the "misery of everyday life" with "its tedious tasks, humiliations reflected in the lives of the working classes and especially of women, upon whom the conditions of everyday life bear heaviest—childbearing and child-rearing, basic preoccupations with bare necessities, money, tradesmen, provisions, the realm of numbers, a sort of intimate knowledge of things outside the sphere of material reality: health, desire, spontaneity, vitality; recurrence, the survival of

poverty and the endlessness of want, a climate of economy, absti-
nence, hardship, repressed desires, meanness and avarice."

In the "positive" panel, Lefebvre praises "the power of everyday
life":

> its continuity, the permanence of life rooted in the soil, the *adapta-*
> *tion* of the body, time, space, desire; environment and the home; the
> unpredictable and immeasurable tragedy forever lurking in everyday
> life; the power of women, crushed and overwhelmed, 'object' of his-
> tory and society but also the inevitable 'subject' and foundation; cre-
> ation from recurrent gestures of a world of sensory experience; the
> coincidence of need with satisfaction and, more rarely, with pleasure;
> work and works of art; the ability to create in terms of everyday life
> from its solids and its spaces—to make something lasting for the indi-
> vidual, the community, the class; the re-production of essential rela-
> tions, the feed-back already mentioned between culture and
> productivity, understanding and ideologies, which is at the bottom of
> all the contradictions among these terms, the battlefield where wars
> are waged between the sexes, generations, communities, ideologies;
> the struggle between the adapted and the non-adapted, the shapeless-
> ness of subjective experience and the chaos of nature; mediations
> between these terms and their aftermath of emptiness, where antago-
> nisms are bred that break out in the 'higher' spheres (institutions,
> super-structures).[47]

Lefebvre's dual panels are neither homogeneous nor self-evident,
yet they do capture the multiple potentialities of the everyday as it
weighs on everyone, but especially on women. Refusing to situate
women's daily life in just one camp or the other (nature versus culture, subject versus object), Lefebvre juggles the terms to create a
double portrait in which positive and negative values can be assigned
to almost any trait, child-rearing being one of the most obvious.
Lefebvre's "use" of women as the primary illustrator of everyday
survival runs parallel to what we are suggesting happens in postwar
films about the war.

Viewed through the fictional memory of film, female characters
repeatedly embody France's uneasy relationship to a past in which
"collaborators" and "resisters" inhabit the same space and sometimes the same body. To collaborate temporarily in order (ultimately) to resist, or to resist and then collaborate; to support
collaboration (initially) and then switch to resistance; or simply to
act without assurances of the moral weight of one's initiatives—such

are some of the twists of shifting allegiances as the French tried to sort through Occupation politics.[48] Women's depictions in films on the Occupation bring together the hero and the traitor, the executioner and the victim—and everything in between. The prominence of these polyvalent figures problematizes clear-cut political distinctions between the Left and the Right, but it also makes us question the ties between women's *actual* activities during the war and their fictive renderings in film. Let us consider briefly some of the sociopolitical conditions of women's lives between 1940 and 1944, and the ways they have or have not been emphasized in public consciousness. This will help to ground subsequent arguments about women as cinematic symbols of occupied France.

EVENTS AND ICONS: WOMEN REAL AND INVENTED

In beginning research several years ago on potential connections between the strong role of the character Marion Steiner in François Truffaut's *The Last Metro* and women's accomplishments during the war, I decided to look into how French women got the vote (obtained on April 21, 1944). As I gathered information, I came across a curious phenomenon: it was as if this historical occurrence had somehow escaped the notice of many historians. Checking through various databases, I could find few references about the conditions in which women obtained the right to vote in France (which was first put into action in the municipal elections of April 29, 1945). Was the omission an oversight, an embarrassment that the vote came so late in France compared to other Western countries, or an acknowledgment that French women's rise to social and legal equality was part of a slow, gradual process rather than bound to a single event? (Amazingly, married French women did not obtain the right to enter a profession or to open their own independent bank accounts without their husband's consent until 1965.[49]) When the history books I consulted did consider French women's legal rights, they emphasized the *unsuccessful* suffrage movement in the early part of the century before World War I. A deliberate treatment of the actual gain of the vote was, however, sorely lacking in several general histories about the period. Jean-Pierre Rioux's *La France de la Quatrième République* (*The Fourth Republic 1944–1958*) in the popular history collection "Points," does not even include a footnote about it, nor does *Etudes sur la France de 1939 à nos jours*

("Studies of France from 1939 to Our Time"), in the same collection. *The European Women's Almanac* erroneously says that women obtained the right to vote in France in 1907 (the year when women were finally permitted to spend their own salaries as they saw fit, but still could not vote).[50] In a work devoted to statistical data on women's lives in Europe, this kind of mistake is surprising, to say the least. In more recent histories of French women's rights, the lacuna has been remedied, but obtaining the right to vote is still shrouded in mystery and elicits conflicting interpretations.

The Vichy government, which continually harkened back nostalgically to "family values" of a bygone (mythical) era through its childless spokesman, Pétain, had actually blamed women for the decline of France and for losing the war. While Vichy had paid lip service to women's issues, women's right to vote was, in fact, closely associated with the liberation of France at the end of the war. In a work on women and the vote, Albert and Nicole Du Roy quote from *Belle jeunesse* ("Beautiful Youth"), a Vichy weekly magazine devoted to "young French women," which made the following outrageous claim: "All French women who showed a lack of courage during peacetime, through misconduct, flightiness, and egoism, are somewhat responsible for the war."[51] In the rightist publication *Le Franciste*, we read on July 21, 1941: "French women killed France not only through blind vanity, through self-centered passion, but also through a dogmatic will to avoid the most imperious duty to the race and national survival."[52] Accused of immorality and of refusing to procreate for the good of the country (and the "race," no doubt French Aryan?), women under Vichy were often defined according to the stereotypical extremes of prostitute (the "loose" woman) and of saint (the fertile, self-sacrificing mother).

Vichy's only concessions to women's rights arose from necessity: because so many husbands were absent, and thus not around to provide for their families, Vichy put into action (September 22, 1942) a law allowing women to administer communal property and to represent an absent husband.[53] But the double binds for women under Vichy remained evident: in caring for home and children, waiting for the men's return from war prisons and forced labor or concentration camps, women had to face the daunting task of economic survival. Vichy's supposed concerns for the well-being of women and their families eventually revealed their hollowness. In order to ensure French *men's* employment in 1940, the law of October 11 prohibited married women from working in administrative positions.

Between 1940 and 1942, vast numbers of women were consigned to the ranks of the unemployed (60% in 1942 versus 25% in 1940), in order to ensure employment for French men. At the same time, with Hitler's pressure to replenish the German labor force, Prime Minister Laval declared in 1942 that "nothing should keep married women any longer from working, even women whose husbands can meet the family's needs."[54] This bogus enfranchisement allowed women to be forced to work in Germany.

While the Socialist government of Léon Blum during the Popular Front in the 1930s did manage to *appoint* three women ministers,[55] it took, ironically, the national disaster of the Occupation to prove both the bankruptcy of Pétain's traditional assignations for women in wartime and the logic of including women in universal suffrage (if not yet recognizing them as legal equals). It is more than likely that women's actions during the war helped secure the recognition that they should be counted as participants in the political process. With so many men eliminated from their traditional functions, it became clear that "women's work" could, and had to, include responsibilities and rights that only men had previously assumed. During the most treacherous times, they proved themselves faithful patriots in their many roles: as resistance fighters against Vichy and the Nazis, and as resourceful survivors and breadwinners.[56] Laure Adler, in her book devoted to "political women," notes, however, the hush surrounding both the role of women in the resistance and the actual attainment of voting rights (which would explain historians' frequent overlooking of the event).[57] Because women did not fill the top functions in the resistance networks, and because the resistance was by its very nature clandestine, women's participation was less visible than that of male counterparts. Paula Schwartz has pointed out that official, scholarly documentation of the resistance tended to follow party lines, full-time activists, or official members, with the result that women resisters were placed at the margins of formal definitions and structures.[58]

De Gaulle, although raised in a conservative family that staunchly upheld traditional values,[59] is generally credited with initiating in one quick turn of phrase, almost parenthetically, the inclusion of women amongst the future voting public at the time of the liberation. The liberation of France and of disenfranchised French women seemed to go hand in hand for de Gaulle. As Sarah Fishman has astutely pointed out, "the myth of 'Forty Million Resisters' was powerful enough to benefit women. Women's notable contributions to the resistance prompted the idea that women, politically imma- ture and undeserving of the vote before the war, had proven them- selves worthy of the vote through their resistance activities."[60] Viewed as a sort of "rite of passage to full citizenship after the war,"[61] women's participation in the resistance took on an impor- tance that was politically useful for them, even if it was based on false or biased suppositions. The consecration of women's newly gained rights at the end of the war was quickly subsumed however, by the new political struggles for power in the post Vichy governments of the Fourth Republic. Laure Adler points out that even the "fact" of granting the vote is still a point of contention: arguments continue about whether it was the communists or de Gaulle who actually gave women the right to vote.[62]

For Pétain, the feminine was associated with a threat. As of July 10, 1940 his regime actually encouraged the removal of all the busts of Marianne, the traditional female symbol of the French Republic, from town halls. He also removed Marianne's portrait on French stamps and replaced it with his own. As Florence Montreynaud has said: "Whereas a robust young woman embodied the Republic, it is an eighty-four year old with a white mustache who, identifying him- self with the 'cruelly wounded homeland' (Patrie), proposes himself as the national symbol . . . Very quickly, the rupture is total: the insti- tutions of the Third Republic are swept away, with the motto *Free- dom–Equality–Fraternity* replaced by *Work–Family–Fatherland*. The cult of the Marshal is instituted. Moreover Pétain only likes women at home, preferably pregnant. He chases them from the world of work . . . revives Mother's Day . . . praises the Virgin Mary and Joan of Arc."[63]

A master of self-promotional symbols, Pétain willingly stepped into the limelight and welcomed the proliferation of his own photo- graph in public as well as private spaces, from the classroom to the walls of individuals' homes. An adamant anti-republican, Pétain was skillful at covering over the traces of the republic with his French state iconography. In his own version of Louis XIV's adage, "L'Etat, c'est moi" ("I am the State"), he fostered his own personality cult offering France the "gift of his person," to save the country.[64] Robert Paxton notes that Pétain began "each new law with the quasi royal: "We, Philippe Pétain, Marshal of France, Head of the French State, decree . . . "[65] Perhaps it is not altogether by chance that one passes from the republic whose gender in French is feminine (with "nation" and "France" also feminine), to the masculine French state that Pétain embodies. In this context, female symbols (the Virgin Mary, Joan of Arc, women on pedestals) were at the service of an autocratic state.

It is certainly true, however, that the conservative, pro-collaboration Vichy government was not the only one to adapt feminine symbols to its political needs during the war. De Gaulle's call for resistance was expressed in gendered terms: "'France, tied and gagged, is fighting against the rape that was negotiated by her oppressors,' declares General de Gaulle in a speech on Radio-London, December 16, 1940."[66] The beginning of his memoirs generalizes this metaphor in the now famous passage: "All my life I have thought of France in a certain way. This is inspired by sentiment as much as by reason. The emotional side of me tends to imagine France, *like the princess in the fairy stories or the Madonna in the frescoes*, as dedicated to an exalted and exceptional destiny . . . France cannot be France without greatness" (my emphasis).[67] Under the Fifth Republic, de Gaulle would think of himself as the (masculine) *head of state* safeguarding "la belle France." His own symbol would be distinct from that of the woman-nation. On the presidential medal made in his honor as the Fifth Republic's new president in 1958, de Gaulle did not use the traditional female figure of Marianne as had his predecessors. Instead, he chose for his medal the Cross of Lorraine framed by a victory V, thus evoking his own role in saving the country from Hitler.[68]

France possesses, of course, a long tradition of using female figures to represent itself, either historically, as with Joan of Arc, or symbolically, as with Marianne. Whether on coins, statues, paintings, engravings, or public monuments, Marianne, with her characteristic Phrygian cap,[69] has been the primary embodiment of France since the Revolution. Maurice Agulhon's exhaustive study of France's female iconography underscores Marianne's manifestations in terms of *visual representations*, and paves the way for studying female cinematic symbols of France. Agulhon begins with Marianne as a political symbol of the nascent republic in 1792, but emphasizes that she also represents through the next centuries "Liberty" and "France-as-nation" (either separately or concurrently).[70] Significantly enough, Marianne's origins as symbol of the French republic retain the kind of ambiguities that we will be studying in cinematic form: initially used pejoratively, the name came to swing back and forth between "the language of the counter-revolution and that of the Republic, between the language of the populace and that of educated people and between a colloquial and an official tone."[71] Our examples of official lore—from Pétain and de Gaulle—offer just such oscillations between positive and negative poles of female representation. Marianne has been associated historically much more with the political Left (as a manifestation of the *republic*) than with the Right, although this tendency has become attenuated in the postwar years. De Gaulle's position—combining paternalism and patriotism without eschewing republicanism—suggests some of the complications in attitude. For a host of reasons, as notes Agulhon, feminists have not appropriated Marianne as *their* symbol[72]. Suffice it to say that the sexualization of Marianne in modern times, as well as her infantilization, have not made her a particularly useful symbol for women's movements.

Prior to the Fifth Republic, the incarnations of Marianne tended to be anonymous, idealized, abstract, often wearing Roman style robes and bearing a solemn demeanor to imply civic duty and determination[73]. In the 1960s, however, she became particularized when actual celebrity women became the recognized models for Marianne's representations on stamps, town hall statues, and monuments. Some of the most famous have been movie stars Brigitte Bardot, Catherine Deneuve, and Isabelle Adjani, as well as singer Mireille Mathieu, and ice skater Marie-José Perec. Model Laetitia Casta and TV celebrity and singer, Evelyn Thomas, have also been chosen. Brigitte Bardot is the first in this line of living symbols to lend her image to Marianne. The switch to a live model began primarily as a joke by sculptor Aslan who, in 1969, made an eroticized bust—ever so busty—of a Marianne with Bardot's features but with the somewhat stiff bearing of a typical Marianne facing straight ahead, wearing the Phrygian cap.[74] As a successful star in 1969, Bardot was already a French icon in her own right, so the transition to official status was relatively seamless. Bardot's hedonism and free ways deprived the image of some of its previous gravity that, Agulhon astutely argues, was in turn transferred to the president of the Fifth Republic. With this change, the significance of the "town hall Marianne" was radically altered: "The Gaullist regime values to the extreme the respect due the President, supposedly 'in charge' of the national State, the supreme value; as a result, it demotes to a

secondary position the institutional Republic, the laws and the system. One can smile at or chat with Marianne, because it's with the
chief that one is serious."[75] There is slippage from the "Republic as
political ideal of a liberal democracy" to the "Republic-Nation-
France"[76]. For external consumption, Bardot as Marianne promoted
the stereotype of France as a seductive culture and a world center for
pleasure.

A salient example of Marianne's iconography in films about the
war from the Gaullist period can be found in Christian-Jaque's
(1959) *Babette s'en va-t-en guerre* (*Babette Goes to War*), starring,
appropriately enough, Brigitte Bardot. It is almost as if the actress
were rehearsing, a decade early, her future official role as representative of France. Following in the wake of André Bazin, who argued
that eroticism was a basic component of cinema,[77] Antoine de
Baecque notes the close association in the 1950s between erotoma-
nia and cinephilia, with the longing and desire for the images of
female stars on the screen nurturing the love of cinema itself. This
was especially the case for a whole generation of young New Wave
filmmakers (Truffaut, Godard, Chabrol, Rivette, and Rohmer) who
would go on to showcase women in their own films.[78] Bardot was
France's equivalent of Marilyn Monroe, and her picture filled the
pages of popular film magazines. One of the typical paradoxes of
Bardot's cinematic roles, as Ginette Vincendeau has noted, is that
she is both the object of a male gaze *and* a desiring subject who
"takes active pleasure in her body and expresses her own desire."[79]

Although Christian-Jaque's Babette offers one of the less politically ambivalent instances of Marianne's postwar career in film, even
this version has its double-sided moments. Christian-Jaque's slap-
stick resistance comedy features Brigitte Bardot not so much as the
sexy bombshell of Vadim's (1957) *Et Dieu créa la femme* (*And God
Created Woman*), but rather as an ignorant working class girl, who
first appears with braided pigtails. The star's expressly childlike
demeanor at the beginning of this film matches her initials
(BB=bébé=baby), connoting the woman-child, and coincides with
what was to become a tradition in the last half of the twentieth century of turning Marianne into a child. This ingénue's down-to-earth
resourcefulness (and stunning looks) allow her to successfully incarnate a fighting, resisting France, under the leadership of that other
major icon of the Fifth Republic, General de Gaulle. If the film's
slight irreverence vis-à-vis the resistance seems to poke fun at foibles

(for example, high ranking military officials receive medals for work done by their subordinates, Babette, and her boyfriend), the overall joviality and stereotyping bolsters the Gaullist myth of generalized popular French Resistance, with the role of the Free French in London being emphasized. De Gaulle is even seen briefly from the back in a comical scene: a French captain thinks he's speaking to his English girlfriend on the phone, but the lines have been crossed (by Babette, ineptly working as a phone operator), and it's the general who answers at the other end of the line instead of the girlfriend.[80]

The film promotes Brigitte Bardot's already mercurial rise to stardom, as the new (commercial) figure of Frenchness (resourcefulness combined with beauty), and aligns her aspirations with de Gaulle's fighting forces in London. The suggestion that the two form the quintessential French couple is made explicit in the dialogue when one of de Gaulle's soldiers at headquarters remarks: "In military issues, we answer to the General; in domestic issues, we answer to Babette." With its goal of reaching a broad audience, *Babette* is devoid of nudity and realistic violence.[81] Its only explosions are caused by exploding cigars and cigarettes, a recurring gag throughout. The film's idealized France has no Jews and no real collaborators. The German officers and Gestapo are comical caricatures of monstrous killers or inept subordinates, and Babette is the stereotypical unwilling hero.[82] Her co-fighter and future fiancé shows complete disdain for Babette's intellect, but must acknowledge in the end her effective work as . . . an espionage agent! Babette must work her way up the military ladder, moving from potato peeler and floor washer to parachutist, radio operator, and spy.

It is in Babette's mission that the safe resistance themes become somewhat more complicated, and the woman's ambivalent role in battle is highlighted. A comic, resistance version of Mata Hari, Babette is sent over to the Germans to bring back a certain Von Arenberg because he has the plans for a German attack on England. Her ability to carry out her mission is facilitated by the fact she closely resembles Von Arenberg's ex-girlfriend, also played by Bardot (with a brunette wig), so the differences between opposing camps are diminished through female resemblance. The Gestapo also enlists Babette to spy on Von Arenberg because they do not trust him. Although Babette's alliances remain clearly with the resistance, she nevertheless fills the role of double agent and bait, manipulated by both sides, resistance and Gestapo. But Babette *also* performs her own maneuvers on all sides in order to fulfill her mission. Through her charm and inventiveness, she manipulates Gestapo agents, resisters, and Von Arenberg.

Babette's role as assistant to de Gaulle in this patriotic comedy matches up perfectly with Agulhon's description of an informal Marianne in counterpoint to the august Head of Fighting France. Babette is a likeable character, a "working girl" of the people, flighty, but unthreatening, whereas the grand chief of the resistance (and future head of the republic) remains an imposing figure in the shadows, and is viewed from a respectful distance.

I have been describing, thus far, the perception of women's roles and rights during the Occupation primarily as a function of the actions of heads of state and the symbolism they wished to promote. But it is equally true that the creation of such perceptions are dependent upon implicit and explicit cultural traits and values that circulate among the general population, the "mentality" of a period as reflected—whether consciously or not—in France's cultural representations of itself. What is noteworthy in film is that the greater visibility of women in postwar accounts of the Occupation duplicates their actual prominence in the films made *during* the war. With a paucity of male actors, both acting jobs and dramatic roles for women greatly increased.[83] Since most of the postwar French filmmakers who made films about the war were either children or young adults who lived through it and watched its films, these gender representations from the Occupation are crucial to the directors' memories of the period and their cinematic renderings of it. What we will see in postwar films is a double reflection, with contemporary preoccupations coloring the portrayal of the past, and shades of the past providing contour to the directors' cinematic choices.

Geneviève Sellier and Noël Burch's account of the French "imaginaire social" in *La Drôle de guerre des sexes du cinéma français, 1930–1956* ("The Phony War of the Sexes in French Cinema, 1930–1956") provides an invaluable basis for understanding the psychic repetition in postwar films of certain family scenarios that reflect both women's changing social roles in general *and* the specificity of the war period.[84] The term "imaginaire social" refers to the collective imagination or mindset of a period, but does not necessarily entail a conscious awareness of its characteristics by those living in it.

Burch and Sellier argue that French women's right to vote, which should logically have come about much earlier, only became viable after a certain unconscious reworking of gender roles that the Occupation helped effectuate. They explain that after the turbulent 1920s, in which sexual identity and gender roles were challenged, the 1930s brought about a normalizing repression to fend off the rise of the "modern woman," whose androgyny and increasing financial and moral freedom threatened masculinity, the authority of the father ("the Law of the father"), and the patriarchal regime in general. Burch and Sellier read the national portrait of France through its unconscious Oedipal scenarios in film. The unconscious script of the 1930s embodies a denied phantasm of paternal incest that constitutes "a plea . . . in favor of threatened privileges," embodied in the "father" (symbolic or actual), who has lost or is losing control over women, especially the younger generation.[85] It is, of course, not a matter of a literal incest, but rather of an impossible but manifest desire of the father, often presented through displacements and seemingly innocent paternal affection toward daughters and young women. Three types of incestuous phantasms can be identified: that of "the tranquil father," "the sacrificed father," and "the bad father." The progression of these three types runs through the films of the 1930s, with the "bad father" arising in the post-Popular Front era as the antagonist to a good, younger man.

As women's accession to certain rights began to seem increasingly inevitable, there arose a need to reaffirm patriarchal authority that the films of the 1930s bring to light through a phantasm of threatened paternal supremacy and desire. This danger to the "father" is associated with other patriarchal anxieties: the threat to "l'Ordre patronal," the authority of industrial bosses, as well as the xenophobic, often racist, fear of an "invasion" of immigrant workers flooding into France. All these fears are also connected with a threat to national identity. Clearly, many films of the prewar period respond to these threats with more or less covert misogyny and anti-Semitism, often resorting to a schizophrenic splitting of groups: the modern, "good" woman is represented alongside the shrew; the "good," assimilated Jew resides next to the foreigner with shifty values. This schema parallels François Garçon's arguments that films of the 1930s were more anti-Semitic than those of the Occupation, and that the treatment of female characters during the Occupation was more extensive and more positive than in the 1930s.[86]

The period of the Occupation brings about a profound change in the cinematic treatment of gender and family configurations. With

the accession to power of Marshal Pétain, an old, revered father figure (even if never a father himself), the public witnesses the increasing decline and ineptitude of Pétain as leader. In film, a new
concurrent figure arises, that of the "castrated father," likeable but
destined to be discredited, chastised for incestuous desires upon
"daughters" or younger women, and overrun by the course of
events. In the films of this period, female protagonists are more
prevalent than before, and their roles are more active. Let us look
briefly at the story lines of three Occupation films that Burch and
Sellier discuss in their model. This will serve to set the stage for our
discussion of postwar national icons combining female strength and
duplicity. These Occupation stories capture the tendencies of the
period (its "mentality"), without dealing with the war head-on.[87]
They also shape and reflect the viewing public's sense of itself—at
the first airings, but also as collective memories that circulate in the
postwar films.[88]

   Two adaptations of Balzacian novels offer particularly compelling
examples of the strong woman/weak father pattern. It is not hard to
see the feminist side of Jean Giraudoux's 1941 adaptation of Balzac's
novella, *La Duchesse de Langeais*, compared to the misogynistic original: the Occupation duchess is made a symbol of all women trying
to take revenge against male domination and control over their
lives.[89] She is even a friend of the poor working classes. In great contrast to her cold, conniving Balzacian precedent, the duchess of Jean
Giraudoux and director Jean de Baroncelli is a sympathetic figure,
who in dying, becomes "a martyr in the battle of the sexes."[90]

   Similarly, in René Le Hénaff's 1943 film adaptation of Balzac's
1832 short novel *Le Colonel Chabert*, the eponymous hero is a fee-
ble, old soldier, endearing but incapable of controlling the situation
or his much younger wife. He is attached to an old regime and old
values that no longer seem viable: he is a Pétain type who, like the
Vichy leader, has no children of his own and is in total decline. In
fact, Le Hénaff makes him an invalid by depriving him of an arm.
The colonel's ex-wife, now the Countess Ferraud, is portrayed much
more sympathetically than her original scheming counterpart in the
novel. The cinematic countess is a survivor who has managed to rise
out of the poverty in which she was born, and who seeks to protect
her own and her children's security when she sees Count Ferraud
detaching himself from her. The spectator witnesses a sympathetic

young female (the countess) helping out and taking charge of the helpless father figure (Chabert).

In the clearly politicized pro-Vichy films of the Occupation, women's increased prominence in active roles becomes quite often that of the victim—the icon of France's suffering and valor. The quintessential example of selfless female devotion can be found in Jean Stelli's tearjerker of 1942, *Le Voile bleu* ("The Blue Veil"), in which a governess repeatedly sacrifices her personal happiness and wellbeing to care for other people's children. In the Vichy framework, the price of women becoming idealized national icons is that they are deprived of the possibility of being desiring humans, since their desire would be considered too threatening to men's virility. In order to revitalize France's men, Vichy's female film icons must renounce their own desire. In those films not advocating the Vichy ideology, women are still active and even express their own desire. What is most compelling about the Burch and Sellier transformational model is that it presents a scenario common to the vast majority of the films, *regardless of their political leanings*. As we look at postwar films on the Occupation, we will be returning to the Burch-Sellier model because it offers both a grounding in the Occupation's historical events *and* in the period's films (addressing conditions of work, gender roles, and the difficulties of survival).

In a paradoxical twist, the cinema of the Occupation is often referred to as the "golden era" of a specifically French cinema. Those who made films in France during the war were assured of a French public without the tough competition of commercial Hollywood films. They made quality films within the constraints of difficult production circumstances, including censorship and the lack of physical and human resources, including directors, writers, and crews—many of whom were Jewish—who fled for their safety and/or to avoid moral compromise. The inherent moral ambiguities of a situation so full of compromises—with French cinema under Vichy devoid of its many of its participants (especially, but not exclusively its Jewish ones)—will mark the general iconography of postwar films returning to this period for their inspiration. The prominence of women characters in the cinematic recreations of wartime France recalls their presence in films made during the Occupation, but it also figures into postwar anxieties about France's ethical choices and about the new social roles of women.

For the postwar generation of filmmakers, the Occupation proved to be a source of fascination and of artistic inspiration. This was particularly the case for young New Wave filmmakers like Claude Chabrol and François Truffaut, who were ten and eight years old, respectively, at the outbreak of the war. Already enthusiastic film viewers in the 1940s, both were marked by this initial viewing experience, at a time when French films were predominant (with American and British films banned). As *male* filmmakers having watched Occupation films that were devoid of the Occupation itself and that featured *women* characters, they offer intriguing reflections through their works of gendered icons of desire, and their connections to national portraits.

Tangential to the New Wave, Louis Malle (who was eight years old in 1940), Claude Berri (six years old in 1940), and Michel Drach (nine years old in 1940) also fell sway to the autobiographical urge to portray a period that helped to shape their tastes, characters, and world views. For the most part, the turn to the Occupation years only became possible after the airing of *The Sorrow and the Pity*.[91] The tendency of France's New Wave films (and New Novels) to challenge the possibility of realistic representation of large scale events paralleled the general public's desire, in the decades immediately following the war, to turn away from disconcerting memories and collective or personal responsibility concerning France's complicity with Nazism. Just as the postwar generation of filmmakers eventually returned to their personal attachments to the Occupation in their films (especially from the 1970s on), the general French public began to obsessively review national and personal accountability regarding wartime experience. But we will see that, in fact, certain key films of the *early* postwar years already bore the strains, tensions, and complications that exploded with full force later on.

Writer St. Exupéry once commented that one comes from childhood the way one comes from a country. This remark seems particularly pertinent to our study because it implicitly binds childhood memories, historical moment, and national identity. For the majority of the filmmakers considered here, the Occupation was a defining moment of their youth. Our effort will be to grasp the effects of history on these postwar filmmakers and, in turn, their effect on our collective understanding of history. Given the prominence of the New Wave in the history of French filmmaking, the New Wave's contributions to war films will be especially important.

Film critic Jean Douchet divides New Wave filmmakers into two generational groups—those who were adults during the war and who had already been politicized (for example, Bazin, Rohmer, Resnais, and Marker), and those who were still children during the war and whose early experiences of Occupation life and film viewing were crucial to their developing worldviews (Godard, Truffaut, Chabrol, and Demy).[92] Of this younger group, Truffaut and Chabrol both made films about the war. And while they have often seemed distanced from a political cause in their filmmaking, they *have* been associated with the "Right Bank" of the New Wave, in contrast, for example, with the older Resnais, whose leftist political commitment was early and clearly delineated in his films on the war, from *Night and Fog* (1956) to *Hiroshima mon amour* (1959). Because Chabrol, Truffaut, Malle, Drach, and Berri were so young during the Occupation, and because there were no French films made then in which the actual Occupation was represented (other than crude propaganda films promoted by Vichy and the Germans), their views of the Occupation tended to develop through the indirect perspective of children reading an often opaque situation that seemed distant from them. Their passion for films at this time could not lead to a political understanding of the events. I argue that in the case of the younger filmmakers, their recreations of the period effectively perform in the viewer an ethical reckoning that makes us witness, judge, and participant on history's sidelines, much in the way the filmmakers were during the war. The opacity that each brings to the ethical dilemmas presented—with few interpretative cues to guide us through the moral mine field—reproduces in us the bystander's bewilderment.

Our repertory of films shares in some of the issues pertaining to literary autobiography and to the construction of a textual self. The relationships between fictive creation and faithful account, between individual uniqueness and generalized types (and the level at which historical truths are considered typical), all enter into the mix of postwar films on the Occupation, and have made of them lightning rods of critical reception. Part of my task is to explore how the interactions between individual and collectivity become enmeshed in heated arguments about national conscience. The particularity of Marianne as a gendered symbol of material existence runs parallel to the autobiographical impulse in postwar filmmakers to identify particular (individual) memories with a collective reckoning of the past.

Several of the films examined involve self-conscious stagings of cinematic scopophilia, that is, they feature the illicit pleasures of watching without being seen. For the younger postwar filmmakers, the structure of film viewing and the memory of the Occupation offer up a sort of primal scene: in both, a (hidden) witness spies on adults' actions. Lacanian film theorist Christian Metz has shown that all film viewing carries an erotic, taboo charge, occasioned through the secret visual and auditory pleasures of the individual subject as voyeur (excluded from any reciprocity with the screen object). Metz insists that conventional narrative cinema, by ignoring that what is on screen is seen, allows the viewer to ignore himself or herself as voyeur: "Certain precise features of the institution contribute to this affinity: the obscurity surrounding the onlooker, the aperture of the screen with its inevitable keyhole effect."[93] The filmmaker who portrays "the Occupation" on screen invites the spectator to share in a particular framing of human events. The situation is akin to Lacan's "mirror stage," in which the child develops a notion of himself (the ego) when he recognizes his image in a mirror: it is a moment of identification ("there I am!") and alienation ("that image is not myself"), and it precedes the child's entry into language (the Symbolic). The filmmaker (reminiscent of the parent) holds up the cinematic mirror for the spectators to recognize the camera's particular "take" on the Occupation story as their own.

Metz underscores the film viewer's isolation—from the screen, from the other members of the audience, from the filmmaker. His psychoanalytic model clearly minimizes the notion of any common experience (good or bad) in film viewing. To my mind, however, this is an unnecessarily reductive way of constructing subjectivity that neglects the subject's positions in the viewing community (as he/she is traversed by the *imaginaire social*). Maurice Halbwachs's early groundbreaking work on collective memory, which apprehends individual memory as constructed by one's interactions within a community (or sets of communities), offers a counterbalance to the isolated psychoanalytic model of the individual, without, however, subverting its insights.[94] Rather than thinking of film as either the production of a self-enclosed object (unrelated to the viewer), or as the interpretative understanding (meaning) of each individual viewer, I prefer to consider it an intersection of signifying practices that include evolving social interactions over time, as well as individual prototypes of the viewer's psychic relation to the screen-as-mirror.

Concurrently, my recourse to biographical and historical data surrounding Occupation events and each filmmaker's life is less a search
for the "origins" of the film than an extension of its intertexts, as it
assembles an historical object. The exploration of the viewer's position or point of view will involve less a singular interpretation than
an effort to apprehend conditions that allow a gaze to be constructed through identification with the camera and characters.

Although we will be taking a look at some key films where women
do not occupy center stage, for the most part Marianne will figure
prominently in our discussions. In almost all cases, she is seen
through the eyes of male directors. In several instances, their films
are based on the works of women (fiction, memoirs, or scripts), but
on the whole, there are very few women *cinéastes* who have chosen
the Occupation as either foreground or background for their films.
The primary exception is Josée Yanne, whose 1993 film *Boulevard
des hirondelles* (about Lucie Aubrac) we will consider briefly in Chapter 5. The conventional nature of this film does little to distinguish it
from the work of Yanne's male counterparts. Two much less obvious
films that allude to the war without actually making it their topic are
Diane Kurys's (1983) *Entre nous* and Chantal Akerman's (1978) *Les
Rendez-vous d'Anna*. Although neither film is really "about" the
Occupation *per se*, Lynn Higgins has convincingly shown that these
films do suggest ways in which generations born after the war self-
consciously ask questions about their relationship to a past they
never knew. Higgins argues that rather than telling a story of the
Occupation, "dramatizing public history," these feminist films
explore memory in terms of "relationships that are the consequence
of the catastrophe."[95] Their connections to historical events are,
however, sometimes so subtle that most spectators would not identify them with the Occupation.

My own focus will be more on films that manipulate various conventional tropes of historical representation that call upon the public
to rethink the past, to be a witness/accomplice, as well as a judge.
The French audience for these feature films includes, of course, both
those who had experienced the war during their lifetimes, and those
who were born afterwards, so that issues of remembering, questioning, and teaching history's lessons are intertwined in a format also
designed to entertain. Our mix of films will include both uncritical
films portraying a "truth," as well as those that question that very
possibility while still telling a story. Some films posit the past as lived

action in a virtual present (consciously or unselfconsciously), while others concentrate on the construction and deconstruction of Occupation memory in the present. Given the inherently conserving, conservative nature of trying to represent a national event, it is not surprising that a "truth effect" will be constantly at issue in our discussion.

Although I allude to documentaries in several instances—one cannot avoid discussing *The Sorrow and the Pity*—I concentrate on feature films that present a fiction that is more or less based in actual events. The figure of Marianne walks on the borderline of fiction and historical account, between myth and fact. Marc Ferro has argued that "if it is true that the not-said and the imaginary have as much historical value as History, then the cinema, and especially the fictional film, open a royal way to psycho-socio-historical zones never reached by the analysis of documents."[96] Fictional stories create a juncture between document and dream, political vision, and the unconscious air or mentality of a period. What makes them so fascinating is that their vision remains double, with the past shaping the present and vice versa.

For the most part, I discuss films in chronological order, trying to show the layering of new material over old (in contrast to, in dialogue with, or in ignorance of, earlier films). In Chapter 2, I concentrate on a short period—between 1959 and 1962—when French films on the war began to offer more complex, morally ambiguous renditions of Occupation daily life, rather than tales of heroism. Films of this transitional period between the Fourth and Fifth Republics challenge or nuance resistance myths, explore the psychology of collaboration and of repressed memory, and offer an array of representations of an ambiguous Marianne, whether on the Left or on the Right. Alain Resnais's *Hiroshima mon amour* provides us with a quintessential articulation of an ambiguous Marianne. In the chapter's final section, we consider three films about the war by Jean-Pierre Melville, precursor to the New Wave. A comparison of Melville's films will allow us to take stock of the transitional period's most prevalent characteristics.

Chapters 3, 4, and 5 devote extended analysis to three "Right Bank" films on the war that spotlight national identity. Louis Malle's 1974 *Lacombe Lucien*, François Truffaut's 1980 *Le Dernier Métro* (*The Last Metro*), and Claude Chabrol's 1987 *Une Affaire de femmes* (*Story of Women*) not only thematize France's role in collaboration, they dramatically "perform" the issue for the spectators who are called upon to judge the protagonists' actions, and potentially themselves. At issue is the extent to which these films are representative of French wartime comportment. Malle's film occasioned passionate critical responses that attest to the high stakes involved in featuring French collaboration. I argue that the heated critical controversies surrounding Malle's film are emblematic of France's identity crisis. Shown during a period of intense political polarization, *Lacombe Lucien*'s representation of "accidental collaboration" met with fervent reactions from all sides, but particularly from the Left. At stake in our discussion of Malle (as well as in our analysis of Truffaut and Chabrol) will be the degree to which Malle's film is either typical of, or faithful to, the specifics of the historical period portrayed, since many of the attacks on it have to do with its exemplarity. *Lacombe Lucien*'s evocative portrayal of the facility of collaboration establishes a model for other films in the 1980s and 1990s, as we will discuss in the first section of Chapter 6.

Truffaut's and Chabrol's films offer two of the most striking examples of feminine national icons. Truffaut's *The Last Metro* showcases a magnificent Catherine Deneuve in the role of a theater director who, like all the theatrical troupe's participants, is forced to conduct a balancing act between resistance to, and cooperation with, the occupiers. Like Malle, Truffaut also broaches the topic of collaboration, but with a much more sympathetic attitude toward the characters' compromises. Although this film was well received critically when it first aired—it *is* after all a beautiful film with a gripping story—I argue that its forgiving attitude toward collaboration, and its emphasis on an esthetic triumph over a political understanding of events, is in fact more problematic than Malle's more outwardly controversial film.

Contrary to Malle's and Truffaut's films, Chabrol's *Story of Women* finds its inspiration in actual events that cover the life and execution of a female abortionist during the war. Chabrol makes his heroine the icon of French duplicity, simultaneously a symbol of treachery and victimization. *Story of Women* is no doubt the film that most clearly thematizes the issue of judging the past, while also feeding the contemporary debate on abortion.

It is generally accepted that most French films of the 1980s are less innovative and more conformist than those of a decade earlier. The numerous films on the Occupation from this period tend to adhere to this schema as well. (Chabrol's film may well be the exception confirming the rule.) The 1980s' move toward conventionality coincides with a change in political climate, as the clear-cut divisions between the Left and the Right were breaking down in France. In Chapter 6, we will see that the provocative ambiguities that had inflected films on the Occupation in the 1970s become virtually codified in the 1980s and beyond. For our purposes, however, the codification only serves to show just how strong the link between ambiguous female icons and national identity has remained.

The last sections of Chapter 6 take into consideration two very different kinds of films. First, I discuss Claude Berri's relatively conventional feature film on resister Lucie Aubrac, as well as the controversies surrounding her memoirs and the film. Clearly, even in 1997, when *Lucie Aubrac* first played in movie theaters, and during the following months when a round table of historians tried to establish the truth about what "really" happened to Lucie and Raymond Aubrac during the war, their personal history became invested with the task of rescuing French national identity.

Given conventional film narrative's frequent failures to account for multiple, sometimes incompatible versions of the past, we end Chapter 6 with a reading of postmodern films of the 1990s, in particular Jacques Audiard's *Un Héros très discret* (*A Self-Made Hero*), as well as Robert Guédiguian's 2004 *Le Promeneur du Champ de Mars* (*The Last Mitterrand*). I will consider whether a non-traditional, postmodern approach to events could take stock of history's conflicting versions without sacrificing its intelligibility. Ultimately, what these films reveal is less an *interpretation* of the past than a ludic portrait of how memory is constructed, what conventions and tropes it uses to fabricate the past, whether at the individual or collective levels. Such works point to what Lynn Higgins and others have frequently noted, namely that "history is not in the past" because "the past is always viewed through the eyes, the languages, and the rhetoric of the present."[97]

In the past couple of years, the audience for French films on the Occupation has expanded worldwide. For example, Jean Dewever's 1960 *Les Honneurs de la guerre* (*The Honors of War*), an initially controversial film due to its sympathetic portrayals of German soldiers in a French village, was re-released in 2006 to acclaim in French theaters. Previously unattainable films in the United States, such as *Lacombe Lucien*, are now distributed on DVD. Jean-Pierre Melville's

1969 masterpiece *L'Armée des ombres* (*The Army of Shadows*), about the French Resistance, started making the rounds at local movie houses in the United States in 2006. This renewed interest and accessibility on both sides of the Atlantic attests to the ongoing fascination with, and reappraisals of, World War II. Also in the public eye are the contemporary lawsuits against the French state by families of Jewish holocaust victims. These legal battles keep France's official responsibility in the headlines. For some, issues surrounding the U.S. occupation of Iraq echo those raised by occupied France's internal struggles. Whether fanciful or relevant, the potential ties between memory and present events seem unavoidable.

Some of the films selected here are great works of art; others are popular fare, but they all share in the construction of French national identity via the representation of the Occupation. I do not assume that my readers necessarily know French or that they are familiar with the films I am considering. For this reason, a certain amount of storytelling is necessary in order to flesh out the scenarios of national identity crisis that I explore. I emphasize the ways specific narrative strategies produce a certain historical vision of the nation, taking into account film's formal properties in the construction of historical significance. For those already familiar with the films, I hope to offer a fresh perspective; for those who have never seen them, I hope to either awaken an interest in the films themselves or to demonstrate their particular place in the history of portraying a wartime Marianne.

Some of the fictional feature films discussed are heavily anchored in archival information; some borrow from personal experience or from historical novels; still others are wholly fictional scripts with a dusting of historical detail to situate them. All of them, however, share in the construction of "a certain idea of France," to recall de Gaulle's now hackneyed expression. France's obsession with its past and its cinematic embodiments have received the attention of a number of important works in the last ten years. In France, Sylvie Lindeperg's 1997 *Les Ecrans de l'ombre: La Seconde Guerre mondiale dans le cinéma français (1944–1969)*, skillfully details both popular and professional reception to French films about the war up to 1969, paying special attention to the relationships among cinematic production, biographical data of the filmmakers, and construction of the historical narrative. *L'Histoire de France au cinéma* (1993), by Philippe Guibert and Michel Oms, affords a general overview of the way the French have turned to film to portray their past. Lynn Higgins's remarkable *New Novel, New Wave, New Politics: Fiction and the Representation of History in Postwar France* (1996) considers the treatment of World War II in both the French New Novel and New Wave film, and pays particular attention to issues of national identity, as does Naomi Greene's *Landscapes of Loss: The National Past in Postwar French Cinema*. Greene's work devotes one chapter to films about Vichy. *France in Focus: Film and National Identity* (2000), edited by Elizabeth Ezra and Sue Harris, is a collection of short essays that emphasize the economic, historical, and political conditions of the notion of a French national cinema. My own work's orientation differs from these in at least three ways: I offer a more distinct focus on films about the Occupation than Guibert, Oms, Higgins, Greene, and Ezra/Harris, whose works deal with films portraying several historical periods; my study extends well beyond the time period that Lindeperg considers to include recent films and new historical concerns; finally, I have articulated the issue of national identity in film via a sustained discussion of the female icon of Marianne. I am indebted to these predecessors, but hope to provide my readers with a new understanding of the intersections between French national identity, a collective autobiography of the Occupation, and women's roles in films on World War II.

CHAPTER 2

—⊰⊱—

TRANSITIONS BEFORE THE "SORROW": CRITICISM AND MYTH IN THE LATE 1950S AND EARLY 1960S

In the first decade after the war, "reconstruction" in France included rebuilding its economy, its film industry, and its image. As Jean-Pierre Jeancolas has noted, in 1945, de Gaulle's interim government created a "Ministry of Reconstruction" that became a "Ministry of Construction" under the Fifth Republic's first government. In addition to rebuilding the physical sites of destroyed movie theaters and studios, "the most pressing concern was to revive an ethos of creation, as much a matter of public morale—and thus of politics—as of aesthetics."[1]

In the immediate postwar period (1944–1946), an abundance of films about the war appeared before the French public. They emphasized French heroism in battle or in the underground resistance, portraying France as having "won the war." As part of the rhetoric for rebuilding national identity, this early period's films reaffirmed French men's authority, strength, and courage.[2] After the initial outpouring of heroic war films (twenty made in 1945), the Fourth Republic remained relatively quiet on the subject, as if issues about the war had been laid to rest (although clearly that would prove not to be the case).[3] By the time of de Gaulle's return to power in 1958, France was already undergoing a renewed interest in films about the events of 1939–1945. Between 1946 and 1958, France averaged only about three films per year on the topic, but in 1959 alone, ten films were made, and in 1960, that number increased to fifteen.[4]

While some of the films from the late 1950s have a Gaullist (heroic) bent, there is a prominence of films between 1958 and 1962 that cover a much broader range of topics than the early postwar films. Because France no longer felt so vulnerable about its status as a nation, the films are much less Manichean,[5] with all the shades of gray between resisters and collaborators being added, as well as new portraitures (prisoners of war, the defeat of 1940, more tempered or varied representations of Germans, and the like).

Although one might have thought that the fable of a generalized French resistance was not disputed in France until the early 1970s, in fact, it had already been challenged in the late 1950s and early 1960s, as de Gaulle was coming to power. In the passage from one republic to another, before the myth of a generalized resistance among the French population had taken full hold (or concurrently with that myth's formation), several films were featuring nuanced, frequently complex, portrayals of the less idealistic, more controversial acts and positions of the French during the Occupation. It is these uneasy representations of occupied France, with their social contradictions and political anxieties, that will be our focus as we explore the ways political and gender tensions articulate images of a France at war with itself. Although it is true that these intermediary films between the Fourth and Fifth Republics did not attach a political status to the phenomenon of collaboration, and to Vichy as the French government of the period, their attention to collaborators, traitors, and the messy ambiguities of everyday survival became topics to be explored.[6] Whereas male characters had populated the early postwar heroic films, female characters figure prominently in these more morally complex films. One of our tasks will be to assess the ways the transitional films, sandwiched between two heroic male modes, articulate national identity via "women's issues."

HIROSHIMA MON AMOUR

Of the French films from the late 1950s and early 1960s, no other film staged more forcefully, and also more self-consciously, the issue of representing World War II as collective and individual trauma than *Hiroshima mon amour*. Alain Resnais's famous film from 1959, based on Marguerite Duras's haunting script, inaugurates the best of New Wave film and perhaps the postmodern period in general. It looks at history as discourse, an evocation-trace of what is no longer; the "past" becomes a repeated performance in the act of storytelling, in words and images.[7] The film implicates the spectator in the problematic act of remembering and representing the war through a series of interlocking stories that frame and mirror each other. It is more about the difficulties of representing the war than about the war "itself." To put it another way, there is no historical event outside its narrations and its various versions, collective and individual. *Hiroshima mon amour* is also, no doubt, the film that most powerfully features a French woman to problematize the war's moral dimensions. In the to and fro between individual and collective, between Allies and Axis, between men and women, and between races, Duras and Resnais choose unsettling combinations that challenge easy or obvious moral positions on the war.[8]

Resnais's initial project had been to make a documentary on the bombing of Hiroshima, following on the heels of his majestic, moving documentary *Night and Fog* (1956), about the memory of the concentration camps. But as James Monaco has explained, Resnais "was blocked. There seemed to be no way to do the film on the bomb without remaking 'Nuit et Brouillard' [*Night and Fog*]. The facts of the bomb were different enough from the facts of the death camps, it is true, but the perceptual effects were the same: memories, knowledge of incomprehensible suffering, pain, and death. Since it was the perception of it rather than the event that interested Resnais, the two films added up to the same thing."[9] The fictionalization of the Hiroshima project provided a distance—a study in counterpoint—through which collective history and personal experience could become symbols for each other.

Set in Hiroshima in contemporary time (1957), the brief love affair between a French actress and a Japanese architect—both unnamed—is intertwined with a series of scenes that evoke the war through its formal representations: we are spectators to portions of a (fictitious) anti-war documentary in which the actress has a role, a film that Duras qualifies (somewhat ironically) as "edifying," suggesting its inadequacy to make us fully grasp the impact of the bomb. Also included are shots of Hiroshima's war museums and its hospitals, as well as photos and film clips of the mangled and burned bodies in the wake of the bombing of Hiroshima. All of these images are designed to evoke the horrors of war, but ultimately Resnais also suggests the sheer impossibility of that evocation. We are constantly made aware that we are looking at a reconstruction that emphasizes *re*presentation rather than presentation—that with the bombing of Hiroshima, there is literally *nothing* left of the event's *presence*. The impossibility of "knowing," or even accounting for, such large scale, methodical human destruction is evoked through the film's self-conscious reconstruction of Hiroshima's destruction. There is no representation adequate to render this horrific past that defies rational understanding. When the actress repeatedly asserts that she has seen everything at Hiroshima (that is, all the commemorations, all the traces), the Japanese man retorts that she has seen nothing of Hiroshima (the event in the past is out of reach, an unknowable experience).

Resnais defends against the temptation to make the suffering at Hiroshima an "object" of our knowledge. The fictitious documentary within the film relies on facts to enlighten: statistics about the strength of the bomb or the number of the dead are useful, but they do not allow us to know the event as a lived experience. On the other hand, Resnais also resists playing upon our emotions to accentuate the bomb's effects. Our potential fascination with horror is undermined by his emphasis on the reconstruction. For example, the director shows us the makeup of an actor playing a burn victim, and portrays the faces in a hospital ward as curiously devoid of expression, rather than expressing intense suffering as we might have expected in a piece of fictional realism. Background music sometimes seems to clash with what is shown: the cues to read the emotional investment of a scene are thus lacking. In addition, because the images of Hiroshima's destruction are disturbingly interwoven with the scenes of the couple's love-making, it is not always possible to tell what we are seeing: physical love or burned dead bodies. This confusion reinforces the connections between private and collective stories, but it also undermines the idea that a clear view or understanding of Hiroshima's annihilation would be representable. Resnais, in fact, decided to eliminate the mushroom cloud of the bomb that Duras had placed at the beginning of her scenario. The exclusion of this notorious image, says Nancy Lane, points to the idea that the suffering the bomb caused is beyond figuration.[10]

The French actress's love affair with the Japanese man is a relationship that disregards marriage vows and symbolically crosses "enemy lines," transgressing wartime divisions between Allied and Axis countries (see Figure 2.1). The affair triggers, in turn, from the

Figure 2.1. Hiroshima *mon amour*, Alain Resnais, 1958. "Elle" and her Japanese lover embrace.

actress's repressed memory, the resurgence of another, illicit love affair across enemy lines.[11] Again, the spectator is witness, this time to a past-resurrected-in-the-present via the flashback, as the woman narrates for her Japanese lover the previously forgotten memory of her love for a young German soldier who died in her arms in 1944, shot by a French Resistance sniper. The parallel between the dead lover and the new one arises from their dual roles as aggressors (fighting for the "wrong" side—Germany and Japan) and victims (of the French Resistance and the American bomb). The anonymous French woman, who was twenty in 1944, also straddles the division between traitor and victim: we watch in dismay her punishment by the local community of Nevers for this "traitorous" love with the enemy, including the ritualized shaving of her head for "horizontal collaboration," and her confinement in her family's cellar where she temporarily goes mad. Embodying the shame of her family and community, the young woman is symbolically "buried" with the Marseillaise resounding in the street over her head as the liberation proceeds.

The French actress's story is framed by Hiroshima, both in its telling (to a Japanese man from Hiroshima whom she simply calls "Hiroshima") and in its remembrance (she flees Nevers for Paris on the day the bomb is dropped). Told as a voice-over by the autobiographical subject/object of these events, the account places the community's actions at fault, favors the personal over the national, and love over war. The French woman's ability to narrate this buried story is a reenactment of the madness it brought her (she re-lives the pain through narrative), and a coming to terms with her loss of the lover and herself, but also of the experience's privileged status outside recounted memory, for it can, in fact, be told. The story is about the dual necessity of remembering and forgetting. The film concludes as the French woman is about to return home to France. If one could speak of closure in this film that continually muddles clear-cut meaning at every turn, it might reside in the sense of a salutary, although wrenching, repetition of the buried memory, a repeated "performance" that is paralleled and doubled by the peace film-within-the-film on the bombing of Hiroshima.

This extraordinarily dense, visually striking film calls into play a number of theoretical domains—psychoanalysis, historiography, cinematography, and autobiography—and manages to involve us in their web so that insides and outsides, and pasts and presents crisscross.[12] As we watch the peace procession within the film, it is possible to confound (if only temporarily) the fictitious anti-nuclear film and the one we are watching. In the personal love story, no one is given a proper name, so that the story transcends specific identities. Critics have frequently resorted to calling the unnamed French actress by the name of Resnais's actress, Emmanuelle Riva, in order to identify her—thus somewhat paradoxically confusing the insides and outsides of fiction. As the French actress (simply referred to here as "Elle"[13]) retells her love for the dead German soldier, and addresses him directly as "you" (the familiar form of "tu" in French), the Japanese lover responds by taking on the German's role. The Japanese lover becomes complicit in this reenactment: "When you are in the cellar, am I dead?" he asks, and then continues to respond as the dead lover when the woman relives her traumatic loss. The Japanese lover even replicates the community's past violence against her when he smacks "Elle," who, in a paroxysmal fit, yells that this was her first love. For us, it is unclear whether we are to condemn the violence or whether it allows her to escape the madness that her memory dredges up after a night of drinking.

What is particularly striking to me is the way the Resnais-Duras collaboration brings to the screen anonymous characters who, by their very anonymity, by the banality of the illicit love, and by the constant transgression of national, ethnic, and social boundaries, are able to suggest more than individualistic stories. There are no heroes and heroines in this work, even if the Durasian scenario decants the cliché of love to make it anew. The anonymous "Elle" of Duras's story bears the symbolic weight of something typical about the process of trauma, repression, and memory. I would also argue that *Hiroshima mon amour* adroitly anticipates Henry Rousso's Vichy Syndrome in its ability to articulate a troubled national history through a transnational psychoanalytic model of the individual. Rousso and the Resnais/Duras team account for the way the wartime history had to be remembered if it was to be transcended. What critic Nancy Lane has said of "Elle" could easily describe France's difficulties: "Paradoxically, she must recover the past before she can put it aside."[14]

Students of Occupation history are familiar with Rousso's four stages to explain the continual resurfacing of the Occupation in French postwar society. The first one, a period of "unfinished mourning" (1944–1954), is marked by a general political turmoil: after the "guerre franco-française" (the Franco-French war) come proclamations of victory, and concurrently, denunciations, black lists, trials, pardons, and purges of collaborators. The original trauma of the anonymous "Elle" in *Hiroshima mon amour* is emblematic of this chaos in psychic and collective terms: she is overwhelmed by the loss of her German lover and loses her sense of self when she is ostracized by her family and community. The liberation is turned on its head here, transformed into a moment of collective repression, embodied by this young woman who first becomes the spectacle of public humiliation, and then is hidden from sight. Is she guilty of collaboration, a symbol of treachery, the internal enemy, or a victim of collective revenge? Using René Girard's theory of social sacrifice, Lynn Higgins has drawn attention to the French woman's role as scapegoat for communal, and by extension, national guilt: "her expulsion protects [the community] from its own violence."[15] "Elle" is the quintessential "guilty" victim, the surrogate for the national dilemma.[16]

In Rousso's second stage, following the Freudian model, repression takes over. The (national) community turns away from remembering the war: in film, we have noted the relative paucity of works about the Occupation during the Fourth Republic. In *Hiroshima mon amour*, repression sets in as "Elle" "forgets" the traumatic shock of her youth (the death of her German lover, her public disgrace, and her psychosis). Her return to "health," that is, to a normal, normative existence—marriage, children, a career—is at the price of repression. Parallel to the Gaullist myth that "forgets" routine collaboration in favor of an image of a resisting France, Duras's young French woman "forgets" the pain of having lost her first lover, and a portion of her memory.[17] No one in her new life in Paris after the war, not even her husband, she says, is aware of this dark past.

It is of course Ophüls's documentary *The Sorrow and the Pity* that is credited with shattering the uniform Gaullist myth and that constitutes the "broken mirror" of Rousso's third stage (1971–1974). Through interviews with a wide array of the war's participants from several countries, varying backgrounds, classes, and political affiliations (all shades of resisters, collaborators, Nazis, and everything between), Ophüls explodes the smooth image of national harmony concerning the war. In Resnais's film, Hiroshima symbolizes the pulverizing explosion that ended the war in 1945 through the destruction of the Japanese city, but it is also the blast that rips open the scars, both personal and collective, of the war on the French scene. By framing the flashback of the French past with Hiroshima (as place, bomb, lover), the political tidiness of specular oppositions (French/German, victor/victim, traitors/good citizens) is rendered problematic. In one of the later scenes in the film, the French woman addresses her dead German lover as she looks at herself in a mirror and bemoans the fact that her remembering will now allow (cause?) her to forget him (the German lover). Telling their story is thus a betrayal of the memory, even at it is its consecration. In the historical realm, telling the complicated memory of the Franco-French war during the Fifth Republic represents a betrayal of the simplified Gaullist myth that had enabled France to get back on its feet after the war.

In Rousso's historical analysis, the return of Vichy and the Occupation in contemporary politics bears a double connotation. The return confirms that the past was too quickly buried and must resurface to be adequately dealt with, but it also becomes a pretext or tool to articulate political positions in the present. The political battles keep the memories constantly recirculating. This is particularly the case in the "obsessive phase" (from 1974 on) of Rousso's syndrome, but it is also operative in all the postwar periods. The most notable example from the 1950s and 1960s—the Algerian war—provides "a useful catalog of the various ways in which the past [World War II] can be mobilized for political purposes."[18] In the "obsessive phase" the syndrome is played out as a function of Jewish memory, as a struggle for survivors to tell their stories despite attempts to silence them, with the extreme being negationism—denying the Jewish Holocaust altogether.

Although the deportation of Jews and the Holocaust are not specifically mentioned in *Hiroshima mon amour*, their memory is like a haunting absence in the film. In the wartime love story, details such as the young girl clawing the walls of her cellar-prison recall the concentration camp victims' bloody scratches on the walls of the gas chambers. Her shorn hair—the symbolic castration of the female traitor—reminds us, on screen, of the bomb victims of Hiroshima who lose their hair due to radiation poisoning, and off screen, of the concentration camp victims whose hair was cut off and made into fabric after they were killed. (Resnais's *Night and Fog* shows the enormous piles of victims' hair from the concentration camps.) Such examples of a continual triangulation between the representations of the two collective cataclysms and "Elle"'s personal tragedy abound. It is in the reverberating echoes from one to the other that the absent center of human catastrophe and suffering takes on a virtual shape.

The attempt to silence Jewish survivors is not the only difficulty they experience during the obsessive phase of the Vichy Syndrome. In the reemergence of the survivors' memories, a set of contradictory desires arises for them: "As prolific and detailed as the deportees' accounts may be, their words remain in a sense shrouded in silence . . . [Memory] *wants to make the event contemporary and yet maintain it beyond our grasp; it wants to welcome it without assimilating it*" (my emphasis).[19] "Elle" embodies similar conflicting desires to share her story (its love, but also its horror and shame), and to remain silent about it, to preserve it from banalization (while acknowledging its similarities to other experiences). "Elle"'s ambivalence about telling her past, betraying love's memory, is connected to the belief that this love is unique, so that no repetition (in discourse, in action) would be conceivable. And, yet, as "Elle" admits, it is possible after all, perhaps even necessary, to tell the story, to love others, just as it is necessary for the survivors' experience to find expression while preserving some silence around the experience.[20]

But does the traumatic memory's repetition in the present signal the possibility of "putting it aside"?[21] Rousso saw no specific end to the Vichy Syndrome: the return of references to Vichy does not resolve the issues the war elicited about guilt, responsibility, and citizenship, either in present political concerns or in the interpretation of the past event. Consensus has not been achieved. Similarly, the final scenes of *Hiroshima mon amour* leave the question open about whether "Elle" will go beyond mnemonic obsession, forever reliving in the present what she cannot actively forget as a past. We are left in a sort of limbo: between the necessity of remembering and of forgetting, or, in practical terms, between a return to France or the abandonment of "Elle"'s prior life for her Japanese lover. Although the peace film on Hiroshima will have been made (both the fictitious one and Resnais's), the spectator experiences no finality in these events. By refusing closure on both the personal and collective versions of the war, the film transfers to the spectator-witness the task of rethinking the possibility of representing—and judging—wartime actions, individual and collective. James Monaco even goes so far as to claim: "Your reaction is the subject of the film, and its objective. Some of us see nothing in *Hiroshima*. Nothing. Others see *everything*. *Everything*. That is the point."[22] Or as Lynn Higgins says, "the film constitutes a community of spectators," and we belong to it.[23]

I have been describing *Hiroshima mon amour* as an esthetic triumph that captures personal and collective histories in an international framework, and chooses a female character to embody the complicated betrayals and victimizations involved in France's wartime experience. But it should also be noted that because this film touched nerves about Franco-German relations, and about collaboration and the purges, it had its share of detractors, controversy, and unusual convergences of opinion from the Left and the Right. This was particularly the case when it first aired. The reactions (its "subject," as Monaco said) show how its contradictions and twists sowed confusion in orderly political distinctions and revealed disconcerting affinities.[24] No doubt the parallels suggested between the suffering of a French girl who has loved a German soldier, and that of Hiroshima's victims (or the Holocaust's), were bound to be provocative. For those wishing to view the work through a political grid, extracting political or ethical positions, the film discomfits. One viewer bemoaned the fact that Resnais did not make it easy to identify a comfortable moral position: why did he not choose as lovers a scarred burn victim from Hiroshima and a young French woman tortured by the Gestapo? [25] Of course, Resnais's point was precisely *not* to make it too easy for the spectator who should struggle with the complexities. In agreement with the New Novel's call for thoughtful participation on the part of the reader, Resnais welcomes the active spectator who imaginatively works through the film.

Although Resnais's affinities with the political Left were quite strong, some ex-resisters were scandalized by the film, while others defended it. The same could be said of critics on the Right. Much of the controversy centered on the memory of the French "purge scene" (the shaving of "Elle's" head) in Nevers. Given that for most viewers the love story overtakes the war story and that our sympathies go toward the victimized woman, we end up siding with her against the community's representatives, and are thus led to disapprove of those associated with carrying out the purge (potentially resisters, although Resnais identifies them in his film as shopkeepers). On the extreme Right, for pro-fascist film critic Maurice Bardèche, the hair clipping was the key scene of the film because it showed the victimization of a young girl by the "liberators."[26] Bardèche implicitly connects the portrayal of the girl's victimization with the ultra-Right's claims of persecution during the purges—a faulty resemblance given that the girl is uninterested in the political divides that separate her and her German lover. Those on the Left who applauded the film's anti-war message saw the girl's situation as a particular case rather than a generalized characterization and endorsement of collaborators' actions.

Hiroshima mon amour is, no doubt, more a *critical* film than one that proposes a political agenda. Duras's influence is strongly felt in this refusal to allow politics to overtake human sensibilities, although it can be said that *Hiroshima* is clearly an anti-war film. She reads her own script's articulation of political and ethical determinants in terms of circumstance and chance rather than conscious deliberation.[27] If her script and its introduction raised more eyebrows than the actual film, it is probably due to the categorical nature of her pronouncements: "To shave the head of a girl because she loved an official enemy of her country, is the height of horror and stupidity."[28] Geneviève Sellier has linked *Hiroshima*'s insistence on a non-aggressive anti-war message to the fact that its script was written by a woman who presents "valued unheroic soldiers, [such as] Emmanuelle Riva's German lover" who appears more as a victim than a hero or an assailant.[29] Given the non-aggressive, anti-heroic peace stance Resnais had already brought forth with *Night and Fog*, I think it fair to give dual credit here. It does seem significant, however, that Duras's specific contribution to the story, that is, the French actress's love affair with the German soldier, is the primary focal point for challenging standard heroic rhetoric, perhaps more so than the fictive documentary. It is undeniable that *Hiroshima mon amour* bears the mark of Duras's particular affinity for deconstructing the Manichean oppositions that are the necessary ground for justifying war. Through the Romeo and Juliet-style love story, she portrays the radical Other—a German *and* a soldier—in affective, not belligerent terms. By privileging the (international) love story over national values, and chance over choice, Duras frames the documentary that Resnais couldn't make, but nevertheless represents in *Hiroshima mon amour*. Art and politics do converge in this tale in a way that doesn't erect heroes, but does evoke pacifist politics. The complication or twist that Duras brings is to tie a woman's individual victimization to collective protest. The choice of a *woman's* story particularizes the events, but her case of "amnesia," and subsequent obsession with the past, is illustrative of an entire nation's.

A very different rendering of female roles, as well as Franco-German relations in the war, arises in Jean Renoir's *Le Caporal épinglé* (*The Elusive Corporal*), which came out in 1962. Renoir's film about French prisoners of war in Germany reflects the anxieties of the postwar period as it thinks back on the war. Rather than depictions of French women's heroism against the occupier or against collaboration, Renoir features *German* women who are sympathetic to French men and who push them to resist German aggression. Since the German women are shown in a positive light (pragmatic, smart, courageous), the effect is to destabilize any absolute opposition between Germans and French.[30] Whereas *Hiroshima mon amour* provided an international framework in which to contest wartime oppositions—with the German character remaining deliberately *vague*—*The Elusive Corporal* chips away at French nationalism by humanizing the (German) Other—in the form of female German civilians (rather than male German soldiers).[31] The refusal to make a French woman the icon of France seems to go hand in hand with

Renoir's undercutting of nationalism. In *The Elusive Corporal*, a German dentist and her pretty daughter are strong female characters associated with the fear and alleviation of pain (extracting the protagonist's abscessed tooth), and with the urge to escape: "I love a man who isn't a slave," announces the German daughter to the French corporal who will then muster his courage to flee the German prison camp (aided by the young German woman).[32] While the French men in the camps are often vulnerable and weak, French women are described by the prisoners as threatening: an ex-café waiter declares his will to escape because he's heard talk that women are going to replace men as servers. The fear of women entering the work force to take over men's jobs is tangible in this film, and is consonant with the way Burch and Sellier have described men's postwar unease about women's new socio-political status. Renoir's prison camp is a microcosm revealing the *postwar* anxieties and humiliations of French men. Although the film itself does not have to be read as misogynistic, the way it makes visible male vulnerability without providing an understanding of French women's suffering seems lopsided. French women's aptitudes and abilities take on a frightening quality as they are seen through downtrodden French male characters.

The Elusive Corporal predicts the postwar situation within the context of the war's depiction: in a proleptic vision, we see that the end of the war will not eliminate class differences, will not free French men of their problems, and the changes the end of the war *will* bring—such as the enfranchisement of women—loom ahead in scary ways.[33] This is why being stuck in a prison camp even feels comforting to some of the men who, temporarily at least, do not have to contend with the new complexities of a postwar French society. Like Stendhal's romantic hero Fabrizio del Dongo in *The Charterhouse of Parma*, who appears happiest when imprisoned in his tower, the French prisoners find solace in their confinement, for it protects them from the menaces of a crass and changing society.

Akin to a photographic negative, the *absence* of French women protagonists on the screen, and their threatening (negative) image in the minds of Frenchmen, constitute the traces of a deconstructed image of French nationalism in Renoir's film. Instead of thinking through France's status as a nation in terms of internal resolution or a settling of accounts in the postwar era, Renoir thinks of it as a reconciliation *across* national boundaries. Toward the end of the film, the escaped corporal encounters another Frenchman who has decided to stay in Germany with the German widow who helped him escape. Their union symbolically points to reconciliation between nations, but it also underscores the Frenchman's feelings of disenfranchisement: he has nothing to return to in France—no property, no job—so why go back? Renoir's film is undoubtedly a critique of postwar French society, but it is clearly read through a man's eyes.

It is perhaps appropriate to close this discussion of transitional films with a look at Jean-Pierre Melville (1917–1970), whose three films about the war embody the changing optics of their periods and span almost twenty years. The evolution of women's roles in these films is of particular interest because the plots deviate from the Romeo and Juliet model of conflict (that is, love across political affiliation, as in *Hiroshima mon amour* and *The Elusive Corporal*). Or rather, this model is already marked as impossible or displaced by political exigency. From his stark, beautifully stylized rendering of Vercors' *Le Silence de la mer* (*The Silence of the Sea*, 1947), about a Frenchman and his niece who resist, via their silence, the German officer who occupies their home, to the "middle" period with *Leon Morin, Priest* (awarded the Venice Prize, 1961), with its ambiguities and broad range of responses to the German occupation, and finally, to his Gaullist film of a heroic resistance in *L'Armée des ombres* (*Army of Shadows*, 1969), Melville's *oeuvre* offers us the chance to frame the complex transitional period with the two heroic periods on either side of it.

In many ways Melville was a transitional figure in his own right. Belonging neither to the "Tradition of Quality" filmmakers who became famous, or were already so during the war,[34] nor to the younger New Wave, Melville spanned both.[35] Initially, he accepted the adulation of the New Wave, taking on an avuncular role for the younger group of filmmakers (Truffaut, Godard, Chabrol, and Rohmer, for example). His virtually clandestine making of *The Silence of the Sea* turned him into an exemplary figure for the creators of "*auteur* cinema." As an independent, paying close attention to the materiality of his craft, with no union card, little money (producing his own film), and without the rights to Vercors' book, he cut the bold figure of a renegade that was bound to please the younger crowd.[36] His prodigious speed—taking only twenty-seven days—and his daring to film in Vercors' own house (when the latter wasn't home!) completed the audacious image.[37] Melville even agreed later on to play the role of a jovial, lecherous, and pretentious author in Jean-Luc Godard's *Breathless*, as if he were unafraid to risk parodying himself. But, eventually, his predilection for studio film-ing, his tight control over scripts and actors, his desire to draw a large public (without sacrificing the intellectual quality of his work),[38] and his political stances as an ex-resistance fighter and Gaullist, all reveal the distance between him and the young New Wave filmmakers who initially admired him. As Jean-Michel Frodon has aptly pointed out, Melville's early career as a "clandestine film-maker" working in the shadows, without funding or legitimacy, appropriately matches his own participation in the clandestine actions of the resistance during the war. Frodon suggests that Melville's initial association with the New Wave, as well as his fre-quent choice of the popular *film noir* or gangster genres, were so many camouflages for his real work as an independent, virtuoso *auteur*. Even the cloaking of his Jewish identity (changing his name from Jean-Pierre Grumbach to Jean-Pierre Melville, his alias during the war), was maintained after the liberation, and became part of his persona.[39] This leads us to ask: to what extent does Melville's clan-destine resistance not only articulate a self-image, but also one of national identity?

Although Melville's first work, *The Silence of the Sea*, appears at first glance to belong to the heroic period of resistance films, it is really more a precursor to the triumphant renditions of armed resist-ance: Vercors' book was written well before the end of the war (cir-culated clandestinely in 1942) and before the resistance networks had formally organized to any great extent. Its subtle form of resist-ance—a refusal to communicate in the face of a humanized enemy (a rather sympathetic German Francophile)—seems quite meek when compared with the later spirited accounts of armed resistance in 1943–1944 (embodied cinematically by René Clément's 1946 *La Bataille du rail*). Actress Nicole Stéphane, who played the niece in Melville's film, and who had been an active member of the fighting French, was, in fact, initially uncomfortable with her character's pas-sive role[40]: the niece's heroism consists solely of a mute resistance to the German officer Von Ebrennac, for whom she harbors an unspo-ken attraction (see Figure 2.2). Contrary to the book, which was uniformly praised, Melville's faithful adaptation stirred up its share of controversy, particularly on the Left: weren't the French too com-plicit with the occupier, not resisting enough; wasn't the German too

Figure 2.2. *The Silence of the Sea*, Jean-Pierre Melville, 1947. The niece avoids looking at the German soldier.

sympathetic? Nicole Stéphane, reevaluating the film in hindsight, has said that her role represented, for many French, a worthy portrait of themselves as "proud and noble people who hadn't acted but who had still maintained during the ordeal a stately dignity."[41] The typicality (as was the case in *Hiroshima mon amour*) is reinforced by the anonymity of the French characters (whereas the German possesses a proper name and is thus more particularized, perhaps less representative of his nationality).

Melville's contributions to Vercors' story tend, if anything, to strengthen the icon of French resistance. Faithful to the writer's self-sacrificing model of the niece, Melville intensifies the clarity of the dramatic lines. A loud ticking clock in the house measures the depth and discomfort of the silence, as if an explosion of feeling could burst forth at any moment. The stark, high-contrast lighting, low angle shots on Von Ebrennac, and high angle shots on the niece and uncle, set up the implicit power struggle. Von Ebrennac himself refers to speech as a means of "vanquishing" silence, and tells the tale of *The Beauty and the Beast* to suggest the wedding of France and Germany, and of the niece and himself. In the face of Von Ebrennac's narratives of national conciliation and personal seduction, the niece's only weapon to disrupt the double allegory is her unresponsive muteness.

In an added outdoor scene, Melville increases the potential for interaction when he has the niece and the German officer cross paths. The brief passage is visually striking: in a snowy landscape setting off the characters' silhouettes, the niece stalwartly refuses to acknowledge the German's presence as she passes him by. This is a moment when, away from her uncle's gaze, she might have felt free to express her feelings for the German without recrimination. But the niece remains steadfast in her silence, thus showing that it is *her* decision, not just one imposed by an older paternal authority. When asked about this scene's differential shots of the two figures—the reverse angles of the niece are filmed with a fix-focus, and those of the officer with a tracking shot—Melville explains: "because he is walking towards her wanting to *do* something [greet her, speak with her], whereas she is holding herself in check."[42] She is like a frozen icon in the wintry countryside; her resistance lies in *arrested* movement rather than in action. As she advances, she is also physically holding back her dog on a leash, and their tug of war reinforces the conflicted image in which the animal (perhaps a symbol of forbidden desire) tries to free itself.

Melville has said he wanted to make *The Silence of the Sea* precisely because it was such an anti-cinematographic book. His own esthetic takes hold in the niece's resistance as he seeks to create "a language composed entirely of images and sounds, and from which movement and action would be more or less banished."[43] Resistance (to action) becomes both a political symbol and a cinematic strategy. If Nicole Stéphane was right about the niece's ability to represent the French, then this *fixed* image of the niece's movement is Melville's privileged icon of occupied France.

What also strikes me about the Melvillian heroine is the uncanny way she resembles women in pro-Vichy films. As we noted earlier, in the Vichy framework the price of women becoming an idealized national symbol is that they are deprived of the possibility of being desiring humans. Writing his book in the early 1940s, Vercors creates a female figure that harmonizes with the Vichy prototype. The niece becomes an icon precisely because she has been able to betray her own desire.[44] As Burch and Sellier have shown, during the war the female image of self-sacrifice remains operative, whether used by Vichy or by the resistance, just as later films' postwar negativity toward women is independent of the filmmakers' political proclivities.

Melville's transitional film of 1961, *Leon Morin, Priest*, is populated primarily with a cast of female characters working in a correspondence school in Grenoble, and is more a reconstruction of Occupation survival and resistance than a film about *remembering* the past. The script follows very closely the autobiographical novel by Béatrix Beck, which won the prestigious Goncourt prize in 1952.

Beck was, in fact, only the second woman to be awarded this prize. Interestingly enough, the first woman's literary work to win the Goncourt, Elsa Triolet's *A Fine of 200 Francs* (*Le Premier Accroc coûte 200 francs*, 1945), also dealt with World War II and resistance. It is not much of a stretch to link women's active participation in the war and their literary renderings of that experience to the concurrent acknowledgments, albeit tardy, of their abilities as creative artists and of their worthiness to be part of the French electorate. And, yet, even this recognition of women's undertakings during the war holds its own share of ironies. After the Editions de Minuit (Vercors' publishing house) circulated Triolet's work clandestinely during the war, it was ultimately published by the collaborationist publishing house Denoël, which thus got all the credit for publishing a Goncourt Prize recipient.[45]

Leon Morin, Priest's wartime story showcases the young widow, Barny (played by Emmanuelle Riva),[46] whose infatuation with her young priest (an engaging Jean-Paul Belmondo, already famous from Godard's *Breathless*) coincides with/causes her conversion to Catholicism. Barny's first person voice-over orients our attention, provides a point of view, but without offering critical commentary through which to judge the actions presented. The war is featured specifically as *occupation*, that is, as it permeates personal relations and daily existence, but without the immediacy of battle. Although the dialogue is didactic at times, as when communist Barny (widow of a Jew, and newly converted to Catholicism) argues with her pro-Vichy friend Christine about Pétain, collaboration, Jews, and the "French race," the film (like the book) leaves the viewer/reader to draw conclusions and make value judgments. To be sure, Barny's position, which uses Christian arguments to chip away at Christine's collaborationist attitude, easily overcomes the latter:

> Christine: By resisting, you attract reprisals, and that's all you get.
> Barny: In other words, you, a Catholic, consent to having my daughter deported so that yours can have her portion of milk? [Barny's daughter is half Jewish.]
> Christine: Do you think that it's necessary to sacrifice the lives of one's family members even if it's useless?
> Barny: Those who are carted off are just as much your family as the others.
> Christine: They're Jews! So hardly!

Barny: Well, precisely, our Lord is a Jew.[47]

As Joseph Daniel has pointed out, such polemical conversations in 1961 were a means to explore the issue of collaboration, to understand how people might have chosen the wrong path, without excusing it.[48] Beck herself describes the lack of moral commentary as an *esthetic* issue (no doubt wishing to avoid propaganda).[49] Both Beck and Melville keep a relatively light touch, or distance, in presenting a broad array of political positions amongst the women who include supporters of Pétain and of collaboration, as well as Anti-Semites, but also communists, Catholics, Jews, and the wives of *Maquis* resistance fighters. Although their political differences are very real, their daily difficulties (such as work, and the care of children, finding food, safe lodging, and heat) seem to loom larger. This is why it is possible to envision a friendship between resistance supporter Barny and Pétainist Christine (who share a religious and personal interest in Léon Morin).

But of equal importance to the dialogue (and this is no doubt Melville's own imprimatur on the story) are physical objects and material spaces, lighting and sound, which claim our visual and auditory attention,[50] as if to announce their own importance in the human effort to endure. A wood stove, a pear, a gesture, or a noise not only support the dialogue, but also challenge its importance at times. For example, while playing the piano loudly, Léon tells Barny about a sniper who had been shooting from the church tower at the *Miliciens* occupying the hotel across the street. The sniper is never caught, however, because Léon says he opened up the church ever so slowly for the officials, and the "culprit" escaped. The importance of the event recounted is diminished by its competing status for our attention. Not only do we not see the resistance action, its verbal account leaves interpretation up to the listener(s), whose understanding must compete with the music and the visual attributes of Léon playing the piano in his little room. Melville's rivaling sounds, images, and Léon's monologue metaphorically keep us at arm's length from a description of committed resistance. It is perhaps another way of portraying the hidden side of the Occupation, where things often seem to happen without agency, or can only be referred to indirectly. A certain "static" breaks up the message, just as Léon had provided a delay (static) in the search for the resistance sniper.

Melville and Beck both emphasize the *effects* of the Occupation, rather than direct actions, for such is the situation of an occupied town: explosions are heard at night without our knowing exactly where the bombs hit, nor to whom they belong; the priest casually remarks that there are always Jews sleeping in his bed, and that he's turning out new baptism certificates like hot cakes (presumably to hide Jewish identities). The indirection renders the heroic acts that each commits devoid of any heroic aura. On the other side, traitors are handled in the shadows and Vichy sympathizers are taken in stride: two elderly sisters (who have cared for Barny's daughter) nonchalantly explain that while they're in town, they plan to catch a glimpse of the "tondues" (the women accused of "horizontal collaboration") being paraded through the streets with their heads shorn. Barny doesn't register any particular reaction to the spinsters' *Schadenfreude*. Similarly, we watch—without moral commentary— German soldiers identify their victims for roundup by spying their reflections in shop windows. While the spectator *qua* judge has little trouble reading the frightening implications of these reflections, the roundabout way that such actions are represented underscores their sense of unreality: the war-as-occupation is both omnipresent and no where in particular.

This matter-of-fact attitude and the understated sense of drama tend to reduce the war's mythic dimensions. Also used to convey the various political positions of occupied France are satire, caricature, and comedy: a secondary character, Marion, has trouble keeping up the morale of her five lovers, whose political ties cover every group: two are in the resistance, one in the *Milice*, another in the black market, and the last one is a German! Even the military occupation is portrayed with a sense of humor by Beck and Melville: the Italian soldiers' elaborate plumed hats are a source of discreet merriment for the local population. In the film, the successive occupations of this southern town (Grenoble) by regiments of Italians, Germans, and finally, Americans, are each accompanied by an identifying background music that verges on the stereotype (light orchestra for the Italians; ponderous music for the Germans; jazz for the Americans). When the Italians and the Germans cross paths in the street, there is a musical joust between their two presences. Again, this does not mean that a sense of danger is absent from the film, but rather that it is taken as a matter of course in the effort to carry out daily activities.

In contrast to Renoir's *Elusive Corporal* that had concentrated on the male society of a German prison camp in order to think about French identity, Melville's second war film represents occupied France through a female microcosm. "French identity" is no doubt problematic in Beck's case, since the author was Belgian, and the widow of a Polish-Russian Jew, Naum Szapiro. Beck's autobiographical heroine, Barny, whose Jewish husband (like Beck's) died in the war, names her young daughter *France*, as if to anchor her French identity more forcefully, especially at a time when a foreign name, or a Jewish name, would place the child in danger.[51] In the film and book, children's wellbeing is a constant source of concern and reason for action. France, the daughter of communists and half Jewish, must be "Christianized" in order to be safe. In a comical scene, Barny and her women friends (communists, Jews, and other resisters) assign to one another and their spouses the feigned roles of godmothers and godfathers for their various children, but the women get confused about who is supposed to be what to whom, and have to write it all down. The masquerade, with its manufactured marks of faith, is both comical and serious. Resistance identity here involves the construction of *fake* religious ties, but the activity itself develops *real* social bonds amongst the women.

Given that the Occupation is portrayed as a multi-national affair, the film plays with the obvious symbolism of the name of Barny's daughter to suggest an image of the French as shaped by their transnational encounters, by their ability to cope, whoever the occupying force may be. In separate scenes, little France first befriends a German soldier, and then at the liberation is carried playfully on the shoulders of an American GI. The Franco-German rapprochement in the film is in keeping with the early Fifth Republic's developing relations with Germany (working toward European pacifism and the Common Market), all of which tend to loosen the hold of zealous patriotism in favor of interrelations and cross-border cooperation. Joseph Daniel points out that in 1961, "the time was past when one referred to Germans and Nazis interchangeably."[52] The inclusion of the American soldier as part of another occupying, though friendly, force tends to underplay differences between foreign forces: Germans and Americans are both occupiers. In Beck's novel, both sets of soldiers also take on sinister aspects in other scenes: the Germans arrest and deport people; a GI makes unwelcome advances toward Barny. Melville omits this last equalizing detail of the threatening

American, thus politicizing the film more than its literary equivalent, in which the threat of male violence is less a function of political stripe or nationality. Even the "good guys" can be threatening to a woman in Beck's novel.

While Barny's story focuses on her relationship with the priest, it is important to emphasize that the film's ambiguities and paradoxes reside more in the ongoing negotiations with wartime politics, and with the materiality of daily life, than in the conversion/love story. Even if Barny must ultimately renounce her desire for the young priest, her political and ethical positions in the wartime situation are not a source of personal conflict.

As artists, Melville and Beck were particularly well suited to each other. While they both thrived on ambiguities, dualities, and betrayals in their works, both were steadfast in their support of resistance during the war. Beck, whose character Barny keeps personal friendships and political affiliations distinct, recounts in her own memoirs an even greater dissociation between personal attraction and social commitment: although a certain magnetism existed in the 1950s between her and Roger Nimier, the rebellious young dandy of the Right, she and he tactfully avoided discussing politics together, for both realized that they were at opposite ends of the political spectrum.[53] This compartmentalization of interests recalls "Elle"'s dissociation of love and war (or love and patriotism) in *Hiroshima mon amour*. But Melville's recycling of actress Emmanuelle Riva in *Leon Morin, Priest* marks the differences between the characters just as much as their similarities. Whereas "Elle's" trauma is structured as a confrontation between individual and community (or country), Barny belongs to a community of women, and her unrealized romantic longings for the priest merely underscore the typical solitude of women during the war. While marriages and romantic heterosexual relationships suffer with the absence of eligible men, new friendships and rapports, sometimes odd ones, arise in the interval. Melville is known for shunning the representation of romantic love. Beck's female microcosm, with all its compromises, betrayals, friendships, and generosities, is well suited to Melville's light-handed treatment of the twists of Occupation politics. *Leon Morin, Priest* often registers a smile at the abundance of complications and details about the French and their occupiers that *The Silence of the Sea* could not have shown in 1946. Beck's and Melville's women are the sign of French society's multiplicity in response to the war.

* * *

"As I grow older, I look back with nostalgia on the years from 1940 to 1944, because they are part of my youth.[54]

Melville's third war film, *Army of Shadows*, aired four months after De Gaulle's resignation in 1969, so it comes at the tail end of the Gaullist period of heroic war films. It is based on the 1944 book of the same name by Joseph Kessel, who has been called "Free France's hagiographer."[55] Kessel's book is a resounding tribute to the men and women who worked in the Gaullist ranks of resistance, and who risked their lives daily. The "army of shadows" fights a war of secret attacks and hasty executions with stalwart courage. Jean-Michel Frodon has described Melville's film as "one of the best French films on the Resistance,"[56] and "the first stone for the posthumous statue of 'France's savior.'"[57] De Gaulle (played by an actor) even appears on screen in a London scene. In a silent moment full of pomp and patriotic emotion, the figure of the towering Général leans forward (his back to the camera) to pin a medal on a resistance group leader whose face seems to bathe in the beatific light of Free France's leader. The image is more than a tad maudlin and would certainly seem to guarantee this film's credentials as a stereotype for resistance cinema.[58]

Despite such clichés, however, the film as a whole confounds the over-simplified image of the resistance, and tends to shun picturesque details in favor of a suspenseful drama. I would argue that Melville's collective portrait of resistance continually emphasizes the necessarily hidden side of resistance fighting, and tends to darken, in symbolic and visual modes, any clean, bright image of heroic action. Many of the scenes take place in the dark, with the shadowy night figures accomplishing their tasks in quasi-anonymity. To have one's identity known is to risk one's own or one's friends' death. The higher one rises in the hierarchy, the more one's identity must be protected. Melville draws attention to this compartmentalization of the group through the structure of the plot. Through the juxtaposition of scenes, the viewer gradually develops an overview of the organization and the characters' interactions, whereas the characters themselves frequently remain in the dark (literally and figuratively). We watch, for example, an episode in which the young ex-aviator Jean-François prepares to die in prison, unbeknownst to his network.

We piece together from prior scenes that he has let himself be arrested in order to help out a fellow member of his network, Félix, who is being tortured in prison by the Germans. (Jean-François will offer his only cyanide pill to the dying friend.) Although the spectator understands Jean-François' disappearance, the other characters never find out what happens to him, and remain puzzled. Similarly, Jean-François dies not knowing that his older brother, Luc Jardie, who appears to be a gentle intellectual with his head in the clouds, is actually the chief of the network, the great "Boss" with nerves of steel.

Identity is a function of disguises and masks for Melville. He also plays with the substitutability of resistance identities, as if to underscore the organic unit of the network over its individual members. In one scene, a character nicknamed "the Mask" enters a café to meet with Mathilde, who is also a member of the same network. After the camera films the Mask's face upon coming through the door into the café, the next shot switches to Mathilde and the reflection in the mirror behind her. But in the reflection, we are now looking at Jean-François, not the Mask. In a third shot of the same café scene, Mathilde is speaking to a third member, nicknamed "the Bison," in the same seat that the Mask and Jean-François had previously occupied. To add to the confusion, we don't actually hear Mathilde speak; instead, we recognize the voice of a fourth man, the group's leader, Philippe Gerbier, who is introducing Mathilde to the viewer, not the men. The switch in characters and the competing subject matter of the voice-over underscore the confusion about identities, but we also are made aware that the rank and file men are interchangeable, and that the scene emphasizes a *collective* operation.

Several critics have noted Melville's tendency to insist on ambiguities and on instances when cops and robbers look alike. His propensity for American gangster movies and *film noir* is well known. As Jacques Zimmer and Chantal de Béchade point out: "Melville didn't wait for *Lacombe Lucien* to pose the problem of 'chance and necessity' and to make us feel how fragile the border between traitor and hero, lawman and outlaw, is. *Army of Shadows* bears witness to this uncertainty of destinies and methods."[59] The political emphasis, however, is entirely different, given that Malle features an anti-hero (a Frenchmen working for the German police), whereas Melville spotlights heroes of the underground. Nevertheless, in both, simple oppositions between good and evil are disrupted by the exploration in depth of one of the poles. Although the Germans remain within the standard repertory of representations (soldiers, Nazis, and torturers), and Vichy officials do not figure prominently,[60] the resistance is painted in a variety of tones and attitudes, and frequently takes on sinister traits as the camera explores at length the actions of one network.

Resistance leader Philippe Gerbier is expertly played by actor Lino Ventura, whose rugged features and prior gangster roles make him the quintessential grim, tough guy. In this instance, however, he is also a stalwart, committed hero. The courageous image becomes seriously complicated, and even tainted, when his singularly focused dedication to resistance causes the death of the innocent. In an early scene that Melville added, Gerbier manages to escape the Gestapo by having another detained Frenchman flee before him. The German soldiers quickly run after the other guy, and we hear shots in that direction, attesting to the other's probable death. Because the soldiers run after the first escapee, Gerbier is able to get away, unharmed. Although he has not meant to hurt the other Frenchman, his actions produce this result.

The next episode shows Gerbier's little group picking up an informant, the young Dounat, who had caused Gerbier's detention in the first place. In a particularly disconcerting, graphic scene, three resistance members, including Gerbier, execute Dounat by strangling him to death. The sinister settling of accounts by these men resembles too closely the Nazi executions of partisans and civilians. The executed informant looks more like a victim than an aggressor in Melville's story: the spectator as witness winces at the ugly side of resistance action. Later on, Gerbier takes refuge at the palatial estate of the Baron de Ferté Talloire, who jokes with Gerbier about his prewar past as an anti-Republican, ready to storm the *préfecture* on horseback were there to be a royalist takeover. Clearly this man has come a long way in his views to be able to fully support the resistance against the anti-Republican government of Vichy. But as the camera focuses on the Baron occupied with his horses, Gerbier's voice informs the spectator that the Baron and his household were executed by the Germans just after Gerbier left. This is "collateral damage" about which Gerbier only expresses his feeling of good fortune at having gotten away soon enough. Melville has intensified the image of unmitigated dedication to the point that Gerbier starts to resemble his foes.

Although Gerbier is clearly a prototypical hero whose directness signifies his commitment, it is Mathilde, magnificently played by Simone Signoret, who occupies the film's center, not because she is on camera more than the other network members—she is featured relatively late in the film—but because she embodies *different kinds of resistance*, is the only one to suffer the dilemma of choosing between family and network, and is the only one to become the ambiguous victim of the network. She offers another version of heroism that ultimately seems incompatible with her male counterparts' understanding.

Mathilde is the quiet hero of resistance who provides a perfect counterpoint to Gerbier. Whereas *he* is "poorly equipped for role-playing,"[61] *she* is flexible and thrives on disguises and new identities. This unassuming mother and wife works without her husband's knowledge, and can metamorphose herself at will. The vamp, the widow, the elderly matron or nurse—are all part of her repertory, which Melville presents in a quick series of mini-scenes in which Mathilde changes disguises (with the explanatory voice-over of Gerbier). Looking into a mirror as she adjusts each outfit, Mathilde appears not as a narcissist reveling in her image, but rather as a theatrical performer gauging the verisimilitude of a costume. In effect, her role is *to be seen*, whereas the evaluative gaze is Gerbier's (and ours).

The nature of the differences between Mathilde and Gerbier is already indicated by the way they are referred to: a first name for her (connoting familiarity), a last name for him. Whereas Gerbier tends to be abrupt, especially with those under his command, Mathilde is egalitarian and inspires confidence: Jean-François feels more camaraderie and understanding with her in two minutes than he does in a lifetime with his older brother Luc. Both Gerbier and Luc (the "Boss") recognize in her "an extraordinary woman," "made to command as much as to obey." She is described as a superb organizer and a methodical, patient tactician. The opinions in Gerbier's voice-over and dialogue are ratified by action that we see on screen.[62] She masterminds a last-minute rescue of Gerbier, who is about to be executed by the Germans. When Félix is caught by the Gestapo, she presents a cogent plan for getting Félix out *alive*, whereas Gerbier's first thought is to kill Félix off so he won't suffer under torture. Later, when Mathilde's plan ripens, Gerbier is adamant about being part of it, but Mathilde argues correctly that his participation would be too dangerous (putting others in jeopardy), and that the network can hardly afford to lose him. Her logic is confirmed during the plan's realization when she notices, in the German prison, Gerbier's photo among the most wanted resisters. At each turn, Mathilde's finesse, wisdom, and warmth trump Gerbier's obtuseness. Her protection of life contrasts with Gerbier's readiness to kill.

Mathilde has all the qualities of an inspiring leader, but she also bears the classical hero's "tragic fault." While Gerbier appears to have no private life, and Jean-François is detached from his brother, Mathilde carries on family commitments and lives a double life, only half of which do we witness.[63] Her love for her daughter, whose photo she carries with her, is her Achilles' heel.[64] The Gestapo arrests Mathilde, identifies the photo, and threatens to prostitute Mathilde's daughter if she doesn't reveal names and places pertaining to the network. This time, there is no one to proclaim ingenuity and life over the "necessity" of eradication as she had done for Gerbier and Félix, so Mathilde will be gunned down by her compatriots. The "Boss" even makes an eloquent argument about how Mathilde would want them to kill her, although he admits in private that he has invented these remarks and doesn't know what she would think. When they drive up and the Bison pulls the trigger, it is impossible to read anything other than recognition in Mathilde's expression. Melville refuses to exonerate the male members of the network in this execution (see Figure 2.3).

Now it is certainly true that *all* members of this network are eventually killed, and we sense early on that this story is primarily about *dead* heroes. The final photo-portraits of each of the remaining characters are accompanied by the time, place, and manner of their deaths. But it is Mathilde's death that is showcased via the action, for she is the one to be killed by her own group as a traitor. It is as if the price for this woman's incarnation of the ultimate symbol of what the resistance ought to be is an un-heroic death at the hands of her friends. The choice between family and public combat is deemed impossible; the woman's qualities, while laudable, can only be held up for adulation in the recounting of her eventual demise.[65] Although this film may belong to the period in which patriarchal authority is in full force (De Gaulle's brief but commanding presence in the film should attest to that), the female icon of national resistance retains the same kind of ambiguity that we have seen in films of the transition period. Mathilde's death is a function of her inability

Figure 2.3. *The Army of Shadows*, Jean-Pierre Melville, 1969. Mathilde stares at her executioners.

to negotiate the public/private split—a complication that none of her colleagues confront. Her martyrdom hinges upon that duality, and makes her an ambiguous heroic symbol.

Henry Rousso has said that Melville's masterpiece could not really fill the bill as the official myth of resistance because "too much concerned with individual fates, the film lacked political punch."[66] I would argue instead that its "lack of political punch" is less a matter of individual fates diminishing the power of myth. Melville has, in fact, said that characters such as Gerbier, as well as Luc Jardie, represent composites of men he had known during the Occupation. His portraits offer a typicality that exceeds individual fates. Rather, the smooth surface of myth is eroded because Melville gives *such close scrutiny* to this "army of shadows." It is similar to a cinematic close-up, when the beauty (or even recognition) of a face begins to disintegrate because of previously unnoticed flaws, or from a loss of proportion, or because the head is cut off from its bodily moorings. Mary Ann Doane's description of the close-up's properties uncannily describes Melville's individual resistance network in relation to the resistance as a whole, and still more generally, to French society: "The close-up performs the inextricability of these two seemingly opposed formulations, simultaneously posing as both microcosm and macrocosm, detail and whole . . . Faced with an accelerating rationalization, specialization, and disintegration of the sense of a social totality, the subject clings to the hope or simulacra of wholeness. The close-up, with its contradictory status (as both detail of a larger scene and totality in its own right—a spectacle of scale with its own integrity) responds to this need . . . The scale of the close-up transforms the face into an instance of the gigantic, the monstrous: it overwhelms."[67] In Melville's film, the discomforting resemblance between resistance tactics and those of its enemy give the resistance a gruesome quality. The closer one looks at it, the less it is recognizable, so that the myth is deconstructed from within. What better image than the sacrifice of Mathilde, one of the resistance's own and one of its best, to symbolize both the glory *and* the nastiness of resistance fighting? In the moments when Melville's film *resists* the more simplistic aspects of myth, when it turns away from political dogma, the work is at its strongest. This doesn't mean that it is without political import; rather, its impact derives precisely from the competing versions of resistance in Gerbier and Mathilde. Recalling the niece's arrested movement in *The Silence of the Sea*, Mathilde's final gaze at the camera just before she is gunned down leaves us with another image frozen in time. But, whereas the niece's decision to resist was her own, Mathilde's static image carries with it doubts about who chooses her death.

Margaret Atack has convincingly argued that the treatment of the resistance in *Army of Shadows* reflects the end of the Gaullist era when it was made.[68] According to her, this post-May 1968 film emphasizes a peculiar form of anti-establishment resistance: Melville focuses on transgressive resistance, a shadowy underground that evades recognized institutions such as the state, the army, the nation, and traditional political parties, much in the way May 1968 student and worker revolts challenged those institutions. I would add that the double image of heroism present in Melville's film also coincides with the unraveling of masculinist versions of heroism in the late 1960s. Although patriarchal authority triumphs in the name of the collective cause in *Army of Shadows*, Mathilde's final head-on gaze at the camera (and hence at us) carries with it an implicit interrogation/ accusation. In a Freudian vein, we might ask: "What does this woman want?" with the understanding that this "dark continent"— woman—wears an impenetrable look that is precisely the sign of the "army of shadows." The spectator is left to ponder the *two* versions of resistance that Gerbier and Mathilde provide.

From muted, singular resistance, to a surviving community, and finally to heroic collective resistance, Melville highlights three female images to portray the ways in which France endured and resisted the Occupation. His personal style of nuanced, ambiguous portraits from all three eras associates him most closely with the particularities of the transitional period. His attention to detail, and to complication in the negotiation between daily existence and historic events of the war, accompanies a focus on women's lives as models for the dilemmas of occupied life. *Army of Shadows* resists much of the facile stereotyping and conformism to be found in popular, comedic films of the late 1950s and 1960s, such as *Babette Goes to War* and *La Grande Vadrouille* (*Don't Look Now, We've Been Shot at*, Gérard Oury, 1966). Although all his war films emphasize France's resistance to occupation more than complacent collaboration, thereby exonerating the French for the most part, his female icons still retain equivocal poses that reveal both the changing character of women's social roles and the problematic nature of French identity during the war. If the latter two issues are not identical, they nevertheless seem intricately intertwined.

CHAPTER 3

IDENTITY POLITICS IN
FILMS OF THE 1970S

FILM AND POLITICS

In the France of the early 1970s, on the heels of the "events of May 1968," with their worker strikes and student protests, political culture and political analysis increasingly infused the understanding and creation of art forms. On the Left, artists and critics alike sought to explore what were perceived as the necessary links between new art forms and political representations of the real. During this "Maoist period" at France's leading film journal, *Les Cahiers du cinéma*, films, if they were to be worthy of respect, needed to exhibit a commitment to a clear political viewpoint, and many filmmakers wished to make themselves the agents of political change. The re-release of Jean Renoir's 1936 communist sponsored film *La Vie est à nous* ("Life Is Ours"), with its collective authorship (Renoir, André Zwobada, Jacques Becker, Jean-Paul Dreyfus, Jacques B. Brunius, Pierre Unik) and forthright militancy, confirms the political aura of the period. The reviews of a Pascal Bonitzer or a Christian Zimmer in the *Cahiers* of the early 1970s adhered to a Marxist critical perspective in which ideology inevitably played a key role (with nothing escaping the political). Set against successive regimes of conservative political leaders (Presidents Georges Pompidou and Valéry Giscard d'Estaing), much of the critical theory of the period was informed by the (post)structuralist Marxist political theory of Louis Althusser and Pierre Macherey. With the release of Marcel Ophüls's documentary *The Sorrow and the Pity* in 1969, the political stage was set for the flood of feature films reviewing France's collaboration with the Nazis at individual and collective levels. On the Right, the *mode rétro*, the vogue of 1940s nostalgia, held sway in fiction and memoirs, with many of the children of ex-collaborators writing about their parents, and in some instances justifying them.

The early 1970s were thus a self-conscious period when politics and esthetics were often called upon to form a unity of vision. "The problem is not how to make *political* films but to make films *politically*," declared Jean-Luc Godard's radical film collective, the Dziga-Vertov group, in 1968. As critic Colin MacCabe notes, Godard insisted that the political nature of film should arise from the cinematic creation itself, not through the importation of a political topic into the filmmaking.[1] Godard explored the politics of the image in order to determine, as Jill Forbes puts it in her discussion of Godard's *Tout va bien* ("All Is Well") and Marin Karmitz's *Coup sur coup* ("One after the Other"), "whether different things should be filmed or whether things should be filmed differently."[2] Both films deal with a workers' strike, but Forbes makes a clear distinction between Karmitz, the traditional militant leftist filmmaker (for whom artistic expression serves a political message) and Godard, whose self-conscious artistry (pointing out the film's own production, and its focus on multiple frames) tends to supersede any unequivocal political content in the "main" story of the workers' strike. Forbes argues that in *Tout va bien* this quintessentially political topic becomes an exercise in "formal audacity" with a multiplicity of points of view that ultimately results in a film that is "politically incoherent."[3] In either instance (Karmitz or Godard), the interaction between politics and esthetics never quite forms a unified vision.

Feature films about the Occupation made during the early 1970s are certainly not immune to this urge to weave together artistic and political threads. Several fictional films shown to French audiences in the mid 1970s offer prime instances—in their making and reception—of thoughtful, creative articulations of art and politics. Among them are Michel Drach's *Les Violons du bal* ("The Violins at the Ball") and Louis Malle's *Lacombe Lucien*.[4] Although we will be focusing on *Lacombe Lucien* because of its broad audience and the intense reactions the film elicited, Michel Drach's autobiographical film is perhaps the 1970s film that most insistently frames the representation of the past—Drach's Occupation childhood—with a representation of the present (Drach's making of the film). This self-reflexive personal film emphasizes that the construction of the past is articulated through memory rather than through impersonal, "objective" facts. It interweaves Drach's passion for the techniques of his craft, his obsession with a Jewish childhood lived under the threat of deportation, and a political attention to the relationship between past and present (including the "May '68 generation"). Drach implicitly responds to Godard's injunction to explore how to "make a film politically," and his film embodies the obsession of the 1970s to recall a past that had previously been buried, that the public did not want to hear about (which is what potential producers keep telling Drach *in* his film). *Les Violons du bal* is no doubt a precursor to later, postmodern films of the 1990s, such as *Un Héros très discret* (*A Self-Made Hero*), while also recalling earlier films that frame a buried past, such as Duvivier's *Marie Octobre* and Resnais's *Hiroshima mon amour*. Its focus on the child of the Occupation belongs to an autobiographical tradition, including Claude Berri's *The Two of Us* (*Le Vieil Homme et l'enfant*, 1966) and Louis Malle's *Goodbye Children* (*Au Revoir les enfants*, 1987). But while *Les Violons du bal* intersects with a number of important cinematic trends in representing the Occupation, it is nevertheless *Lacombe Lucien* that has generated the most impassioned reactions among the 1970s feature films on the Occupation.

SALUBRIOUS SCANDALS / EFFECTIVE PROVOCATIONS: IDENTITY POLITICS SURROUNDING *LACOMBE LUCIEN*

Relatively small numbers of the French public actually saw Marcel Ophüls's *The Sorrow and the Pity* in a movie theater in 1971, when it was first released in France, and its television airing was blocked by French government officials until 1981. So it is somewhat of a paradox that this film came to represent a crucial turning point in the way the French public would remember the Occupation. What is clear, however, is that the film's emphasis on collaboration, countering more than a decade of official insistence on the Gaullist myth of a national, generalized heroic resistance to the Germans and to the Vichy government, triggered an explosion of critical re-evaluations of French citizens' involvement in collaboration, betrayal, and anti-Semitism in a way no other French film or book had previously done.

A strong supporter of Ophüls's film, Louis Malle had been instrumental in the distribution of *The Sorrow and the Pity* to French movie theaters when it was refused for state owned French television because of the controversial nature of its content. Malle's own 1974 film, *Lacombe Lucien*, was one of the first commercially successful films to pass through the floodgate opened up by Ophüls and his co-producers, André Harris and Alain de Sédouy. It can be argued that, for the general public in the 1970s, *Lacombe Lucien* had a greater impact in changing the understanding/memory of the past than *The Sorrow and the Pity*. Malle's film was seen by more spectators, and as a feature film, captured the public's imagination through the highly provocative story of a rough adolescent peasant, Lucien Lacombe, who, more by accident than by conscious choice, ends up on the wrong side, as a thug working for the German police in 1944.[5] Although Ophüls's use of numerous interwoven interviews from the present, and actual film clips from the Occupation, was no doubt highly effective as a political critique of collaboration and Pétainism, the controversial allure of Malle's storytelling goes a step further. Whereas Ophüls's interviews offer a relatively balanced proportion of time and of numbers of interviews to resisters and collaborators, Malle's fiction focuses more on French collaborators and a range of forms of collaboration.[6] Based on a script created by Patrick Modiano, but anchored in historical anecdote, *Lacombe Lucien*'s power lies in a dramatic fiction that seems opaque on moral issues, and as such, makes of it a lightning rod for political discussions dealing with commitment, free choice, and collaboration.

The notoriety of *Lacombe Lucien* in the 1970s can, to a certain extent, be understood in terms of the relationships between historical event and fictive creation, along the precarious borders between unlikely facts and realistic stories, and between documentary and fiction. But its questionable reputation is also a function of the general climactic change on the 1970s cultural scene, as political criticism permeated all domains (with the phrase "work of art" sometimes becoming a term of derision for the Left).

Where does Malle figure in the debates on political film, however one defines it (as a realistic content or a questioning of representation)? Can one make a political film about collaboration that is not invariably complicit with iniquitous political choices? For many on the Left, the answer in the 1970s was clearly "no." Unlike Michel Drach, Malle also does not offer up Godard-style, self-conscious framing devices that would emphasize film's ability to *construct* reality rather than to give us a fiction as if it were real. Nevertheless, we will see that the interplay between fiction and reality in Malle's film, the profound ambivalence that the story harbors concerning questions of personal and collective identity, and the crucial role of spectator as decipherer and judge, all make it closer to Godard's vision of filmmaking than one might have thought.[7] No single political message arises in Malle's portrait of collaboration.

Given the polarized political situation of the 1970s, it is not surprising that many of the Left/Right political battles were being funneled through references to the war. As the Left laid claim to the Resistance, and the Right held on to Vichy and a politics of "reconciliation" (often a handy euphemism for justifying collaboration), Malle's film became a center of controversy. Marc Ferro includes *Lacombe Lucien* among the important films that "reveal an independence vis-à-vis dominant ideological currents. They create and offer a vision of an unseen world, a world of their own which arouses a new awareness with such force that existing ideological institutions (political parties, churches . . . etc.) struggle with and back away from these works as if these institutions and they alone had the right to express themselves in the name of God, the nation, or the proletariat."[8]

The particular ways *Lacombe Lucien* has shocked and incensed so many of its critics in the 1970s—and continues to do so now for some—are to my mind revelatory, not just of the ideological debates of the 1970s, but also of France's ongoing identity crisis. As the obsession with the memory of the Holocaust intensified from the mid-1970s on, literature, film, and art in general, have often become suspect because of their ability to shape events and thus alter or falsify history. As late as 1992, Stanley Hoffmann accused *Lacombe Lucien* of making its own false myth of the Occupation (with French collaborationism too prominently portrayed).[9] The tardy public revelations of ex-President François Mitterrand in the early 1990s about his own ties to collaboration during the war no doubt helped feed the flames of debate much longer than one might have expected. But the renewed commitment to be "faithful" to the truth of the past by such imminent historians as Henry Rousso has also generated a false sense of security in the historian's ability *over* the creative work to state *the* (only) truth about the past. My contention is that the "faults" that render *Lacombe Lucien* "more provocative than thought-provoking" (to use Rousso's critical evaluation)[10] are the mark of artistic strategies that have produced two major effects: first, these strategies are instrumental in breaking down the official, "clean" memory of the Occupation for a large public; second, they have triggered defensive reactions among critics that reveal some of the most sensitive, unresolved issues in reviewing France's ethical responsibilities (individually and collectively) during the war. It is in this way that Malle's film may be seen as connected to Godard's project of "filming politically."

Like Ophüls's *The Sorrow and the Pity*, *Lacombe Lucien* was not just a representation or account of the issue of collaboration in the past, but rather its performance for the spectator, that is, a reworking in the present of the issue of collaboration. As Richard J. Golsan pointed out: "The film is less a symptom of what Henry Rousso has labeled the Vichy Syndrome than its victim."[11] *Lacombe Lucien* was in effect less involved in repressing or twisting truths about the Occupation than some critics have claimed. Critics' political agendas have, in fact, often hampered rather than helped their evaluations of the film, particularly on issues of collaboration. Rather than simply identifying *Lacombe Lucien* as one more myth about France's wartime years, we will be looking at how Malle and Modiano's film turns to fiction and art to account more forcefully for historical facts concerning French collaboration—often in ways that were difficult for critics to accept because the recognition of these facts was too painful, too threatening (because potentially generalizable), or too well hidden by "clean" (unambiguous) versions of events.

Setting aside an oppositional model of history versus fiction, I'd like to stress the ways in which *Lacombe Lucien* dramatizes the calamity of collaboration, without excusing it. There is no doubt a relatively abundant literature from the *mode rétro* period that *does* absolve collaborators in the act of telling, particularly in the case of children writing about their parents' wartime activities. Pascal Jardin's *La Guerre à neuf ans* ("The War at Age Nine"), Marie Chaix's *Les Lauriers du Lac de Constance* ("The Laurels of Lake Constance"), and Jean-Pierre Maxence's *L'Ombre d'un père* ("The Shadow of a Father") are the most notable, but there are many others.[12] In these works, a first person narrator—each the child of a collaborator—interprets a father's past with a sympathetic eye. I hope to argue, however, that *Lacombe Lucien* does not follow the same pattern of exoneration through understanding.

In Malle's film, the nation's duplicity during the war is articulated through ethnic, class, and gender issues. The cultured, bourgeois, Jewish woman who falls in love with Lucien, the young peasant working for the German police, is named *France*, as if to underscore ironically questions of national identity as they are tied to anti-Semitism, class and gender difference, and betrayal (political, ethnic, and social).[13] At the same time, naming the Jewish girl "France" renders manifest the parental desire to affirm the child's right to French identity, to belong to French society. We remember the little daughter of Jewish origin in Melville's *Leon Morin, Priest*, who is also named France and who befriends a German soldier. In both Malle's and Melville's films, the patriotic tenor of this female name ambiguously hides one identity (ethnic) in favor of another (national).[14] To the irritation and anguish of some, *Lacombe Lucien* shows French identity as performance, a rehearsing of traits and names whose evolution is subject to the arbitrariness of the sign, as well as to chance and unexpected twists, rather than as a portrayal of the innate or static.

If I have chosen to study in detail Malle's first film about the Occupation instead of the later, more directly autobiographical film, *Goodbye, Children* (1987), that deals with a child's vision of collaboration and personal complicity (a version of Malle's own), it is because both the later film and the period in which it appeared no longer carried within them the *intense scandal* of collaboration. By 1987, the portrayal of collaboration had become more commonplace, acceptable, and was less inclined to challenge the meaning of French identity. Nevertheless, *Lacombe Lucien is* somewhat of an ambiguous screen memory for Malle; it readies him to retell later a childhood memory[15] that he describes as "the most significant event of [his] childhood," a sort of primal scene, but it also keeps him from dealing with that personal memory more immediately.[16] The delay is key in that the second film will indirectly implicate the filmmaker-child in an act of collaboration. Whereas Truffaut had concentrated on, in *Four Hundred Blows* (1959), a personal story whose wartime context was not brought forth until *The Last Metro* (1980), Malle writes himself into the scene of the war (*Goodbye, Children*) only after portraying a harsher version of youthful complicity (*Lacombe Lucien*). I will return in the final section of this chapter to the autobiographical dimension of *Goodbye, Children* for Malle (who was age eight at the start of the war) once we have mapped out the issues for *Lacombe Lucien*.

SCANDALOUS FICTIONS

Historical fiction brings together Louis Malle's enduring interests in documentary, autobiographical anecdote, historical event, and the creative choices of the cinematic storyteller, in this case, the joint effort of Modiano and Malle. It appears freer than a documentary like *The Sorrow and the Pity*, in that its ties to a historical reality remain looser: *Lacombe Lucien*'s fiction focuses on the lives of unknown villains and heroes, with national figures only looming in the background. On the other hand, its creative moves cannot escape the close scrutiny of those concerned with historical meanings involving the dark side of the Occupation. The issue of accountability is always at hand. *Lacombe Lucien*'s mixtures of fact and fiction also cause it to straddle clear-cut generic categories that would confirm its meaning(s). In contrast to Ophüls, who, according to Malle, "wanted to make a point . . . to expose French collaboration . . . making a moral judgement," Malle says that in his own film he "wanted to scrutinize a kind of behaviour that is very hard to understand and was certainly contemptible."[17] While both films explore the historical period, Malle's feature focuses on an individual collaborator in a limited time frame (a few months in 1944). Malle is less concerned with advancing an ideological message than with revealing the plausibility of the implausible, that is, with helping us, via a specific plot, to fathom an iniquitous political choice, with neither ideology nor an evil "nature" providing a (reassuring) explanatory cause. In Hannah Arendt's terms (that Malle himself used to describe his film), *Lacombe Lucien* is a fictive enactment of the "banality of evil."[18] Like Eichmann's crimes, Lucien Lacombe's criminal acts are rooted in conformism and thoughtlessness.

    The scandal that swirled around the film in the first few months of its showing quickly took on a double focus: the film was evaluated (and most often attacked) on the basis of its ambiguity toward its collaborating protagonist, and for its refusal to portray the latter as politically aware. Although prior to *The Sorrow and the Pity* the collaborator had frequently been someone who had sold out to the enemy for personal gain, the documentary set up new expectations about collaboration. The interviews, for example, with Christian de la Mazière, the eloquent, self-assured ex-ideologue who had consciously chosen to be a member of the Charlemagne division of the German Waffen SS, startlingly revealed a political collaboration that was ideologically grounded and had little to do with a Lucien Lacombe. In addition, as Rousso points out, Lucien does not follow the example of Paul Touvier, ex-official of the *Milice*, whose iniquitous deeds during the war were coming to light at about the same time that Malle's film was released.[19] It is thus a "bad" performance of collaboration for some of the 1970s' public, particularly because it does not originate in intention or clear motivation. (Rousso even asserts: "Malle turned his back on history."[20]) But the film also disturbed many in the period because its portrayal seemed *too* realistic, excessively so: the film's colors were too vivid, the attention to historical detail (clothing, cars, styles) was irritatingly too accurate (stressing accuracy over meaning).[21] For most, such care was a sign of the *mode rétro*, which in its more negative senses signaled an unhealthy reveling in the depiction of the Occupation. One may wonder, nevertheless, how much the public's discomfort in the face of this realism was actually due to the effectiveness of the depiction of French collaboration with the Germans, and to the film's implicit links with contemporary politics. With the arrest in Bolivia of Nazi official, Klaus Barbie (the assassin of resistance leader, Jean Moulin), and President Pompidou's pardon of Paul Touvier, polemics surrounding the nature of collaboration were in the air.[22]

The character Lucien was no doubt disturbing to certain critics because he did not replicate conventional patterns of collaboration.[23] Both on the Right and the Left, critics were troubled by the absence of ideological fervor in Malle's protagonist. The filmmaker's apparent unwillingness to make his protagonist's metaphorical black hat appear anything other than an accoutrement, rather than part of a fundamental political identity or nature, brought harsh criticisms, especially, although not exclusively, from the political Left. Even Ophüls was reportedly shocked by the ambiguity of *Lacombe Lucien*.[24]

Historian Paul Jankowski has aptly pointed out that *The Sorrow and the Pity* gives "top billing" to an aristocratic collaborator and a peasant resister, as if to confirm and perhaps widen the class gap between the good guys and the bad, whereas Jankowski notes that

"*Lacombe Lucien* blurred edges."[25] The conviction that class appur-
tenance determined which side one chose (resistance or collaboration) recalls the claims of Sartre and the Left at the end of the war
when they maintained that it was mostly the bourgeoisie and rich
elites who were guilty of collaboration, not the working class or
peasants.[26]

Given Malle's own wealthy bourgeois origins and his family's
Pétainist leanings during the war, some critics have understandably
accused him of hiding bourgeois guilt and complicity under Lucien's
peasant status. His associations in the 1950s with Roger Nimier,
who wrote the script for Malle's 1957 film *Ascenseur pour l'échafaud*
(*Elevator to the Gallows*), also renders Malle's political position suspect when one is evaluating the political and ethical roots of his 1974
film. Contrary to a proven Leftist like novelist Béatrix Beck (*Leon
Morin, Priest*), who flirted with Nimier and Maurrasian Pierre
Boutang, Malle had fewer clear ties to political agendas or parties,
and his family background was resolutely conservative. For my purposes, however, it is not necessary to try to ferret out authorial intentions (whether conscious or not) in reading the film. Malle's
pronouncements about his film can be considered in tandem with
those of critics and historians. What is perhaps most striking about
the critiques of *Lacombe Lucien* is that the politicized analyses frequently complaining about the ambiguity of the protagonist resort
to eliminating some of the ambiguity of various scenes. This elimi-
nation allows critics to make a stronger case for a Manichean reading
of the film (that is, as a film sympathetic to the Right and to collaboration). After reviewing how Lucien's character embodies the
ambiguities of collaboration, we will look at the ways in which the
film's critics have reacted to these ambiguities.

MIXED MESSAGES

Ambiguity is understandably intolerable for the moralist. Its manipulation can contaminate the righteous on the one hand, or attenuate
the guilty's responsibilities on the other. One need only think of
Holocaust negationists to appreciate the noxious effects of refusing
evidence. With the advent of the *mode rétro* in the 1970s, Michel
Foucault described the stakes of films on the Occupation in terms
of a fight to articulate—and thus appropriate—the popular memory

of the war. He pointed out that the Right was turning everybody into a collaborator (with a certain complicity between Gaullists and the Right), while the Left clung to the memory of popular resistance.[27] Clearly, the debate on political ambiguity was a charged one that colored both the making and the viewing of films on the period.[28] And, yet, strategic indeterminacy, as it promotes the play of multiple meanings and interpretations challenging us to rethink the world and its representations, can also be read as the mark of a strong work of art, rather than as a sign of insufficiency or negativity. If we liken one form of thoughtlessness, as Hannah Arendt does, to the "complacent repetition of 'truths' which have become trivial and empty," then a work of art that portrays this—and in the process makes us uncertain of our assumptions about the past—may well help to reopen the prematurely closed doors of meaning.[29] The intolerably ambiguous has the potential to make us review memories that have become too pat. For many French remembering the Occupation in the early 1970s, the Gaullist myth of "resistancialism" had clearly become one of those unexamined, empty truths (that neglected or underplayed the populations' part in collaboration and anti-Semitism). In the case of *Lacombe Lucien*, the burden of interpreting actions is particularly heavy on the spectator, who is compelled to ask questions about the nature of collaboration without a reassuring voice-over or political message to confirm the "proper" way to read the film. This is both the film's strength and its vulnerability. At a time in the early 1970s when the battle lines between political responsibility and a certain estheticism closed in upon itself were well marked, the esthetic opacity of Malle's film, as it enacted murky political questions for the individual, was especially disturbing. At the same time, *Lacombe Lucien* was criticized because the specific collaborations it portrays were taken to represent the French as a whole.[30] At issue here is the relationship of individual to type.

Malle's film does not psychologize the portrait of Lucien Lacombe: the seventeen-year-old's inner thoughts are not presented to the viewer—his choices are not so much explained by the camera as they are performed. Lucien is taciturn, often does not respond to others' remarks, and any causal chain in his actions must be apprehended and worked through by the viewer. When, in the opening scenes, the camera provides a close-up of a songbird, and we hear its idyllic, innocent chirping, followed by Lucien's killing of the little bird with a slingshot, we do not know whether to laugh at a boy's mischief or to be horrified by a cold-blooded killing. Following the action, Lucien looks satisfied with his shot and, making sure no one has seen his feat, he goes back to scrubbing the floor of the Catholic hospice where he is a janitor. Meanwhile, the film's sound track launches into the lilting, light-hearted music of Stéphane Grappelli's fiddle and Django Reinhardt's guitar.[31] There is no dialogue at this moment, and as in so many instances in the film, Lucien's face remains relatively closed, without defining expression, thereby providing us with few clues about motivations, thoughts, or feelings.

This beginning is indicative of the way the film, as a whole, establishes Lucien's individual actions in relation to the historical frame. Just before the slingshot killing of the bird, Lucien dusts lightly around a portrait of Pétain on a bed stand, and while Lucien is taking aim at the bird, we hear the hospice radio broadcasting a speech by the notorious Philippe Henriot, the anti-Semitic propagandist for Vichy in 1944. For the spectator, the sheer proximity of the signs of Vichy seems to relate them to the boy's actions: we are trained by our viewing experience to find metonymical connections, to bind the background detail and the foregrounded action, to suggest that the boy's violent inclinations are consonant with the violent actions of Vichy, as represented by the insinuating tones of Henriot discussing the "propaganda" of Radio London. Annette Insdorf establishes this smooth connection between the boy's violent nature and collaboration: "*Lacombe Lucien* portrays the collaborators as creatures of amoral impulse. Lucien's first action in the film is to shoot a bird with a slingshot; later he shoots rabbits, [and] poaches other animals."[32] Just as Insdorf's two sentences support the implicit connection between collaboration and the killing of the bird, Malle's camera seems to invite us to make the same kinds of visual and auditory links. And, yet, the binding of foreground to frame does not actually work in terms of the character's consciousness, because Lucien's attention is focused exclusively on the bird.[33] The connection between Lucien's pleasure in shooting a bird and acts of collaborators (Pétain, Henriot) is merely incidental rather than natural or necessary. For the peasant that Lucien is, the killing of the bird bears no political impulse, nor is it necessarily sadistic. It is an integral activity in his upbringing, something a peasant does for fun (and/or for food). In the opening scene, Lucien's actions indicate neither resistance nor adherence to Henriot's message: rather, Lucien appears utterly oblivious to the radio broadcast, which, in fact, fades out to a barely audible level when the bird's song is heard, as if our ears temporarily became Lucien's. (Nevertheless, *we* have already identified Henriot's voice by this time). In similar fashion, Lucien's actual entry into the German police later on is a function of proximity: when his bike gets a flat tire in front of the collaborators' headquarters (the Hôtel des Grottes) after curfew, Lucien is picked up by the collaborators, who take him in.

If the film is an enactment of collaboration in the past that triggers strong reactions in the present, it is because the camera in effect calls upon the spectator to perform the role of the witness-judge who will decide upon the extent of Lucien's political guilt in the war. Our function is to weigh what the character lives on a personal level in terms of ethical or public responsibility. Whereas Lucien, as an uneducated, abandoned peasant boy, seems unable to articulate connections between his individual actions and their political or social significance, the camera repeatedly creates patterns that encourage the spectator to do so. For example, the ease and matter-of-factness with which Lucien kills animals for food, or finds sheer pleasure in a hunt, parallels his enjoyment in the hunt for resisters with his collaborator buddies or his amorous pursuit of the young Jewish woman, France. The desire for recognition (and thus, a sense of self) goes hand in hand for the disenfranchised boy with the pleasure of *power* over others. There is a sort of flattening or leveling of experience in Lucien's framework that makes all action and all people dangerously equivalent in ethical terms. It is up to the spectator to determine the nature of the differences.[34] At the end of an article on Malle's *Goodbye, Children*, Stanley Hoffmann provides a real-life equivalent to this leveling that involves French collaboration: "When I was doing research in the French archives, I came across a report from the *préfet* of Belfort to the Minister of the Interior. One part of each *rapport de préfet* was devoted to Franco-German cooperation. In this one, that section was divided in two. One dealt with cooperation in hunting down wild boars; the other, with cooperation in hunting down resisters."[35] These are precisely the kinds of dehumanizing equivalents that Lucien takes for granted. Again, it is the viewer's responsibility to acknowledge the horror of the parallel construction, to see the evil of the routine killing.

For each negative building block in the construction of Lucien's character, there is a concurrent positive one, making it difficult to pigeonhole him. For example, Lucien's delectation in killing animals is balanced by a scene in which he tenderly strokes the head of a horse that has just died (see Figure 3.1). Lucien's awkward, although some-times poignant, wooing of France turns physically rough at one key point, and the camera's visual sequence suggests that Lucien rapes France. And yet, this violence does not end their relationship: in the final scenes they seem to care for each other. The combination of the peasant's brutality and naiveté creates an unsettling image: there is no singular vision of Lucien, and this fact leaves it up to the specta-tor to decide whether the announcement of his execution (written on the screen in the final scene) is just.

What is difficult in this evaluation is that, from an esthetic point of view, the two sides of Lucien, corresponding roughly to good and evil, are visually equivalent (given equal time, equal importance), even if their ethical values are opposed. Although critics alternately criticized the character for being stupid or for being portrayed too sympathetically, I would suggest that it is the fear of a gullible or guilty public that is at issue here, one that would identify with, and then exonerate, the character. Critics on the Left were particularly concerned that the public might not sense strongly enough the necessity of condemning Lucien's actions. At a time in the 1970s when the Right was gaining political power and was promoting a politics of reconciliation (a convenient way to excuse collaboration), the Left's concern was not unfounded. Modiano's choice (over Malle's initial idea) of making Lucien an auxiliary to the German police rather than a member of the *Milice* (with its more formal

Figure 3.1. *Lacombe Lucien*, Louis Malle, 1973. Lucien tenderly strokes a dead horse.

structure, uniform, rules, and hierarchy) intensifies the ambiguity of
the character. Lucien retains more his civilian status and is thus associated with the general population more than a specific organization
of collaboration.[36]

In numerous ways, the seductive nature of Lucien lies in the
unstated, but clearly repeated, moving search of the adolescent for a
father figure who would help him make life choices. Lucien is both
displaced and rejected: as the son of a sharecropper, he belongs to a
rural underclass. In addition, we learn at the beginning of the film
that his father is a prisoner of war, his family's lodging has been taken
over by another share-cropper family, and his mother has moved in
with the farm owner and boss, Mr. Laborit, who makes it clear that
Lucien is an intruder. Although women do not tend to be the center
of attention in *Lacombe Lucien*, they are the ones who embody the
more conventional (passive) forms of collaboration. Lucien's mother
does not hesitate to accept his Gestapo earnings (even if she takes
distance from her collaboration with the Germans). Her sexual infidelity is implicitly associated with her collaboration (making her
doubly guilty), even though Laborit is on the side of the Resistance.
Malle's treatment of poor or working class women in this film is resolutely negative and there are no female characters tied formally to
the Resistance. To my mind, this is the least convincing aspect of
Malle's rendering of the Occupation. It is no doubt because
Lacombe Lucien focuses on the *outcast boy's viewpoint* that women
receive such treatment. This male perspective also informs Claude
Chabrol's later film, *Une Affaire de femmes* (*Story of Women*, 1987).
It would also appear that in a disproportionate number of film scenarios about the war, female infidelity in marriage is associated with
political collaboration, almost as if the films were reproducing
Vichy's belief that the war was attributable to women's immorality.

Like most of the male protagonists in Patrick Modiano's novels,
Lucien searches continually for a substitute to the missing father.[37]
The first potential father figure for Lucien is the schoolteacher,
Peyssac, who is a member of the local *Maquis* Resistance network.[38]
But Peyssac is skeptical of Lucien's reasons for wishing to join the
resistance, suspecting that they may have little to do with ideology,
and offhandedly dismisses Lucien as being too young. Throughout
the film, Lucien seeks to emulate others—principally men—in an
effort to establish who he is, and to belong to some group (first, to his
own family; next, to the Resistance; then, to a group of collaborators;

and, finally, to a Jewish family). Subsequent to his rejection by Peyssac, Lucien is caught after curfew by French Gestapo agents, and he turns to *them* for a father figure. He then imitates their criminal acts that, for him, become associated with power, self-importance, and revenge on those who have rejected him. Although spectators might wish to excuse Lucien's betrayal of Peyssac, whose name he reveals when he is plied with liquor by the French Gestapo, they soon change their minds because Lucien shows no remorse when Peyssac is captured and tortured. The earlier "paternal rejection" is thus repeated by the "son" in a powerful Oedipal drama where the "son" Lucien is instrumental in the "father's" death.

The initial paternal absence troubles Lucien much more (albeit unconsciously) than the nature of the dividing lines between resister and Vichy supporter, or fascists and Jews.[39] When he is introduced later to a Jewish family who is in hiding, the father of the family, Albert Horn, a dignified, accomplished tailor, becomes the paternal model that Lucien will imitate. In psychoanalytic terms, the "place of the father," that is, the symbolic position he would occupy in the boy's identity formation, is repeatedly filled by extraordinarily different men whose ethical stances are irrelevant to the boy.

Ultimately, however, the fact that, for Lucien, it does not matter whether the person filling the role of father is morally deplorable or uplifting *never excuses* the adolescent's choices in the film. When Lucien refuses to bend to the pleas of a captured resistance fighter to switch sides (from collaboration to Resistance), there is no visual justification or moral explanation for Lucien's taping shut the man's mouth, or his capricious drawing of a mouth onto the tape over the man's mouth. He is guilty of cruelty and of actively turning away from a just cause. In one of the curious twists of ill-learned lessons, Lucien's mean reaction to the resister is articulated through his identification with Albert Horn: in an earlier scene, Horn had met the fascist collaborator Faure in Lucien's presence, and the eminently dignified Horn asked why Faure spoke to him with the familiar form of address ("tu"), given that they did not know each other. In this context, Faure clearly wished to manifest his contempt (and feelings of superiority) toward Horn as Jew, and Horn resisted the social insult. Then, in the scene between Lucien and the resister, the latter speaks to Lucien in the familiar form ("tu"), no doubt through a desire to create a bond between them—to win Lucien's trust—but Lucien merely responds to the form of address: "Je n'aime pas qu'on

me tutoie" ("I do not like your using 'tu' [your being familiar] with
me"). Instead of understanding the use of the familiar as a bond,
Lucien repeats Horn's refusal to be placed in an inferior social position, to be treated like a child. But in the identification with the mis-
treated Jew, the disenfranchised peasant lacks the model's ability to
manipulate language to his advantage. Lacking verbal prowess,
Lucien silences the resister by taping his mouth shut. Lucien's linguistic repetition is emptied of its moral, social content, and is
understood as a weapon of power.

When I recently showed *Lacombe Lucien* to undergraduates in a
course on the "Vichy syndrome" in film, none felt that Lucien's execution was unintelligible or outrageous in the context of the historical events portrayed. Young people who might have empathized
with the adolescent character ("saved by love," as some critics have
maintained) did not lose their ability to evaluate his actions critically.
Neither the social oppression Lucien undergoes, nor even the idyllic
love passages in the last section of the film, when Lucien, France,
and her grandmother hide out in the beautiful countryside of Southern France, effaced Lucien's culpability. As we noted earlier, Lucien
Lacombe's criminal acts spring from his conformism and a lack of
reflection that the film displays without commenting on. In the
1970s, the apparent silence of the filmmaker's voice about Lucien's
actions meant collusion with the character, whereas today it is easier
to appreciate the critical distance between camera and character. My
students were also quick to acknowledge Malle's stated connections
between contemporary problems of teenagers and those of Lucien,
an idea that angered critics from the 1970s, for whom comparisons
between periods were impossible or inappropriate (because they lev-
eled the specificity of the period and its issues).

For the 1970s, the "performance" of Pierre Blaise in the role of
Lucien Lacombe was paradoxically *too* good. It is here that the distinctions between acting a role and embodying it begin to blur or at
least to become problematic. The life of Pierre Blaise, a wild, seventeen-year-old boy with no acting experience, whom Malle chose for
the part of Lucien, confirms the connections between past and present in uncanny ways. As an untrained actor, Blaise brought to the
role his own rough, peasant accent, his delight in hunting, his violent inclinations, his ignorance. According to Malle, Blaise had never
seen a film, never read a book, but he possessed a certain understanding of Lucien's psychology. He knew the character did bad

things, but understood how he thought. Like the disenfranchised Lucien, Pierre Blaise was also sensitive to any perceived slights, to the point that Malle had to tell the film crew to treat him like a star, as if he were a Belmondo or an Alain Delon, because he kept threatening to quit. Pierre Blaise, who died in a car accident two years after the film, got Malle into trouble because he was *so* convincing in the role of a power hungry boy.[40] The parallels between Pierre Blaise's life and Lucien Lacombe's provide a stunning example of how the film *represented* the Occupation in a double sense: as portrayal (of a past content) and performance of some of its issues in the present. Both Lucien and Pierre Blaise were involved in play-acting, trying on masks and disguises to see what identities might suit them. Is it any wonder that critics disliked Malle's comments about the close ties between Lucien's bad choices and the difficulties of contemporary youth (connecting gang violence, asocial behavior, and a lack of parental guidance)? For some, to link contemporary problems to the past of the Occupation was again to implicate the present; for others, it constituted a denial of the past's specificity, its absolute difference.

Malle's initial inspirations for making a film about rebellious youth had, in fact, not begun with Lucien Lacombe. Before choosing the Occupation, he had wanted to make a film about Mexican street gangs, about a French soldier who tortures in the Algerian war, as well as about an American Vietnam vet who returns home after committing atrocities.[41] In each case, the portrayal of banal evil is embodied by young, defiant boys who themselves are in search of acceptance. In settling upon *Lacombe Lucien*, he was choosing the embodiment of a type (or set of problems), but its specificities anchored it in France and a portion of his own past.

REREADING THE CRITICS: THE TERROR OF THE TYPICAL

Having sketched out some of the film's key traits, I would like to take a step back now, and consider the ways in which the non-coincidence between personal identity search and ethical choices touched off a flurry of criticisms of *Lacombe Lucien*. Charges most frequently made include the lack of verisimilitude; the obliteration of idealism, ideology, and historical specificity; the atypical quality of the film's portrayal of collaborators and Jews; the lack of a critical attitude toward the collaborating protagonist; and the choice of a peasant (rather than a bourgeois). The early assertion in 1974 by one critic from *Le Monde* that the film was a "work of art" seems to have angered many critics even more.[42] A few months later, another critic from *Le Monde* would be asking whether one should see the film at all.[43] The communist and *Maquis* fighter, René Andrieu, complained in the 1970s that Malle chose actual marginal events and characters over realistic ones.[44] Naomi Greene's essay "*La vie en rose*: Images of the Occupation in French Cinema," offers a very useful review (and endorsement) of many of the critical positions on *Lacombe Lucien* from the Left in the 1970s.[45] I would like to explore, in some detail, these arguments concerning *Lacombe Lucien* because they illustrate, in exemplary fashion, tensions between the esthetic performance of history and national identity. Our own viewpoint from the twenty-first century will obviously color our reading (with its attendant blind spots and peculiar focuses), but within that frame, certain aspects of the film (and our time) can be illuminated.

The first objection to Lucien Lacombe is that he is "a most atypical collaborator," which is tied to the fact that he is not engaged in the fight on ideological grounds.[46] As we noted before, Malle's character does not fit the description of the collaborator who acts according to political beliefs—the figure that audiences in the 1970s were already familiar with (and to some extent, were coming to expect after *The Sorrow and the Pity*). To provide a more contemporary viewpoint about the norms of resistance and collaboration among the young, Greene also quotes Stanley Hoffmann (from a 1988 article), whose own childhood experience of the war was clearly articulated along ideological lines. (On the other hand, historian Emmanuel Le Roy Ladurie remembers his Catholic Pétainist upbringing—well before his communist period—and notes that he was scarcely aware of political divisions within his school during the war.)[47] An argument based on personal experience of the events must, of necessity, carry at least some weight in discussions of historical "types." The problem is: *whose* experience are we to use as model for the type? Greene implicitly acknowledges the problem, since she also cites from the 1970s Jean-Louis Bory (who had won the Goncourt prize in 1945 for his novel *Mon Village à l'heure allemande*, "My Village on German Time"). Bory describes *Lacombe Lucien* in the weekly magazine *Le Nouvel Observateur* as: "the first real film—and the first true film—about the Occupation . . . I know. I was there."[48] But, ultimately, it is Hoffmann's personal remarks that are given more prominence, so that they become the gauge by which to measure the (lack of) plausibility of Malle's collaborators. And, yet, as Hoffmann has so forcefully pointed out elsewhere, there were probably as many forms of collaboration as there were collaborators.[49] Malle himself was surprised to discover, just before shooting *Lacombe Lucien*, just how close to reality his fictive character actually was:

> I was in Limogne, the village next to here, and was talking to the man who owns the garage . . . I described what the story [*Lacombe Lucien*] was about. He said, 'Oh, you're talking about Hercule.' Hercule was a tiny young man with a physical defect; he had one shoulder higher than the other, and he had worked for the Gestapo in Cahors. He was eighteen at the time, and they had sent him to infiltrate one of the Maquis here . . . The garage owner in Limogne confirmed that this young man Hercule had stayed with the Maquis in my house, which was really bizarre! . . . Eventually, Hercule was arrested and executed immediately after the war. So the garage owner said, 'You're telling the story of Hercule.' I said I'd never heard of Hercule before. After all this research, and zeroing in on this region, I find that somebody very close to Lucien Lacombe had actually existed and lived in my house! I thought that it was a sign of fate.[50]

While I do not think that Malle's discovery of an individual equivalent to his character makes Lucien's claim to verisimilitude and to being typical any more imposing than Hoffmann's, I do think that attention to detail and to historical specificity allows us to appreciate how close to the events of the Occupation the portrayal of Lucien might actually be.[51] For instance, Greene finds it completely implausible that Lucien should ask, "What is a Jew?" in 1944.[52] And she would be right, were it not for the fact that Lucien never asks this question.[53] It is a question that the very young boy in Michel Drach's *Les Violons du bal* asks at the beginning of the war. The young child, Julien, in Malle's *Goodbye, Children*, also makes a similar query, but there, it is more a political question than one of complete ignorance, closer to the kind of philosophical question Lucas Steiner, the Jewish theater director in Truffaut's *The Last Metro*, asks as he considers roles, stereotypes, and the layers of propaganda that have piled up against Jews, distorting their images to the point of unintelligibility.[54]

Lucien is also faulted with simply mimicking others' ideas rather than developing his own. This is certainly a valid criticism, but one wonders if it is not true for all youth as they try out new ideas. When Lucien remarks: "Monsieur Faure says that Jews are the enemies of France" (a mimicking quotation that troubles Greene), Lucien is indeed repeating what he has heard. Given that he knows that his interlocutor, Albert Horn, is himself a Jew, the comment looks almost like a challenge, as if he were testing the validity of Faure's statement to see what sort of reaction it will elicit from the Jew.[55] By attributing the remark to another (Faure), rather than saying it as his own, Lucien leaves himself a margin in which to evaluate Faure's statement *through* Horn without direct confrontation.[56] Lucien is portrayed as ignorant, but the adolescent's repetition of others' ideas does not seem particularly unlikely.

Greene extends her criticism to the general portrayal of collaboration in the film, arguing that the collaborators profess no moral or political ideology, that they are all misfits and outcasts. This is not entirely accurate, however; the character Faure harangues those around him with a collaborationist discourse—he asserts faith in Germany, and contempt and hatred for communists, Jews, and the British. De Gaulle is dangerous, according to Faure, because he is surrounded by Bolsheviks and Jews. It is also Faure who has Horn deported (after comparing Jews to proliferating rats) when Horn shows up at the Hôtel des Grottes looking for Lucien.[57] As despicable as Faure's convictions are, they nevertheless constitute sociopolitical beliefs. Along side of Faure, we also find the secretary, Lucienne Chauvelot, who says that if the French had been more disciplined like the Germans ("obliging" and "punctual"), they would have won the war. It *is* true, however, that the group includes an inordinate number of misfits: a washed-up alcoholic cyclist; an ex-(bad) cop; a handsome black rogue from Martinique; an aristocratic, amoral dandy; and a vacuous, mean, would-be actress. It is an unsavory bunch that has chosen Germany over De Gaulle *and* Vichy (the group members practice target shooting with a portrait of Pétain). This is not, as Hoffmann and others have pointed out, the more commonplace kind of passive collaboration (that we noted in Lucien's mother).[58]

Because French collaboration covers a range of groups and activities (from passive to active), and because *Lacombe Lucien* is about specific types, it becomes important to pay attention to the time frame of Malle's and Modiano's story. The scenes take place in the summer of 1944, culminating with Lucien's execution in October of the same year. If we match up the story's events with its historical framework, the collection of odd characters involved in collaboration with the Germans turns out to be quite representative of the period. Michael Marrus and Robert Paxton, in *Vichy France and the Jews*, explain how the nature of collaboration in the French police was already changing in 1943: "The work of French policemen was becoming not only disagreeable but dangerous. Sabotage of rails and pylons begins to appear regularly in the prefects' reports, along with the first armed clashes between police and groups of *maquisards* and the first armed attacks upon police stations . . . Small wonder that recruitment for the French police began to drop off sharply in the summer of 1943 . . . With fewer applicants, the police had to recruit with less selectivity."[59]

By June, 1944 (when the action of *Lacombe Lucien* begins), Hitler was losing on the Eastern front and the Allies were invading France. With the tides changing, there was even less incentive for Frenchmen to join the ranks of those faithful to Franco-German collaboration. Historian Bertram Gordon describes the latter part of the Occupation: "As German pressure for French wealth and manpower intensified, the prospect of increased collaboration offered little to most Frenchmen. The collaborationists remained a small group of ideologues, adventurers, and bandits."[60] Malle's and Modiano's group of torturers, murderers, blackmailers, ideologues, and black market opportunists covers a good part of the spectrum of active collaboration (without claiming to be all inclusive). Modiano's influence may be most strongly felt in this context. In several of his novels, as well as in the script of *Lacombe Lucien*, Modiano explores the underworld of collaboration, one that resembles quite closely actual groups of bandit-fascists, such as the Bonny-Lafont gang, which, as Gordon explains, "blackmailed Frenchmen and served the Germans as an auxiliary police in Paris, usually functioned independently of the political parties, although individuals may have been involved in both. The ranks of those who collaborated with the Germans included criminals in it for the money or for personal revenge, but also . . . personally disinterested warriors who lost their lives at the Eastern front."[61] *Lacombe Lucien*'s gang is located in southwest France, and the same mixture of adventurers and believers make up its group of collaborators. It is even plausible that the character Betty Beaulieu, the starlet/gang moll, was modeled after Corinne Luchaire, an actress and the daughter of fascist journalist,

Jean Luchaire, who headed the Press Corporation in Paris after 1940.[62]

What is no doubt equally as troubling as Lucien's work for the fascist-bandit gang is how typical his situation was for many adolescent boys toward the end of the war. Paul Jankowski has convincingly shown that the fear of the STO (the Service du Travail Obligatoire—Compulsory Labor Service in Germany) was a motive shared by resisters and collaborators alike as they chose a means of escape from the enslaved work force in Germany. Hence, a political solution—the choice of the *Milice* (collaboration) or the *Maquis* (resistance)—was triggered by a human, personal dilemma. Contrary to the Left's belief in the 1970s that almost all collaborators were bourgeois, the youth who joined the ranks of either the *Milice* or the *Maquis* in 1944 frequently came from the poor and working class. And while the reasons for collaborating and resisting did differ—with collaborators tending toward immediate self-interest and resisters toward more abstract, idealistic group goals—the lines between them were far from absolute, and combinations of motives were very frequent.[63] Thus, historians now confirm what politicized film criticism in the 1970s was reluctant to accept as even plausible: first, the resemblance between many collaborators and resisters; second, the representative quality of Lucien's situation and the logic of his "fall" into collaboration.

NATIONAL IDENTITIES

A. France as Gypsy

Lacombe Lucien challenges accepted notions of national, personal, and ethnic identities in France, both during the Occupation (an initial historical content) and in its subsequent return as artistic memory (re)activating identity crises. Even the choice of Django Reinhardt's wonderful music for the film brings these issues to the fore. It is remembered as France's jazz of the 1930s and 1940s, but performed and written by a composer/musician whose origins do not fit the mold of the "authentic" Frenchman. Although the Larousse *Dictionnaire des noms propres* (*Dictionary of Proper Names*) refers to Reinhardt as French, he was born in Belgium, of gypsy origins. With no formal education in his early days (he could barely write), Reinhardt performed his guitar music while wandering through France with a gypsy caravan. Having lost the use of two fingers on his left hand as a result of a burn, Reinhardt developed a highly original, virtuoso style of play to compensate for the handicap. This "French" style, paradoxically the result of his handicap, is the only one to have influenced American jazz artists.[64]

Now it is certainly not uncommon for artists to be recognized as representatives of one country when they were born in another. But in the exploration of identity crises during the Occupation, Reinhardt's mixed origins become crucial to rethinking what it means to be French. With his Romany background, Reinhardt represented one of the numerous targets of Nazi ideology, given that five hundred thousand gypsies died in concentration camps during the war. The lilting music of the film thus carries with it the reminder of the lethal dangers to its composer.[65] As a performer, Reinhardt *also* represents the many ambiguities of Occupation politics, with French, Germans, resisters and collaborators all having been members of his nightclub public.[66] In this sense, his life is "typical," because his musical offering could not resist being caught up in political struggles of the time, despite his desires.[67] Alternately suspected of being a resister and a collaborator, Reinhardt did not really fit either category very well.

This is not, of course, the kind of reflection most spectators might entertain while listening to the film's background music. But in the context of the *mode rétro* during the 1970s—when critics were quick to attack Malle's depiction of the Occupation as one more facile representation of the 1940s that indulged in a very questionable nostalgia for its cars, clothes, and music—these echoes from Reinhardt's life, evoking dangerous identity issues, suggest another kind of political reading of the film's choice of period music.[68]

B. France as Jew

Just as Malle's collaborators raise critical ire because of the filmmaker's specific—rather than stereotypical—choices in representing a story of collaboration, so it is the case for the Jews portrayed in *Lacombe Lucien*. What is revelatory about the reviews' criticisms is that the Horn family members are alternately interpreted negatively, but in opposing terms, either as facile stereotypes or as totally atypical characters. Once again, as the film explores the problematic nature of identity, the ways in which identities are marked or deviate from norms and stereotypes provoke uneasy reactions. The viewing public is forced to think through the relationships between individual and type, between a marked ethnic identity and an assimilated national one. What emerges from the film reviews are the unresolved tensions that continue to be played out in the reading of the film, as if *Lacombe Lucien* were preparing the way for later discussions of ethnic identity in the 1980s and 1990s (particularly Jewish identity).[69]

Contemporary film critic Annette Insdorf is bothered by how "non-Jewish" the blond-haired, blue-eyed young woman France appears, and by the fact that her father thinks of his own identity more in terms of having been the best tailor in Paris than of being Jewish. Insdorf faults him for not taking an active position of solidarity with other (Jewish) victims and resisters and with being complicit with the enemy. (The aristocratic dandy, Jean-Bernard de Voisins, extorts money and clothing from the Horns with the false promise of passage to Spain.) Despite its eloquence, there is a certain self-consciousness to Insdorf's argument concerning *Lacombe Lucien*:

> Filmmakers in the seventies . . . finally addressed themselves to the fatal indifference and complicity of the French, but only with Jewish characters assimilated (or classy) enough to appeal to an audience still subject to anti-Semitism. This not to say that the more "authentic" Jewish characters are or should look unattractive; but rather that the predominance of characters who bear neither external nor internal acknowledgement of their Judaism can offer only a fraction of the historical picture. When physical beauty or social class eclipses all other roots of identity, there is a danger that the aesthetic can become an anesthetic.[70]

While I tend to agree with Insdorf's remarks, what seems somewhat surprising in this quotation is her curious use of "authentic" in referring to physiognomy, as if a blond-haired, blue-eyed person could not be authentically Jewish; or, as if a bourgeois Jew were less "authentic" than a working class one.[71] While there are tendencies that feed a stereotype, the contradictions in this one loom in the background in nasty, heart-wrenching ways: if "authentic" Jews were so recognizable, then the Nazis' imposition of the yellow star on their lapels would have been superfluous. And what does "authenticity" have to do with physical beauty? Would a brown-haired, dark-eyed beauty, or a red-headed one, be an authentic Jew, or would beauty once again efface ethnicity? Is a Sephardic Jew's appearance more genuine than an Ashkenazi's? Given Insdorf's discomfort and that of many other critics, it would seem that Malle's esthetic is anything but anesthetic for a professional audience, even if she may be right about the general public expecting handsome heroes or victims. Insdorf's own quotation marks around the word "authentic" make her discomfort tangible. The fact that France is blue-eyed, blond, and Jewish should make us ponder the issue of ethnic identity and the Diaspora. Additionally, we may note that the actress Aurore Clément, who plays France, later played the role of a Jewish woman in Chantal Akerman's 1978 Les Rendez-vous d'Anna. Akerman's experimental film about a fictitious postwar filmmaker, Anna Silver, also resists easy typologies of national and ethnic identity.

Although Malle's film does not evoke the horrors of the Holocaust (the latter being the topic of Insdorf's book), the threat to the Horns' life hangs over them in tangible fashion.[72] The point may well be that even the supposedly assimilated Jew, the one who does not choose solidarity and does not fit conventions, cannot escape being marked by a vicious Nazi order in 1944. We do not *see* Horn in a concentration camp, but there is little doubt that that is where Faure has him sent. When Marie the maid (who is employed at the Hôtel des Grottes, collaboration headquarters) becomes jealous of France because Lucien courts *her* rather than Marie, the latter does not hesitate to hurl anti-Semitic epithets at France. France cannot avoid being labeled despite her non-Jewish looks.

On the flipside of Insdorf's argument, Mona Ozouf and Naomi Greene take issue with the portrait of the Horns because they are too stereotypical, not assimilated enough. Greene challenges Horn's profession and his refinement: "improbably piling one stereotype on another, Malle depicts M. Horn as both a cultured cosmopolite and a tailor."[73] But in a European society where fashion is a major mark of culture, surely the connection between tailoring and social refinement is not entirely implausible. Ozouf complains that the Horns are too passive, complicit with the enemy, and that they have an accent, "which, in a little town in Aquitaine, makes of them manifest emigrés, wandering Jews, not French citizens."[74] One may wonder to which accent Ozouf is referring, given that the daughter's accent is typically French with no trace of foreignness or regionalism, whereas her father's sounds German or perhaps East European or Scandinavian, at any rate, foreign.[75] (With the exception of one word, the grandmother only speaks German the whole time.) Even if the markings of Lucien's thick southern accent might relate him to some traditional notion of authenticity in which regionalism and property are the signs of social belonging and identity, his social disenfranchisement and displacement make of him an outsider who ill fits the picture of the quintessential Frenchman.[76] In our time at least, France's accent would be closer to the French accent that foreigners learning French might try to copy.

The ironies concerning the link between identity and language continue to accumulate when one takes into account the scene between the fascist Faure and Albert Horn. Faure phones the German *Kommandantur*, his ally (representing "the master race"), to turn Horn in, but Faure can barely make himself understood in German, whereas the man on whom he has heaped his contempt, Albert Horn, speaks impeccable German. We remember, too, that Horn's understanding of the social differences between the familiar and formal forms of address ("tu" and "vous") make him an ill-understood linguistic model for Lucien, the native speaker.

Ozouf's contrast between "French citizens" and "wandering Jews" is an uneasy one. The crisscrosses among language, class, and identity (national and personal) in Malle's treatment of the Occupation challenge the simplicity of such a contrast. The opposition between "French citizen" and "wandering Jew" tends to reestablish— albeit implicitly—a mythical model of French purity, and intimates that the legitimacy of national identity is tied to how one speaks the language (a *particular* French) and to the land. The film's treatment of the Horns' displacement does not make it a matter of choice or nature, but rather an imposition brought about by the fascists. The Horns are not "at home" because they have been forced to flee Paris and to go into hiding.

Christian Zimmer's critique of *Lacombe Lucien* (from the 1970s) is no doubt one of the more vehement indictments of the film. He describes it contemptuously as a reactionary "work of art." ("Work of art," for him, connotes perfection revealing man's imperfection and inalterability).[77] He criticizes the film for suggesting that the personal could escape the political, but he does not connect the personal/political debate to Lucien's demise: Lucien does, after all, pay for his crimes with his life. What is shocking is that his execution by a resistance military tribunal is announced when Lucien looks the least guilty: the information is written over a bucolic image of Lucien lying in the grass, looking at peace with his surroundings. Zimmer interprets the final idyllic scenes, where the collaborator Lucien, the young Jewish woman France, and her grandmother live briefly together in the beautiful countryside—outside of history—as an image of reconciliation (a false one) that the Right was trying to promote in the 1970s. (He follows Mona Ozouf's move in this.) The point is well taken, especially given the politics of the 1970s, when the Left saw, in Giscard d'Estaing's arrival to power, the triumph of an anti-Gaullist, cynical bourgeoisie that could manipulate the images of the Occupation to its advantage. For Zimmer and many others, this film, made by a rich bourgeois, must inevitably perform bourgeois politics of the Right in representing the past.

That the adolescent collaborator and the young Jewish woman care for each other—with each reciprocally providing an image of the radical other—cannot fail to disconcert. But what Zimmer neglects to note is that the potential for violence and discord runs through the last scenes, too, threatening at every moment to topple the idyll *from within*. All is not so harmonious in the final section: at one point the camera shows France standing over Lucien with a big rock in her hands, as if she were about to kill him (see Figure 3.2).

Figure 3.2. *Lacombe Lucien*, Louis Malle, 1973. France holds a rock menacingly, potentially ready to strike Lucien.

Even a love game of "hide and seek" between the two takes on almost sinister tones: as boy chases girl in the attic of an abandoned house, we hear their voices before seeing them, and for a split second it is not clear whether France's shrieks are in jest or in fear. The game recalls Lucien's pleasure in hunting down animals and resisters (with the emphasis on the *hunt* rather than on any particular *object*). By reproducing the same struggles and ambiguities of events in history, the back-to-nature episode reveals its own precariousness, and destroys any notion of a simple harmony between the two. The power dynamics between them continue to underscore cultural, class, and gender differences.[78]

In order to place Malle's film more solidly in the camp of the Right, Zimmer paradoxically has to eliminate the very ambiguity that he was initially criticizing (as a function of the film's Rightist tendencies). The final scene has to be a pure idyll in nature that bears no violent or ambiguous undercurrents, in order to confirm the "Reconciliation" theme that does appear to run through the final section. Zimmer acknowledges, of course, that collaboration took place during the Occupation, but even this smart critic is more comfortable with a clear-cut past, with good guys and bad guys and nothing in between: he mourns the good ol' days of "virtuous indignation, intransigence, faithfulness," when there were still "*great designs*: the Resistance was one, Gaullism too."[79] The problem is that the film does not deny these worthy designs. It portrays resistance fighters who are faithful to their cause to the end (the teacher Peyssac is one example).

The film also shows much more subtle forms of *female* resistance that the eyes of the 1970s critic have trouble identifying. For example, one character who remains faithful to a principle of resistance throughout the film is the old grandmother, Bella Horn (superbly played by Therese Giehse). Although her age and frailty do not permit her to resist in active, overt ways, the grandmother is clearly hostile to collaborators. She willingly retreats into silence when either Germans or French collaborators are around, and at one point she tries to keep Lucien out of the Horn's apartment after her son has disappeared. Her games of solitaire are a retreat from the untenable situation in which her family finds itself, and her silence recalls the subtle resistance of the niece in Melville's film (and Vercors' novel) *The Silence of the Sea*. Interestingly enough, the grandmother comes to provide a counterpoint to Lucien in one of the last scenes in the country. As she plays solitaire, Lucien lays out his money as if he were copying her play, and then utters an awkward "good night" in German when he leaves the room, as if to seal the bond between them. Bella resists the linguistic connivance, murmuring "bonsoir" back to Lucien, in a spirit of contrariness. This is the only French word she utters during the entire film, and it is in response to Lucien's German.

Now it is certainly true that the grandmother's action in this scene can be read in a jocular or playful way, and one might even see it as a form of cross-cultural bonding between her and Lucien. The characteristic opacity of the film leaves room for both personal and political interpretations, just as the niece's silence in Melville's film ambiguously connoted resistance, but also attraction. Although Malle's film offers a new vision of the Occupation, it holds certain aspects in common with the tradition of films on the war. Zimmer's political reading, however, reduces the grandmother to a one-dimensional character who is indifferent to everything around her, and thus overlooks the subtle aspects of her resistance (as well as her playfulness and will to survive).

The frequency of critical blind spots and strong reactions to Malle's treatment of France's collaborationist past allows us to appreciate the extent of the postwar repression. Although critics on the Left were concerned that the Right was using ambiguity to recast events so that resisters and collaborators looked alike, thereby excusing the latter, many critics on the Right were actually critical of *Lacombe Lucien* because the protagonist was not politically aware. Thus, Left and Right harbored the same criticism.

The controversies surrounding *Lacombe Lucien* recall the much earlier case of Henri-Georges Clouzot's *The Raven*, made during the Occupation and produced by the German company, the "Continental."[80] Clouzot's film is a story of a French village ripped apart by anonymous letters accusing inhabitants of various crimes and immoral acts. It was opposed by Vichy and the Catholic church during the Occupation (because the film supposedly mocked their family values), was reproached by the German *Kommandantur* because it discouraged French letters of denunciation, and then was banned by the resistance forces in power after the liberation because of its indictment of French citizens' comportment. Thus, Left and Right both were displeased by the film. But whereas Clouzot's film affords a nihilistic social critique with no one's actions entirely worthy of respect, Malle's film never challenges the values of the Resistance, and his treatment of the victims—the Horn family—is certainly sympathetic (although not idealized). It is no doubt Malle's refusal to portray characters unequivocally (all good or all bad) that disconcerts most.

THE CLASS/ETHNIC CLASH

Whereas *The Raven* sustains a strong class critique of the *haute bourgeoisie*, Malle's film complicates the class issue by crossing it with ethnic concerns. The relationship between Lucien and the Horn family is no doubt the focal point where Occupation politics are most tenaciously performed through the interplay among ethnicity, nationality, class, and gender. Class difference between Lucien and the Horns makes the spectator all the more ill at ease in determining who is victim and who is aggressor. On the one hand, Lucien is a class victim who joins the ranks of the German auxiliary police in part as a means to gain respect and power over a class that has humiliated him. (We remember that Lucien has been ejected from his home and that his share-cropper father has been replaced by the farm owner in his mother's bed.) Malle gives an uncompromising portrait of the rural underclass, its betrayals (sexual and political), and the adolescent's revenge over the bourgeoisie. This revenge is particularly visible in the scenes where the bourgeois resistance family—the Vaugeois (whose very name echoes its class)—is taken prisoner by the French Gestapo. Lucien takes pleasure in destroying the model ship of the son of the family.

The Horn family also belongs to the bourgeois cultural elite that is implicitly Lucien's enemy. It is unsettling that the cultured Albert Horn remains unshaven and clad in a rich looking smoking jacket in several interior scenes, because it gives him a decadent quality that makes it difficult to think of him as a typical victim. The family's refinement and knowledge of high culture set it apart from Lucien. (France is a somewhat accomplished classical pianist).[81] When Albert Horn is given the task of making Lucien's first suit, he makes Lucien a pair of fashionable "golf pants" (knickers) instead of long pants. Lucien does not quite know what to make of this fashion (a style of the 1930s and 1940s), and is suspicious of it. On the other side, Lucien does not hesitate to order the Horn family around to assert his power over them. Malle performs a series of disconcerting switches that force the viewer to rethink assumptions: where we might have looked for the sympathetic victim—Lucien as lowly peasant, tied to French roots and nature—we find, instead, (or as well) an ignorant, power-thirsty French *gestapiste*. The urban viewer is frequently tempted to make of Lucien's peasant roots a sign of brutality instead of rural culture. Where we might have expected an idealized portrait of the Horns as courageous Jewish victims, we find, instead, a troubled, relatively well-to-do bourgeois family that has not joined the resistance.

Familial and gender interactions gradually cloud the class conflict. Lucien wishes to "adopt" the Horns, gaining a father, grandmother, and lover all at once, and awkwardly brings flowers and champagne in the hope of gaining entry into their world and class. France is repulsed by, and attracted to, Lucien, who is alternately a rough man, physically dominating her, and a clumsy suitor who protects her. Both she and Lucien are victimized by society because of their origins—France for being Jewish and Lucien for being a peasant. But there *are* political differences: although France is attracted to Lucien as a handsome young man (perhaps as an earthy peasant, too), she resists his political complicity with the Germans. This is illustrated in a scene where, rather than undergo verbal abuse by other shoppers, she declines to let Lucien use his political clout with the Germans to move her to the head of a food line in front of a shop.

Whereas Lucien's identifications with others are dramatically enacted (rather than explicitly stated), the Horn's dilemmas often tend to be articulated verbally as well, with ethnic identity clearly superseding class identity as a problematic issue. When France—facing anti-Semitic epithets from a working class woman, Marie—cries out to Lucien "I'm fed up with being a Jew," we sense the young woman's desperation, her adolescent desire to belong, to be invulnerable to ethnic attacks that break through standard class hierarchy. It *is* a betrayal of her ethnic origins, in the sense that France (and here I am playing on the confusion of the individual/nation name) cannot envision, in this horrific era, a way to acknowledge ethnic and national identities simultaneously. Class and ethnic hierarchical switches are again performed when, on a visit to her son, Lucien's mother (a peasant) asks if the Horns are from the area (realizing that they are not). Albert Horn answers that they are from Paris, but given his obvious foreign accent, his response seems humorous, even playful.[82] When, however, Lucien's mother insists that Horn is not French, the scene turns from humorous resistance to a poignant, proud assertion of national identity: "Thérèse [Lucien's mother]: You're not French, are you? Horn: More or less . . . My daughter is *really* French" ("Ma fille est une *vraie* Française"). France's identity again depends on who is doing the defining. But are we not always uneasily working through what it means to be "authentically" French, Jewish, a French-Jew, a French-Arab, or any other hyphenated identity? Identity is no doubt always hyphenated, plural, and contextual. The young Jewish character, France, the "vraie Française," would appear to embody France's situation during the war in much more than just name. Alternately resisting Lucien as collaborator, uneducated lout, and brutal enemy, and being pulled toward him as handsome, resourceful individual and poignant naïf, France performs her citizenship with all the attendant ambiguities that go into public/private splits. These are the kinds of ambiguities made so obvious during the Occupation, when personal survival and desire did not mesh with moral, political stances involving national/ ethnic commitment. Both she and Lucien ("opposites" in terms of gender, class, ethnicity, and politics) turn out, in the end—despite all the critical disclaimers—to actualize the dilemma of individual responsibility in occupied France, even though they do not fit normative definitions of "Frenchness" (or for that matter, typical norms of collaborationism and "Jewishness"). That *Lacombe Lucien* continues to stir up controversy about its artistic choices in articulating this view of the Occupation and collaboration may well point to the longevity of the Vichy Syndrome's obsessive phase.

* * *

TURN OF THE CENTURY TAKES— HISTORY, POLITICS, AND AUTOBIOGRAPHY

I would like to close this discussion of *Lacombe Lucien* by noting briefly two essays that came out after a preliminary version of this chapter had been published. It is clear in Jean-Michel Frodon's recent book, *La Projection Nationale: Cinéma et Nation*, that *Lacombe Lucien* still gets under the skin of serious critics. Frodon lambastes *Lacombe Lucien* as a superficial work that reduces real historical and ethical differences.[83] He also contrasts Malle's film with Claude Lanzmann's nine-hour documentary masterpiece *Shoah* (1985) on the memory of the Holocaust. There is no arguing that Lanzmann's film is one of the most potent testimonials to the act of bearing witness to the death camps. But the comparison can only go so far because *Shoah* is not about *France's* responsibility in the deportations to Nazi death camps. However impressive Lanzmann's art is (I believe it is truly great), his work does not address the specific issues of France's wartime involvement.

H. R. Kedward recently affirmed (quoting Michel Sineux in the film journal *Positif*, from 1974)[84] that historians today applaud Malle and Modiano for "giving their characters 'an opacity, an ambiguity, a depth and complexity which in no way blurs the political lessons of history,' the whole film being 'a credible representation of an exceptionally ambiguous moment in history.'"[85] Clearly, my own efforts here have headed in this direction in critiquing certain distortions in 1970s political readings of the film, relying on historians' accounts of the war to inflect my analysis.

Kedward's recent essay ingeniously ties together Malle's autobiographical impulse to make a film about his own experiences as the child of a bourgeois family during the war, and some of the particularities of Lucien Lacombe. In Malle's two films about the war, the figures of collaboration bear important resemblances: in *Goodbye, Children*, Joseph, a poor, discontented kitchen boy employed at a rich Catholic boarding school, is fired for black market activities by the school priests (whereas the rich school boys go unpunished). Joseph takes his revenge by informing the Gestapo that the priests are hiding a Jewish boy, Jean. Malle's own viewpoint is filtered through the eyes of the little Gentile boy, Julien, who befriends the Jewish boy. Joseph's betrayal of the priests and of Jean recalls Lucien Lacombe's disenfranchisement, his lack of guidance, and traitorous rebellion.[86]

Kedward attaches this layer of Malle's memory to another one from the same year (1944) involving a communist-maquisard-poacher who terrified the lord of the manor where the young Louis Malle was boarding. This resistance member represented for Louis a scary person (a communist was a potential pillager to the rich bourgeoisie), but also a sort of Robin Hood, since the young boy knew that resisters were heroes.[87] As in the words of Kedward: "Lucien is an amalgam of the youthful domestic at Avon and the poacher as rural outlaw in maquis terrain."[88] The melting of these two figures inevitably clouds the political divide. Malle's own relationship to the 1944 incidents was to remain that of a fascinated, troubled witness, an eye drawn to the image of the marginalized outlaw, haunted by an image of rebelliousness and culpability. Following these events, Malle experienced his own forms of revolt (including, says Kedward, his friendship and collaboration with Roger Nimier).

Malle has said that, as a boy, he never really glanced toward the Jewish boy when the Gestapo came for him, as Malle's fictional character Julien does in *Goodbye, Children*. But Julien does dramatize the inevitable feelings of responsibility and guilt on the part of the observer who must "let things happen." With *Lacombe Lucien*, Malle placed his 1970s' public precisely in that position of the complicit gaze: simultaneously condemning and understanding. Is it any wonder that reactions have continued to be strong? We will see in Chapter 6 that *Lacombe Lucien* created its own trend in the 1980s and 1990s with a number of films that implicitly model themselves on Malle's groundbreaking work.[89]

CHAPTER 4

---·≼◆≽·---

OCCUPATIONAL PERFORMANCES IN
TRUFFAUT'S *THE LAST METRO*

PRIVATE VERSUS COLLECTIVE PORTRAITS

Whereas *Lacombe Lucien* turned out to be a *succès de scandale*,
François Truffaut's *The Last Metro*, made six years later (1980), was
rather a *succès tout court*, receiving acclaim from the general public,
as well as from the critics. Henry Rousso ranks it among the top 120
box-office successes in France during the fifteen-year period
between 1972 and 1987. Having carried off ten Césars (the Cannes
film festival's equivalent of the Oscar), as well as an Academy Award
nomination in the United States, Truffaut's film clearly belongs to a
different era in the renewal of Occupation memories. It is a period
less tormented by the past, in which esthetic issues took precedence
over political concerns in discussions of the arts and critical theory.
At a time when the Socialists were finally about to come to power
(with Mitterrand taking office in 1981), a narrower brand of Leftist
political criticism was paradoxically beginning to hold less sway over
literary and film criticism. In feminist theory, advocacy of a politicized "feminine writing" of the body from such writers as Hélène
Cixous was beginning to receive critical scrutiny for its essentialism,
and various forms of Marxism were being attacked by the "New
Philosophers" in the late 1970s. Given that *The Last Metro*'s sole villain, the theater critic Daxiat, is the one to declare that "everything is
political," it is easy to see that Truffaut delighted in taking a rancorous

jab at Leftist critics of the late 1960s and 1970s who read literature and the arts through political grids. What could be more vengeful than to put a slogan from the Left into the mouth of a character based on the pro-fascist, anti-Semitic French theater critic, Alain Laubreaux, who wrote for the French fascist journal *Je suis partout*? In associating the political reading of art with fascism and totalitarianism in *The Last Metro*, Truffaut launches his own attack on potential detractors (of whom there were actually relatively few), and lays claim to his artistic independence.[1]

Given the times, Truffaut was thus spared from political criticism for the most part. Many critics, and Truffaut himself, have described the Occupation as merely a backdrop for *The Last Metro*'s story (written by Truffaut and his collaborator, Suzanne Schiffman) about a theatrical troupe during the Occupation. And, yet, there is too much at stake in the careful manipulation of the spectators' opinion of the French during the period to neglect the nature of the detailed mythology that Truffaut creates. This mere "backdrop" is too integral to the film to be cast off as trivia or external to the story of the various theater characters it portrays. Truffaut and Schiffman researched the period at length, and also gathered memories from their own family experiences to put together a coherent, precise image of the time. The film opens with a documentary style presentation of the period—with a map of a divided France and an official voice-over supplying basic historical facts—and ends with the same newscast voice-over to tie up fictive and historical ends of the story (which are then followed by a fictional epilogue). The primary issue that concerns me here is the way Truffaut's elaborate set of researched facts about the period ultimately shape a complacent attitude of and toward the French public's culpability in the war. Whereas Malle and Modiano's inclusion of unusual, but accurate, accounts from the period lead the spectator to a critical understanding of France's complicity in the deportations and daily collaboration, Truffaut's rendering of collaboration makes it comfortable, even humorous, on occasion. But unlike full-blown comedies (or even tragicomedies), the "look" of *The Last Metro* is too solemn for its political import to be dismissed. It is certainly true that in the working through of wartime memories, it becomes possible in various periods to find its comical sides, but *The Last Metro* does not really belong to a comic genre.

It is an entirely different set of films over the decades that play out, in farce, the ironies of wartime survival, without allowing the spectator to take them too seriously. Claude Autant-Lara's 1956 *La Traversée de Paris* (*Four Bags Full*) depicts a raucous chase across Paris for slaughtered hogs. Gérard Oury's 1966 *La Grande Vadrouille* (*Don't Look Now, We've Been Shot At*, 1966), starring two of France's most famous comedians, Bourvil and Louis de Funès, features this French duo whisking Allied parachutists off to the free zone (as much to get rid of their bothersome presence as to aid the Allied cause). Jean-Marie Poiré's 1983 slapstick comedy, *Papy fait de la résistance*, hilariously satirizes all sides from collaborators to resisters. Claude Berri's 1991 *Uranus*, is a cinematic rendering of Marcel Aymé's 1948 cynical comic novel about the postwar switch from Vichy control to communist control in postwar village politics. All of these films use national stereotyping, a frenetic pace, and the chase, along with numerous sight gags, to capture the spectator's attention. *The Last Metro*, on the other hand, contains a few humorous moments within the context of a serious drama involving resistance, collaboration, and a love triangle.

At issue, then, is whether the ease with which the public accepted Truffaut's portrayal of French collaboration (a portrayal making it palatable without condoning it) is a case of bad faith on the public's and the filmmaker's part. Is the film a new obfuscation of ethical responsibilities, or could it be seen as an effective coming-to-terms with the ambiguities of the Occupation? Taking up, again, the metaphor of the *performance* of Occupation memories that we found in *Lacombe Lucien*, we can explore Truffaut's metaphor of the Occupation *as* theater—a claustrophobic space where role-playing, deception, as well as shifting identities and allegiances, are inherent in the successful performance.

The Last Metro weaves together a personal love story, the lives of actors/characters performing in a play, and the historical events of the war. Marion Steiner, played majestically by Catherine Deneuve, takes charge of a Montmartre theater when her husband Lucas, a German Jew and the theater's director (played by Heinz Bennent), must go into hiding (in the theater's cellar) from the German and French authorities who constantly threaten the troupe. Marion Steiner's personal dilemmas and public actions (along with those of the troupe) incarnate the difficult choices of the French during the Occupation, as all are forced to make compromises with the Occupant (and French police) to avoid personal trouble and to keep the theater open. They enact French complicity as well as remarkable resourcefulness in the face of adversity. Marion's personal dilemma echoes the duplicity and infidelity of the times: while protecting her husband from harm, she nevertheless falls in love with her lead male actor, Bernard Granger (Gérard Depardieu), who is secretly also a resistance fighter (unbeknown to his co-actors until the end). The plot of the play being staged, *La Disparue* (*The Vanished One*), vaguely echoes Marion and Bernard's impossible love, thereby playing upon the tenuous differences between play-acting and genuine action or feeling (a theme throughout the film). While Lucas shadow-directs the play from the cellar, he is also the first to be aware of the nascent love between his wife and Bernard, and seems to foster it. Personal and political secrets, hypocrisy, and facades create a hall of mirrors in which each component (personal, theatrical, and historical) reflects another.

Although the New Wave was no longer operative as a movement in 1980, its motifs are nevertheless functional: Truffaut's self-conscious art, dealing with the mobile lines between art and reality (with art shaping reality rather just reflecting it), and with the inescapability of role-playing in life, becomes more than just a convenient cliché in this film. These motifs allow for the movement between filmmaking, personal and collective histories, and the lives of the players (both actors and spectators) in the present. Given some of the later revelations about Truffaut's origins, notably that his father—whom he never knew—was Jewish, personal questions about the filmmaker's identity point to a whole series of collective, national identity issues that are implicit in the film. We will be looking at the way Truffaut's personal psychodramas hold up—in their transformed, filmic version—a mirror to the French public, revealing a likeness that they can live with, even if it does bear its share of duplicity.

For the New Wave film director who had consistently refused to have his art serve a political cause, or even to tackle a charged political subject, the change in climate in the late 1970s and early 1980s was no doubt a relief. Like Malle before him, Truffaut had longed to make a film set during the Occupation, to take stock of his childhood experience of the war. Between his first feature film, *The Four Hundred Blows* (1959), and *The Last Metro*, echoes of the war stay part of Truffaut's output, but only in allusive or allegorical form. For example, his *Fahrenheit 451* (1966), a science fiction parable about censorship (written by Ray Bradbury), deals with a Nazi-style authoritarian society where books were systematically burned. Like Malle,

Truffaut considered that *The Sorrow and the Pity* gave him leave to portray, in fiction, the concessions and compromises of the French with the German occupying forces, a complicity that the French had to own up to if they were to come to terms with the past. Both directors realized that fiction risked looking too suspicious, too outrageous, or unreal without the initial intervention of documentary to authenticate the dark side of the Occupation. As we noted in the last chapter, Malle was in effect accused of mythifying a "guilty France," and of exaggerating the extent of collaboration.

Although *The Last Metro* portrays the collective response of France to the war through the microcosm of the theatrical troupe, Truffaut's camera tends to focus on the beautiful actress and theater director, Marion Steiner. This emphasis on a strong woman's active participation in the Occupation contrasts greatly with *The Sorrow and the Pity*'s virtual neglect of French women in the documentary's interviews. The only woman to speak at length in Ophüls' film is an alleged *collaborator* who is made to *look* guilty through the way she is filmed (whether she actually *is* guilty is unclear).[2] By 1980, there was a growing awareness of women's roles in the war (as collaborators, but also as resisters), and Truffaut's film embodies this new collective interest. In *The Last Metro*, the issues of resistance and collaboration are enacted within each French person rather than being distributed more tidily (and simply) into camps of good and bad characters (resisters and collaborators). Given that women obtained the right to vote in 1944, Truffaut's focus on a woman can be read as an affirmation of a historical shift regarding women. Early in the film, Marion acknowledges that, with her husband's absence, she has had to take on responsibilities that she would have preferred not to deal with (such as the financial matters of the theater).

Both *The Last Metro* and Malle's later film, *Goodbye, Children* (1987) keep the feel of the child's view of the Occupation[3]: although coming from different social classes (with Malle's family quite well-to-do and Truffaut's more modest), the two future directors were ten years old in 1942; both were later haunted by their memories of the war, although in ways different from the older French public. In Malle's case, the subject matter of his later film deals directly with the child Louis' experience of complicity with the Germans. But in Truffaut's case, the content of his childhood experience and the historical facts of the era were actually kept quite separate: his personal memories as an unwanted, rebellious child, born out of wedlock, were laid out in his early success, *The Four Hundred Blows* (1959), while the actual detailed depiction of the *period* with all its duplicity only came forth much later in *The Last Metro*. It was as if personal experience and historical period could not be told together in the late 1950s.[4] I would argue, however, that although Truffaut deemed his own actions as a child to be detached from the guilty political compromises, lies, and deceptions that he witnessed in adults during the Occupation, it can be said that the ruses the boy in *The Four Hundred Blows* uses to get along in a difficult family situation run parallel to the survival tactics of the French in the period. *The Four Hundred Blows* contains its own share of duplicity and lies (by adults, but also by children), denunciations (one little boy "tells on" the young hero, Antoine Doinel), thefts, desperate searches for shelter and enough to eat (when Antoine runs away from home), ruses against a tyrannical master (in the guise of an unjust French teacher), and betrayals (by Antoine's deceitful, hypocritical mother). If the war is not present as concrete event, the kinds of situations and attitudes that so marked the period for Truffaut are certainly echoed in the hapless life of Antoine Doinel.

The Four Hundred Blows sets itself up as the quintessential *French* film with its opening shots of the Eiffel Tower, symbol of both the capital and the country, but then represses all connections between the nation's character and the period when it was lived by the filmmaker, that is, the Occupation. The erasure of the connections between personal experience and historical moment also hides the fact that Truffaut's own initial inspiration was rooted in French films from the war period when Truffaut was an avid spectator, and when no foreign films (other than German films) were being shown in French theaters. The eradication of the Occupation in *The Four Hundred Blows*, and the disappearance of the central child-hero (Truffaut) in *The Last Metro* present a curious psychic splitting.[5] As a member of the New Wave in the 1950s, did Truffaut avoid historicizing the elements of his own filmic autobiography in *The Four Hundred Blows* for fear of resembling too closely the "Tradition of Quality"? Truffaut ferociously criticized representatives of the latter (epitomized by Claude Autant-Lara) for making *period* films at a time when he himself fell under the sway of American films.[6] Significantly enough, directors such as Autant-Lara were among Truffaut's favorites as a child. Later in his career, Truffaut did claim that budget and his new esthetic (the "New Wave spirit") kept him from undertaking a historical film.[7] But one may wonder whether the decoupling of the personal and the political wasn't *also* an (unconscious) necessary move for the Truffaut of the 1950s, when, as a young, aspiring critic, he associated with the political and artistic Right and took a moralizing, provocative tone toward his French predecessors and the Left. Perhaps Truffaut wanted, too, to keep distinct the faults and deceptions, particularly of his mother (whose fictive representation is embodied by the hypocritical, self-centered character, Mme Doinel, in *The Four Hundred Blows*), from the deceptions of a whole era when complicity and collaboration with the Germans were often entwined with survival for the French? The "purity" of Mme Doinel's duplicity and hypocrisy would have been diminished (thereby disculpating her at least somewhat of her marital infidelity and callousness toward her son) if taken as part of a generalized culpability of French citizens.[8] As we begin to unravel the way *The Last Metro* aligns political ambiguity and personal secrets and deceptions, we will consider how certain aspects of Truffaut's biography inflected this film: First, in what ways did his avid childhood viewing of films during the Occupation have an impact on his apprehension of the period? Second (and tied to the first question), what are the connections between his portrayal of a strong active woman during the war and the actions/representations of women at the time? Third, how do Truffaut's family secrets and political beliefs help articulate a certain mythology of the Occupation that the French could live with comfortably in 1980?

Two precise and somewhat contradictory issues arise from these questions. On the one hand, the combination of accurate historical detail, esthetic prowess, and certain silences about the uglier side of the war eventually makes this film more troubling in its ethical scope than *Lacombe Lucien*. On the other, I am interested in the ways the film creates a positive, if ambivalent, icon of female participation in the war and how this image echoes both Occupation films' female figures and actual women's actions of the war period.[9] Ultimately, it will be necessary to figure out if these two dimensions (positive female representation/ethical complacency) can stand on their own, or whether one subsumes the other. When the lines between necessary facades (pretending to collaborate while resisting) and actual political compromise are blurred, is there still room for a nuanced, critical understanding of the good, the bad, and the beautiful?

ADULT RECREATIONS OF CHILDHOOD'S VIEWS

The Last Metro, as Lynn Higgins has aptly pointed out, finds it sources not only in the war period, but in its films, from Marcel Carné's (1943) *Children of Paradise* and from Ernst Lubitsch's *To Be or Not to Be* (1942). Both are concerned with "a theater troupe and theatricality in life and on the stage," as is *The Last Metro*.[10] But beyond the issue of "interfilmic references" to the periods' works and their theatrical topics (a self-conscious, reflexive move characteristic of the adult New Wave filmmaker), there are other key reasons for portraying Occupation reality via the theater that have to do with the "look" of films made during the Occupation.[11] To begin with, due to production constraints during the war, French films of the "Golden Age" often resembled theater with their closed, inside spaces and greatly reduced sets and decors. This look, in fact, becomes an esthetic that Truffaut's film mimics and that distinguishes it from *The Four Hundred Blows* (which contains many scenes filmed outdoors, a characteristic of New Wave film). The feel and appearance of wartime French film go beyond or at least complement the thematic, self-conscious film references of *The Last Metro*.

The muted look of the nighttime "outdoor" sets, with artificial lighting and shadowy corners, also suggest the oppressive atmosphere of the Occupation, an enclosed world full of clandestine activity. Inside, whether it is the beautiful, very spare decor for the Ibsen-style play that will be performed, or off-stage, the film's light glows with a peach colored radiance, creating a visual tie between acting on and off stage. The stylized decor of the play within the film is reminiscent of the pared-down, elegant sets of Carné's *Les Visiteurs du soir*. Its impeccable, finished *mise en scène*, and historical reconstruction are intriguingly reminiscent of the "Tradition of Quality" that Truffaut criticized so ferociously in the 1950s.

For Truffaut remembering, the dark theaters of his youth bear their share of clandestine activity (he sneaks in without paying) and are no doubt associated with the erotic charge of a secret, taboo experience taking place in the dark. Films made during the Occupation censure the political realities around them—no doubt to avoid the external imposition of censorship by the Germans or Vichy— much in the way the Occupation is erased from Truffaut's own autobiographical drama, *The Four Hundred Blows*. Clearly, the ambiguities and compromises portrayed in *The Last Metro* would have been difficult to air in the Gaullist postwar era of Occupation memories. "Behind-the-scenes" (and beyond official postwar mythology), each character (the lesbian, the resister, the Jew, the blackmarketeer, the traitor) harbors a secret that makes life all the more dangerous to live: effective acting is imperative for survival.

As Alan Williams has pointed out, the "closed settings" for the Occupation films' intense social and family dramas have "served as metaphors for France under the Occupation."[12] To name just a few examples: Christian-Jaque's 1941 *L'Assassinat du Père Noël* (*The Murder of Santa Claus,* 1941) takes place in an isolated mountain village; Carné's and Prévert's 1943 *Les Visiteurs du soir* (*The Night Visitors*) is set in a medieval castle; Bresson's 1943 *Les Anges du péché* (*The Angels of Sin*) is set in a convent; and finally, Clouzot's controversial 1943 *Le Corbeau* (*The Raven*) evokes the stifling atmosphere of a small town in which denunciations amongst the inhabitants run rampant.[13] These are some of the key films of Truffaut's youth: he reportedly saw *The Raven* thirteen times, *The Children of Paradise* nine times, and *The Angels of Sin* was also one of his favorites.[14] Although *The Four Hundred Blows* devotes a fair amount of footage to outdoor scenes filmed on bustling Paris streets and boulevards, and uses natural lighting (in contrast to the Occupation films), the claustrophobic interior of the tiny apartment where the Doinel family lives does recall the closed sets (and family dramas) of the war period. *The Last Metro,* with its dark interiors and artificial outdoor sets, metaphorically aligns internal and external conflicts, family life and political events. Truffaut calls it comically, but quite aptly, a cross between *To Be or Not to Be* and *The Diary of Anne Frank*[15]: with the husband hiding in the cellar and the potentially unfaithful wife on the stage, there are clearly coincidences with the wartime film material. The equation "theater=film=life" is thus an esthetic, emotive, and historical marker for Truffaut's later representation of the Occupation. Using the Occupation's own metaphor, *The Last Metro* is a closed drama enlarged to the scale of the country.

As a young cinephile, Truffaut saw over half the French films produced or shown during the Occupation. Truffaut's biographers, Antoine de Baecque and Serge Toubiana, confirm that the young Truffaut's intense, passionate film viewing during the Occupation—when movies were his escape from unhappy home and school situations into the richer, exciting life of the screen—had a lasting impact on his artistic and moral sensibilities.[16] But films made during the Occupation were not the only ones to influence François's outlook on life. Sacha Guitry's witty, inventive film *Le Roman d'un tricheur* (*The Story of a Cheat*), from 1936, was young François's favorite: he purportedly saw it twelve times at the time of the liberation between 1945 and 1946.[17] The young François no doubt identified with the boy who is caught stealing, is deprived of mushrooms for supper as a punishment, and then survives his family that dies poisoned! The lesson here, according to the video's jacket cover, is "dishonesty is probably the best policy." Guitry, himself, plays the boy turned adult casino croupier and roulette cheat, thus implicitly tying together the resourceful young scamp and the adult actor/filmmaker. To complete the parallels, Truffaut's biographers note: "Guitry is suspect at the Liberation for having resisted very little—that's the least one can say—under the Occupation, but that no doubt reinforces even more the film's power of provocation in the eyes of the young François."[18] Truffaut will describe the film's moral in the following way: "To never expect anything from others, to take what you need and what wouldn't be given to you, to get along without turning to violence, to never become tied or attached to anyone, to learn to count only on oneself, to establish a schedule without constraints, such is the moral of *Le Roman d'un tricheur*."[19] Guitry's wit, skepticism, and artistic talent set a model for living and creating for Truffaut. And, although the film was made in the 1930s, it bears for François the mark of the period when he saw it.

During the Occupation, the cinema offers a "pocket of resistance" to the dramas surrounding the young adolescent (difficult home life, struggles between collaborators and resisters, etc.). The war itself, like the films made at the time, takes on the aura of a theatrical performance that can be viewed at a safe distance, entailing little danger for the young viewer. In a moment we will look at the way this specific view of the war is reproduced in *The Last Metro*.

Thanks to extensive quotations from interviews in the archives of Films du Carrosse (Truffaut's production company), Truffaut's biographers trace the way he remembers his adolescence during the Occupation: it would seem that for both adult and adolescent, the war is a matter of picturesque details, of ceremonies and rituals that are deemed a little silly. There is no investment in the political issues of the day: rather than simply expressing pride for an uncle, Bernard de Monferrand, who fought in the resistance and was caught, Truffaut shows a squeamish uneasiness when faced with the "spectacle" of political resistance in his own family:

> During the whole war, there was a map over the fireplace with little French flags that were supposed to situate Bernard. It was rather ridiculous, this mixture of fear and pride vis-à-vis the Resistance, vis-à-vis a thing that existed a lot less than the contraband of beans and sausages that everyone entered into when returning from the mountains, from the Alps, with 25 kilos of grub in one's pack. I really had the impression that the mountains were for bringing back food on the sly to Paris, and in a certain way, the Resistance resembled for me a trip to the mountains, only a little longer than usual. As for my uncle Bernard, he managed to get out alright. We all went to wait for him for three days at the Gare de l'Est [Paris train station]; it was rather impressive, but it still seemed like a picnic outing in the country, as when I used to come back from camp.[20]

The comical side of the boy's remembrance of the black market, which in turn contaminates his idea of the resistance, recalls Claude Autant-Lara's satirical comedy about the black market in *La Traversée de Paris* (1956). Even if Truffaut, as an adult filmmaker, heaped criticism on Autant-Lara's cynical attitude toward human beings, his rendering of the black market has the same tenor as Truffaut's childhood memories about the "silliness" of the situation. It is significant that the passage above leaves unclear whether the feeling of ridicule in matters concerning the resistance is the adult's or the adolescent's. The reality of the black market and material needs outweighs political action for both the adult and the boy. Pride and political import are tainted by their own theatricality. Truffaut even recognizes that it is impossible for him to separate his personal, youthful vision from the general attitude of the population at the time: "I don't know if that moment is theatrical because it is linked to the perception from my adolescence, or because the French of that period didn't want to look too closely at the reality of things, for if they looked at the real truth, faced it, France would have been a country of resigned people, confronted with the facility of collaboration, with the dangers of resistance."[21]

Play-acting and bad faith are intertwined in the period for the boy, no doubt much in the way that adult behavior is generally viewed as hypocritical and self-serving—in the family as in the public arena. It is not just a matter of the adult imposing his views on the child's experience. In 1945, François writes (for a class assignment) a cynical response to Frank Capra's series of propaganda films, *Why We Fight*, made in the United States at the end of the war: "The film explains how France naively declared war on Germany to save Poland. But benevolent generosity is no longer of this world since individualism and interested aid have replaced it."[22] François is already a blasé skeptic by the time of the liberation, at the age of thirteen, and displays little faith in disinterested collective action. He cannot abide adult self-righteousness, especially in its official forms. In the same class essay, François displays his contempt for the myth of a powerful, effective French Resistance: "our resistance was pathetically weak and couldn't do anything without the help of the Allies."[23] It is not surprising that he receives a very bad grade (4/20) for such a tough (if relatively accurate) appraisal of the French in 1945. France needed to believe that its own contribution to its liberation was crucial. Educators were a key instrument in the rebuilding of the nation, and in the reconstruction of French pride. François refuses to swallow what the adults tell him—to the point that the resistance appears to have very little reality at all.[24]

It is probably not a coincidence that the leading male actor and "hero" in *The Last Metro* bears the name of Truffaut's uncle, Bernard, since both men are associated with resistance work. It also seems befitting, given Truffaut's youthful skepticism, that the character Bernard is portrayed as a somewhat fatuous, ineffectual seducer of women, delivering the same tired line to each woman he meets. His first blunder opens the story, as he tries to pick up Marion's costume designer, who turns out to be a lesbian. And, although Bernard is the clandestine political hero, he makes ethical compromises just as everybody else in the period does: he accepts, for example, working for Marion Steiner even though he has seen her turn away a Jew asking for a job. Although Bernard *is* committed to the resistance, his clandestine activities are glimpsed furtively and indirectly by the spectator so that their impact is reduced. Instead of seeing Bernard plant the bomb that will kill off a German officer, we witness Bernard working on a record player that will become the weapon. The bombing is later announced on the radio. As salient as his secret sabotage work may be, we *see* it less on screen than his awkward chivalry, as when he beats up the fascist critic, Daxiat, because he has insulted Marion's acting ability in a review.[25] In short, Truffaut deconstructs any mythic dimensions of the resistance by showing a resister's foibles. He makes him a rather laughable, almost mediocre, hero.[26]

Jean-Loup Cottins, the gay actor who takes on the direction of *The Vanished One* when Lucas disappears, embodies typical survival politics at the end of the film (and the war), when daily compromises are judged by the resistance. Because he has made various deals with the German and French authorities during the liberation of Paris, in order to keep the theater open, he is arrested because of his suspicious connections, is released because of these same connections, and then rearrested because of them. At a dizzying speed, his contacts alternatively help or sink him. With light-hearted music and a documentary-style voice-over, Truffaut comically portrays the predicament as a sort of revolving door for Jean-Loup: the same scene of his being hauled off to the police station in his bath robe by the FFI (resistance fighters) is repeated. The visual repetition suggests that his action is either justifiable or worthy of incarceration, depending upon which perspective one adopts. The end result is that all actions appear to have more or less the same value: while political authorities judge Jean-Loup, the spectator absolves him.[27]

In the Montmartre theater where the Steiner troupe puts on its plays, German soldiers and Jewish girls alike share in the common raptures of artistic pleasure: the Jewish girl has only to hide the yellow star on her coat lapel to avoid any trouble. Again, we are struck by the childlike, "clean" version of the war, where no one important is ever harmed. Just as no one is deported or tortured in the film,[28] we note that even the evil film critic Daxiat manages to flee: the documentary voice-over tells us that he dies of throat cancer in 1962. Life and theater come together in the last "scene," a *trompe-l'oeil* where, after thinking the film will end unhappily with Bernard wounded in a hospital, turning away from Marion, Truffaut's viewers then realize that they are witnessing a play. The "real" end is a happy finale in a harmonious love triangle: woman and lover (the play's actors—Marion and Bernard) are joined on stage by the director/husband (Lucas) in a triumphant moment. All three cheerfully hold hands to the applause of the play's spectators, an ovation that seems to celebrate the reconciliation in a quintessential happy ending. Truffaut's film of political compromise ends in romantic and esthetic victory.

The "lessons" of the Occupation for François Truffaut (as for other filmmakers like Chabrol and Malle, who were children during the war) run completely counter to those prevalent in the early post-war period, when resistance and heroic action became the symbol of France. For Truffaut, the hypocrisy of these "lessons" leads to cynicism toward civic duties, official authorities, and to a distrust of (French) patriotism. He adds: "I don't feel a hundred percent French and I don't know the whole truth about my origins. I have never tried to obtain a voting card so I can't vote. I would have the impression of accomplishing a very artificial gesture if I voted, as if I were playing a role. So I don't feel an attachment to France and could finish my life in another country. Similarly, the notion of patriotism has no hold on me and I also remain skeptical when people try to explain their religion to me . . . My religion is the cinema."[29]

Truffaut's postwar passion for American films goes hand in hand with his political cynicism about France, and with his ferocious criticism of filmmakers like Claude Autant-Lara, whose film, *Douce*, Truffaut had actually adored in the war years.[30] Significantly enough, what Truffaut, the young film reviewer of the 1950s, will criticize in the "Tradition of Quality" (Autant-Lara, Pierre Bost, Jean Aurenche) is precisely the portrayal of French moral corruption: instead of upholding "family values," they revel—claims Truffaut—in depicting decadence, blasphemy, perversion, and cynicism.[31] In his own portrayal of the period over thirty years after the war, he cleans up this corruption, featuring necessary compromises of the "theatrical family" (made up of basically good people) in difficult times. Each fault is countered with a quality, or at least an explanation: although the heroine, Marion Steiner, falls in love with the sexist, bumbling resister, Bernard, she stills cares deeply for her husband, Lucas. Although the actor and director, Jean-Loup Cottins, dines with Nazi sympathizers and German officials, he only does so to obtain concessions and advantages for the theater and its troupe.[32] Although Marion turns away a Jewish actor from her theater, it is because she must protect her Jewish husband and the theater from the dangers involved in hiring a Jew. (This is no doubt one of the more shocking examples of the characters' compromises.) Although Bernard is a hapless sexist, he loves Marion, is a talented actor, and a sincere resister. Some critics have insisted on the opposition between false facades and true secrets that each character harbors. I would say, instead, that the *combinations* of facades and secrets are integral to the characters. Conforming to the theatrical locale, each character plays at least two roles, on the stage and in life.

The Occupation seems to fully bring out the performative nature of social interaction, for it is the period when acting is a form of survival.

FAMILY SCENARIOS

We have seen that, as both witness to the period *and* to the filmic images it produced of itself, in the *Last Metro*, Truffaut offers his public a double representation involving historical data and filmic self-reference. The arguments of Geneviève Sellier and Noël Burch about the relationships among political moment, family dynamics, and gender representations in French film can help us to understand what repeated scenarios Truffaut was absorbing during his youth, and to compare Truffaut's own female emblem of the Occupation, Marion Steiner, with both period representations of women in film and actual women's actions during the war.

As we have already seen, *La Drôle de Guerre des sexes du cinéma français* identifies a pattern of representations in Occupation films involving strong young women and weak old men. Truffaut's favorite French films in his youth are consistently marked by this prominence of forceful women, and ineffectual or absent father figures. This configuration appears in Autant-Lara's *Douce*, Bresson's *Les Dames du Bois de Boulogne* ("Ladies of the Bois de Boulogne"), and his *Anges du péché* ("Angels of Sin"), as well as Clouzot's *The Raven* and Carné's *Children of Paradise*. The 1940s scenario corresponds to changing attitudes about women. Although women's resourcefulness should have been readily visible prior to the war, it seems that the Occupation made the public more acutely aware of women's ability to take charge of family responsibilities outside, as well as inside, the home, to survive economic, physical, and emotional hardships, and to take part in the struggle. And, with so many men absent, filmmakers tended to give scripts featuring women much more of a chance.

Truffaut's recreations of the family dynamic in *Four Hundred Blows* and *The Last Metro* replicate the Burch/Sellier model. In the earlier film, the beautiful, sexy mother looms large in the life of Antoine Doinel, with the adoptive father appearing weak and dominated by his wife, who lies to him (she has an affair with another man) and orders him around. We know nothing of the boy's biological father. The strong woman in this instance is a self-centered working mother who knows her own desire, and is portrayed as the desired, but wholly unscrupulous, object of the boy's fascination.

The Last Metro brings together the political icon and the family scenario of the Burch/Sellier model. Truffaut's emphasis on Marion Steiner as focal point for representing the Occupation is at once (a) an affirmation of active, courageous women; (b) an alluring portrayal of the collective response of France to the war via the beautiful female icon; and (c) a personal fantasy of the filmmaker who overcomes the Oedipal complex via the fictive happy ending (uniting figures of mother, father, and son). The first of these three characterizations matches historical data quite well: the research of Serge Added on theaters during the Occupation confirms Truffaut's own findings that a rather large number of women actually did run theaters in the period, so Marion's role as theater director is historically accurate.[33] The fact that she protects her Jewish husband reminds one of resister Lucie Aubrac's efforts to rescue *her* Jewish husband during the war (not to mention scores of others who helped Jews to hide or escape). Truffaut's portrayal of women in the film, in general, also includes the picturesque historical details that have now become clichés: for example, women in the film discuss tinting their legs to look like stockings, or how to get a copy of the forbidden, but immensely popular, *Gone with the Wind*. A mother melodramatically washes her son's head after a German soldier has given him a friendly pat. In contrast, Melville's female character, Barny, in *Leon Morin, Priest*, merely laughs when her daughter France says she likes the "Kraut soldier"("Boche") who gives her gifts. Whereas Melville (and novelist Béatrix Beck) seem to dismiss the idea that the young daughter could be contaminated by collaboration through an individual encounter with a German, Truffaut ceremoniously shows parents giving proper lessons of civilian resistance to children. In Chapter 5, we will see that Chabrol, on the other hand, emphasizes how a child does learn corrupting lessons of collaboration through what he is taught at school and home.

The contradictions and tensions in Marion's character make it necessary to question what it might mean to be "strong" during the Occupation, in Truffaut's vision. Strength, here, does not conform to a simple ideal of disinterested heroism. It is more a matter of playing one's life role well, fulfilling the duty to survive through extraordinary times. It involves dissimulation, manipulation, and resourcefulness, as well as the objectionable willingness to sacrifice one Jew (an actor requesting work) for another (her husband). The potentially scandalous nature of such a choice is diminished by the sequence of the presentation: *first*, the viewers think that Marion is an anti-Semite turning away a Jew; *then*, viewers learn that she only does so because she is protecting her Jewish husband.[34]

Marion's force entails both resisting collaboration (she refuses to have dinner with Daxiat), and going along with it (she reluctantly shakes his hand). Although she is quite vulnerable, and not terribly self-aware, Marion routinely displays nerves of steel. To allay her husband's fears before their play's opening performance, she pretends to be completely relaxed, and then secretly rushes to the bathroom to throw up when stage jitters besiege her. When necessary, she adroitly lies to the authorities, including Daxiat, about her husband's whereabouts. Her strength lies in overcoming her own fears, particularly in protecting others. When her husband goes temporarily wild at the thought of having to stay in the cellar indefinitely (the Germans have just invaded the "Free Zone"), Marion does not hesitate to bash him over the head to keep him from rashly trying to leave. Lucas's impetuous desire to go to the authorities to put an end to his waiting recalls Monsieur Horn's final visit to French collaboration headquarters in *Lacombe Lucien*.

Although Marion is not a mother, she plays the role of one in *The Vanished One*, the play they are rehearsing in the film, and this acted function is metaphorically repeated. In many scenes her attitude toward her husband Lucas resembles that of a mother caring for her son. She cuts his hair, consoles him, supplies all his basic needs, and tends to his escape plans. Her attentiveness to Lucas recalls René Le Hénaff's 1943 version of the Balzacian story, *Le Colonel Chabert*, which was mentioned in Chapter 1. In Le Hénaff's film, the young Countess Ferraud, dining with the older, one-armed Colonel Chabert (her ex-husband), cuts up the old man's meat for him in a motherly gesture of kindness. Similarly, Marion Steiner's caring involves love for Lucas, if not passion. This image matches, in some ways, the Vichy portrayals of dutiful women who sacrifice themselves for others, particularly children.[35] Like her Vichy counterparts, Marion Steiner appears to set aside her own desires in the first part of the film. But, as in the anti-Vichy films of the war period, Truffaut's character eventually displays her own desire: toward the end of the film, after Bernard announces he is leaving the theater to fight in the resistance, Marion's passion erupts. First, she slaps him; then, they end up making love on the floor of his dressing room. Truffaut's love scene is indirectly infused with a political flavor that, again, makes Marion a fundamentally ambiguous character: Bernard's choice of the resistance coincides with Marion's liberation in love. Her weakness (in political terms) coincides with the ability to express her own desire—to herself and to someone else. While this is a strength of sorts, it hardly fits a political profile.

Marion's acts, and nearly all those of the people in the Montmartre theater, are dictated by personal exigencies rather than ideology. She is consistently identified as an advocate of practical compromise: avoid the Germans if possible, get along with them when necessary. In a visually stunning scene, Truffaut invites us to measure just how far Marion is willing to go, how far she'll "deal with" the enemy. She shows up in her most elegant attire at Gestapo headquarters to try to persuade (presumably using her "feminine charms") a high ranking German official to keep her theater open and out of the hands of Daxiat. The opening part of the scene foreshadows the end result: when she is yanked out of an elevator in order to make room for a high ranking officer, we sense that German military gallantry is more a convenient pretense than a material reality. As Marion ascends one side of an oval staircase, she stares at another woman descending the other side on the arm of a German officer, a woman named Martine, whom she recognizes as a black marketeer (Marion has purchased a ham through Martine) as well as a thief, someone who is now reaping the benefits of her collaboration. The scene is both majestic and scary, as if dramatizing the ceremony of collaboration, with a sweeping staircase that looks like a theatrical set. The camera shifts back and forth between the two women, suggesting that Marion is about to become (or has already become?) the mirror image of this woman by compromising herself. Even the beginning of their names, *Mar*tine and *Mar*ion, suggests the resemblance. But when Marion actually meets a German official, it is not the contact she sought. In a scene whose music connotes an ever-increasing tension to the point of explosion, the unknown officer takes Marion's hand in his and does not let go until she finally wrenches her hand away and flees in terror (see Figure 4.1). The gesture of an officer's good manners has quickly turned into a sinister clutch. We have barely glimpsed the vicious side of relations with the Occupier, but it is clear that Marion has underestimated the consequences of dealing with the enemy. As an image of collaboration,

Figure 4.1. *The Last Metro*, François Truffaut, 1980. Marion Steiner asks a Nazi officer to help keep her theater open.

presented here as ritualized ceremony, the scene intimates the difference between the theatrical facades of decency that collaboration displays, in contrast to the real dangers it harbors. The hasty flight of Marion undoes the structured resemblance between her and the collaborating Martine. Truffaut is careful to distinguish between hardcore collaboration and a politics of survival.

FAMILY SCENARIOS REVISITED: I AM (NOT) MY FATHER

In Truffaut's script, Lucas Steiner embodies the benevolent, but powerless, father figure that was so prominent in the films of the Occupation. (And, like Pétain, he and Marion have no children.) Lucas appears somewhat older than his wife (certainly much older than his "rival" Bernard), and his position of captive in the cellar leaves him feeling wholly frustrated and helpless. But if Marion is strong, deliberate and protective, it is nevertheless Lucas who realizes well before her that she is in love with Bernard. Listening to them from the cellar while they rehearse on stage, Lucas hears in

Marion's voice a forced coldness toward Bernard, and encourages her to play her romantic role better, in short, implicitly to play out her own feelings toward her co-actor. (Again, we are reminded of the ways Vichy's female characters must renounce their desires.) Lucas-the-husband, who has been in the impotent position of prisoner, becomes symbolically Lucas-the-father, who gains a measure of control over the scenario of love between his wife and Bernard, by intuiting it and then by actually directing it himself.[36] (Concurrently, he has also secretly directed the play *The Vanished One* via copious notes passed on to the replacement director, Jean-Loup Cottins.) Incredibly, it is Lucas who first reveals to Bernard that Marion loves him, rather than Marion herself. Lucas's intervention in the situation of the potential lovers resembles that of a kindly father over his children: with no apparent jealousy or pain, he appears content to manipulate what he cannot entirely control.

Now we know that in middle age, during the late 1960s, Truffaut decided to track down his own biological father, whom he had never met. The detective he hires eventually does uncover his father's whereabouts, at which time Truffaut learns that his father is a pharmacist and that he is Jewish. Truffaut, who cannot quite bring himself to actually meet his father, does secretly watch him enter his apartment building one evening. The creation of Lucas Steiner in the scenario as a benevolent, hidden father figure, who is a director and is Jewish, implicitly brings into play Truffaut's own history, combining his father's ethnic background and his own choice of career as director. His character Lucas declares at one point: "In my cellar, I know everything that's going on in the theater." Here, the father takes on his traditionally omnipotent role, although in many other instances he acknowledges his profound frustration (and impotence) at having to remain cooped up in his hideout.

What is curious, but perhaps all too understandable, is that one key area of creative authority over which Truffaut relinquishes some of his control in the script of *The Last Metro* is Lucas's role. Truffaut cannot seem to find the right words to put in the mouth of his Jewish father-figure, Lucas, and enlists playwright Jean-Claude Grumberg to write the dialogue between Lucas and Marion. As Truffaut's biographers note, it is the speech of a *Jewish* character in a Grumberg play that had attracted Truffaut, for the film director cannot imagine how to make Lucas a viable, convincing character, rather than a literary one or a ponderous, stereotyped illustration of "Jews during the Occupation." Lucas's comments about being Jewish, as he playfully slips on a false hooked nose, measure in theatrical terms both wartime racism and Truffaut's questions about his own identity: "I'm trying to feel Jewish. Playing the Jew is very tricky. If you underplay, they say you're exaggerating; if you overplay, they say you don't look Jewish. What does it mean to look Jewish?"[37] One can imagine Truffaut standing before a mirror, asking just such questions after learning about his father's identity. Elsewhere, Truffaut has linked national identity to the oral (versus the visual): "I feel very French when it comes to dialogue . . . Many of the filmmakers who emigrated to Hollywood could master light, image, working with actors, but I think that deep down they couldn't control what they did because of language."[38] The problematic ties between national and personal identity, and between ethnicity and cinematic language, that Truffaut describes for the filmmaker are embodied in Lucas Steiner's role, as it performs the interrogations about ethnic/national identity. (Steiner is, after all, played with a foreign accent by German actor Heinz Bennent). Lucas Steiner's questions on identity thematize the Occupation's racism in general, Truffaut's hidden Jewish background, *as well as* his own anti-Semitic tendencies. Given Truffaut's brazen defense of fascist, anti-Semite Robert Brasillach, who was executed for collaboration in 1945, his defense of Catholic monarchy, and his ties in the mid-1950s to the anti-Semitic cinema critic Lucien Rebatet, it is small wonder that his own Jewish origins should cause him to put ethnic identity in question. The "Jew-in-the-cellar" is of course Truffaut's own, but he also embodies the hidden stories of France's buried past, a mixed bag of collaboration, resistance, racism, and survival.[39]

What arises from this double reading of Truffaut's biography and *The Last Metro* is the consistent impression that the child's experience and understanding of the war period are crucial to Truffaut's adult interpretations of wartime events. The child's cynicism in having witnessed adult hypocrisy in issues of private morality as well as public or political comportment, lead logically to Truffaut's polemical attitudes toward the French and French politics in the 1950s. His affiliations with the intellectual Right, including ex-collaborators like Lucien Rebatet and the rebellious group of dandies, the "hussards" (Roger Nimier, Jacques Laurent, Michel Déon, Antoine Blondin, and Marcel Brion) are no secret to Truffaut's critics, although these associations have frequently been left unmentioned or underemphasized.

His turn toward the Right in the early 1950s (at a time when the Left was prominent in the arts) coincides with his credo of a "disengaged" art, one that would not serve a political cause. This effort to maintain a noncommitted filmmaking is consistent with *The Last Metro*'s artistic agenda.

But, in the final analysis, no work of art, especially a historical one, can escape political perspectives, and *The Last Metro* is part of the resistance/collaboration polemic. If Truffaut's portrayal of Occupation compromises is plausible (and I think it is), its near total neglect of the ugliest parts of collaboration and Nazism in France places his esthetic choices in a questionable light. The closed atmosphere of the film, the play within a play, and the glossy happy ending ultimately seem designed to detach the story from its historical moorings (to "disengage" it), and even undercut its ties to the present. At the time of *The Last Metro*'s release, French anti-Semitism was running strong, as witnessed by a series of bombings of Jewish synagogues at the beginning of the 1980s. Truffaut's fictive plot pulls historical events into its own world, making them dependent on an esthetic that affirms beauty, desire, and goodness within a fallible (but likable) human nature. The majority of the French population who had awaited the war's outcome would not be jostled by such a portrait of France. The startling disregard for the most tragic dimensions of collaboration (the deportations, torture, and the camps) could be explained in terms of exemplarity: the "average" citizen was neither hero nor villain during the war. In Truffaut's version—associated with childhood remembrance—death and destruction are somewhere else—off screen, out of view—as is heroic idealism. I am not trying to suggest here that Truffaut ought to have made a more politicized film than he did. But, given his and Schiffman's attention to historical details that necessarily involves *interpreting* and *evaluating* the meaning of wartime events, it is clear that the filmmaker's creative program includes a sympathetic eye toward the average citizen trying to survive, with all the compromises that that must include.

In the peculiar twists among autobiography, national icons, and film, *The Last Metro* breaches the lines between fact and fiction in revelatory ways. Its *typical* characterizations of French life during the Occupation are bound together by Catherine Deneuve's roles in and out of fiction. First, her fictional role as the artist's lover (whether actor Bernard or playwright Lucas) follows in the wake of her love affair with Truffaut twelve years before when she starred in his 1968 *Sirène du Mississipi* (*Mississippi Mermaid*). The theatrical lines that the hero of *The Vanished One* in *The Last Metro* repeats suggest the bittersweet memories of Truffaut's affair with Deneuve: "It is joy and suffering," says the character about a lost love. The quotation is also a cinematic nod, since it is a melodramatic reprise of a line from *Mississippi Mermaid* (starring Deneuve). To complete the cross reference, Truffaut names the lead female character Marion in both films.

Deneuve's link with films on the Occupation was already established by 1980, for she had starred in Jean-Paul Rappeneau's 1965 comedy about the Occupation, *La Vie de château* (*A Matter of Resistance*).[40] With *The Last Metro*, her career as an Occupation icon is confirmed. Truffaut described the cinema as a "woman's art" in which there is a "coincidence between the talents of the director and an actress directed by him."[41] Truffaut's shot of Deneuve's legs, viewed from below by her husband Lucas as she ascends a flight of stairs, draws the spectator's attention to the scopophilic pleasures of the woman's body for the desiring director (Lucas/Truffaut) in a self-conscious way: it is not just that we see Lucas peep at Marion's legs, he comments on this pleasure himself. The fetishistic showcasing of Deneuve sexualizes the equation "woman=cinema=Occupation symbol." Five years later, Deneuve was chosen as the new official symbol of France, portraying the traditional "Marianne" on stamps, statues, and in the media. Thus, the network of associations among film, the Occupation, and a female national icon becomes complete. Maurice Agulhon notes that Deneuve was much more of a symbol of "France" than the "French Republic,"[42] that is, a more conservative, less militant version of French identity, which would align her with *The Last Metro*'s comfortable portrayal of a compromised citizenry coming together and enduring hard times under Vichy. Her very name, Marion, which we had tied to Martine the collaborator, also reminds us of Marianne. Surely, Marion's maneuvering between collaboration and survival with integrity embodies the nation's problematic, ambiguous path.

Before concluding, we need to return briefly to our earlier question about the feasibility of affirming a strong female survivor and resister in the context of the political compromises Truffaut depicts. What is again striking about this situation is the way that it echoes debates about the connection between women's gains during the war and the horrible deaths of Jews, soldiers, and political resisters. The temptation for some has been to describe women's advances during the war in terms of costs to others (including the victims of the Holocaust!). It is certainly true that in terms of women's rights, responsibilities, and sheer visibility (as witnessed by the Burch and Sellier film research), the Occupation did provide a historical moment in which women rose to the demands of the roles they needed to play. But re-victimizing women as usurpers of men's roles is clearly wrong-headed. It reminds us of how Vichy ideology set women in double binds, sometimes actually accusing them of causing the war, and sometimes calling upon them to be "real women" safe-guarding home and family, while leaving them few or no material resources to take care of their families' needs.

The Last Metro, like the period it portrays, does not attempt to reconcile the positive and the negative, but rather implicitly invites the viewer to experience the *imaginaire social* of the 1980s, to accept the idea that the heroism during the Occupation, of women or of men, usually took on many shades of gray, and that in the long run, it is the ability to play one's roles well—that is, to survive—that is the most important.

CHAPTER 5

------ ❧❦❧ ------

AMBIGUOUS NATIONAL ICONS IN CHABROL'S *STORY OF WOMEN*

Claude Chabrol opens his 1976 memoirs with an early childhood anecdote that could serve as a sort of primal scene for the filmmaker/viewer who breaks out of the parental shell through film. He tells us that at age four (!) he watched *Anthony Adverse*, a historical film set in eighteenth-century Spain, about an unhappily married woman who falls in love with another man. What strikes the child's imagination and undoes his parents' "belle construction morale" ("fine moral framework," an ironic designation) is the film's ending, in which the doddering old husband kills the handsome young lover. In a paragraph-sentence, Chabrol concludes: "I was surprised, scandalized, shocked."[1] For Chabrol, *Anthony Adverse* is the first film to challenge expectations and automatic judgments of human action. Chabrol's own creative efforts will follow this path of contestation, using scandal to provoke us to respond, breaking comfortable viewing habits (and unexamined values) in the process. The ethical ambiguity of situations, the hallmark of Chabrol's cinematic storytelling, thus arose from a very early experience of film viewing. Whether this recounted event is accurate or invented matters less than its ability to explain the autobiographical connections, for Chabrol, between ethical interrogation and filmmaking.

Chabrol's fascination with the Occupation—he has made four films that portray the period—would appear to coincide with his early attraction to ethical ambiguities rather than to the fact that both his parents worked in the Parisian underground resistance. As a young adolescent during the war, Chabrol was whisked away from the dangers of his parents' resistance life, spending much of the war in the country village of Sardent (in the Creuse region). Ultimately, the hypocrisy and ambiguities of Vichy and the early postwar period led young Claude (he was fourteen in 1944) away from a Leftist, heroic position that his parents' activities might have suggested to him.

In rather categorical terms, Chabrol distances himself from the fray: "The events of History are not points of reference for my personal life."[2] His memories of the *cinéclub* he started in a garage in 1942 at age twelve do, however, attest to the characteristic ethical ambiguity that has marked his work. Chabrol first explains that local authorities required that his club show German propaganda newsreels, and that most of the films in distribution were German. Then the adult filmmaker recalls, with a mixture of sympathy and critical, after-the-fact awareness, the reaction of the local public to the infamous anti-Semitic film, *Le Juif Süss* ("The Jew Süss"): "When the Jew Süss was hanged after committing a stream of thefts, deceptions, murders, and rapes, the audience applauded, even those who were hiding Jews in their homes. They hadn't become anti-Semitic in ninety minutes: they were just happy that the bad guy was punished. But even so, even so, there remained in their minds the trace of an identification between the Jew and Evil."[3] In a sort of seesaw movement, Chabrol's description captures one of the paradoxes of the period, interweaving popular political ambivalence and moral positions. I would suggest that the equivocal situations of the Occupation, when the moral quality of an action was constantly in question, coincide precisely with Chabrol's predilection for a cinema that tests our presuppositions about ethical actions and social choices. Chabrol challenges us by exploring instances when good does not triumph over evil.

It has been noted by many that the New Wave and the New Novel in the 1950s and 1960s emphasized self-conscious, self-enclosed esthetics and artistic experimentation at the expense of clearly politicized, ethically unambiguous or historicized *topoi*. For Truffaut and Chabrol, this meant creating films about the present, about the difficulties of youth, and about Paris landscapes, within an increasingly Americanized contemporary culture. As we saw in the previous chapter, *The Four Hundred Blows* takes up various aspects of Truffaut's childhood without setting it in the period of the Occupation in which it was lived. In the New Wave's credo—"Right Bank" style—to represent the past was considered passé to some extent. The New Wave's esthetic turn away from history and politicized stances is no doubt tied to the postwar repression of the wartime past and to de Gaulle's myth of generalized French resistance in the war.

Pascal Ory lists Claude Chabrol's name at the end of his incisive work about anarchism on the Right. In Chabrol's case, the associations between a youthful, rebellious esthetic, and a certain anarchical Right are more than just casual. In the early 1950s, these ties verge on the outrageous. A rabble-rouser even before becoming part of the *Cahiers du cinéma* group, Chabrol tells in his memoirs of belonging during his one year of law school to a club ("la corpo de droit," "the law society"), of which the president was none other than far-Right conservative, Jean-Marie Le Pen, of whom Chabrol says "his intelligence quotient may not have been that of Einstein, but he wasn't stupid."[4] Chabrol's bad boy posturing in the memoirs makes it difficult to tell just how far things went: although Chabrol says the group was primarily on the extreme Right (particularly opposed to student unions), he describes himself as "more on the Left" ("plutôt de gauche").[5] His 1958 film, *Les Cousins*, portrays a wild, drunken party of a well-heeled "corpo"-style group, with its violence and free sex. The group's racism is suggested in the film when a young black character is told to leave the "corpo" gathering. Just as troubling is the mock Nazism of the Parisian young protagonist who dresses in Nazi uniform at the party, and plays a Wagner recording while sauntering through the party spouting German. At one point, he wakes a sleeping friend by yelling a German command in the boy's ear: the boy is Jewish and is temporarily frightened. Games, practical jokes, fights, the mimicry of evil: the wartime past is a toy box of naughty representations for Chabrol's character. This portrayal of a postwar irreverent youth playing around with the symbols of the war caused an uproar by critics at the journal *Positif*, archrival of the *Cahiers*. Identifying the dramatic portrayal of characters with the filmmaker's own point of view, critics accused Chabrol of Nazi sympathies. The provocative side of Chabrol—that is, his representations of the scandalous without telling us what to think about it—has sometimes, understandably, got him into hot water.

But if Chabrol's historical associations seem bound up with the political Right during his youth, we must also remember that Chabrol was one to keep his distance from French nationalist tendencies in favor of critical views of things French (contrary to extremists like Le Pen, who play the nationalist card with xenophobic fervor). Does he actually fit the image of Ory's "anarchists on the Right?" Is he cynical about human motives, critical of everything, affirming nothing, or at least nothing other than his art? The ties among individual experience, artistic enterprise, and shared public consciousness and conscience are worth exploring, especially when the topic is the Occupation.

In 1999, Chabrol commented on the stakes of remembering the Occupation: "The Occupation is a period that fascinates me a lot, and I am not the only one, because it is one of the periods when political choices not only involved people during their life, but subsequent generations as well."[6] His first two attempts at representing the Occupation were not terribly successful, no doubt because the stories were not entirely of his choosing. And, given that both films focus on Resistance groups, we might also speculate that portraying the parental milieu carried an Oedipal flavor to which Chabrol was particularly recalcitrant.

In the 1960s, Chabrol was asked to make a film dealing with the war that conformed to the heroic stance of the postwar myth. *La Ligne de démarcation* ("The Demarcation Line"), made in 1966, was a pastiche of a typical resistance story based on an account by the relatively conservative resister, Colonel Rémy, an account that was too reductive and unequivocal for the Chabrolian style. In Rémy's story, the inhabitants of a French Jura village are divided up according to their political positions—collaborators and resisters (with the geographical "demarcation line" between occupied and free zones being a river running through the town). Where one might have expected a fair number of complications, with appearances sometimes hiding more complex political choices, one finds instead a series of caricatures. Claude Blanchet notes that the more ambivalent characters are doomed to die in Rémy's simplified schema, presumably because there is no room for ambiguous positions in his narrative.[7] Chabrol has said of this film that it was in "formal contradiction with what [he] think[s] of existence," with only a few "tongue in cheek" moments hinting at his personal touch.[8] Despite Chabrol's reservations—or the spectators'—about this film's merits, we should note that *La Ligne de démarcation* nevertheless presents the familiar model of a tough heroine/weak hero, in this instance, an English countess/nurse (played by Jean Seberg) and her French husband the count

(Maurice Ronet), a French captain. The countess is a valiant, resourceful resister, whereas the count, who has returned from the war a cripple, is a pessimist who sees no way out of defeat.

In 1984, Chabrol was asked to film Simone de Beauvoir's story *Le Sang des autres* (*The Blood of Others*, starring Jodie Foster), that portrays a group of communists and resisters in the years just before the war, as well as during the Occupation. Once again, Chabrol was not satisfied with his film that, despite his efforts, remained too flat, "a crude soap opera," as he says, no doubt still too politically correct for him.[9] Again, despite the faults (the dialogue is flat, Jodie Foster is an unconvincing romantic lead), *The Blood of Others* is typical in the way it focuses on a young, strong woman who has to negotiate individual interest (romantic love) and a political cause (resisting the German occupation). Through her love for a resistance fighter, Hélène moves from political indifference (the war is not *her* concern) to effective action. But the price for uniting personal and collective desires is death: the heroine dies from gunshot wounds after successfully carrying out an underground operation. In this scenario, the woman must be sacrificed if the symbolic synthesis of personal and collective interests is to succeed.

It is in his two later films—*Story of Women* (*Une Affaire de femmes*, 1987) and *The Eye of Vichy* (*L'Oeil de Vichy*, 1993)—that we see Chabrol's own characteristic choices come through in depicting the Occupation. *Story of Women*, which is based on the life of abortionist Marie-Louise Giraud, and her execution by the Vichy government in 1943, is arguably Chabrol's strongest film. *The Eye of Vichy*, his documentary on Vichy, is composed exclusively of Vichy and German propaganda from the Occupation period (made in conjunction with historians Jean-Pierre Azéma and Robert O. Paxton). Both films place the burden of interpretation on the spectator: we must decide where guilt and responsibility lie. Given Chabrol's early ties to the Right, we may wonder whether Pascal Ory's term "anarchist on the Right" does not, in fact, characterize Chabrol's style in these films. The cynicism perceived in the unflattering portrayal of the abortionist in *Story of Women*, or in the relentless presentation of Vichy images in *The Eye of Vichy*, would seem to confirm Ory's opinion. We may note, in addition, that Jean-Pierre Azéma's own family ties to collaboration—his father was a collaborator—could add grist to the accusatory mill. But this is clearly *not* the case. Azéma has spent his professional career studying and contesting the political compromises of those like his father, and Robert Paxton was one of the first historians to bring to light France's responsibility in collaboration and in the Holocaust. In both films, Chabrol uses a certain opacity to shake us up, not to make us feel complacent. Contrary to the memoirs of Marie Chaix, Jean-Luc Maxence, and Pascal Jardin, all children of major collaborators, Chabrol's films do not insidiously rationalize and justify collaboration through "innocent" description and explanation. In *Story of Women*, the filmmaker ultimately shows that Vichy functionaries are the true criminals who victimize the female abortionist and her patients. In *The Eye of Vichy* the contemporary voice-over intervenes at every turn to undermine false claims that the Vichy regime would have purported in the old film footage. Thus, in each instance, the critical voice is corrective, not just cynical.

In what follows, I concentrate on *Story of Women* as a prime example of Chabrol's filmic ambivalence concerning women in the war. This work is particularly crucial to the study of women as a symbol of France because it offers a double focus: it not only allows us to question the ways Vichy's propaganda and forms of collaboration enter into women's lives in the historical period, it also enables us to explore the ways this filmic representation/performance of history shapes the attitudes of the viewing public towards women's issues and toward the nation, when they are filtered through the recreation of France's Vichy.

Near the end of *Story of Women*, we watch Chabrol's protagonist, Marie Latour, as she is led to the guillotine in 1943, for having performed abortions, that is, in Vichy's pro-natalist terms, for having committed "crimes against the State." Chabrol, taking his inspiration from Francis Szpiner's 1986 account of the life and execution of the abortionist Marie-Louise Giraud,[10] has chosen to dramatize an actual historical event from the Occupation that no doubt feeds into ongoing debates in Europe and the United States on the issue of abortion. Tear gas canisters were reportedly thrown by protesters in Europe to keep the film from being shown.[11] The film eventually makes it quite clear that Marie Latour's deeds have been judged by a deceitful, murderous "French State," incapable of hiding the inequities and contradictions in its policies toward women. We come to realize, as do Marie and her defense lawyers, that Marie is a scapegoat accused of creating the ills of occupied France, depriving it of its children, while the government unhesitatingly sends French workers to forced labor camps in Germany (the "Service de Travail

Obligatoire"), and ships out communists, resisters, and Jews of all ages to death camps, when it does not have them killed on French soil. Chabrol creates a stark contrast: on the one hand, abortion is sanctimoniously defined as a state issue of morality—this occurs at the end of the film during Marie's trial. On the other hand, the earlier sections of the film emphasize the individual plight of women, mostly uneducated, poor, working class, who have become pregnant—by their husbands, lovers, or German soldiers—and who cannot afford financially and/or personally to bring the pregnancy to term. Although uneducated herself, Marie astutely remarks to a cellmate at the end that rich women do not have to go through the same difficulties and suffering, because they can buy their way out of the problem. Thus, the law's victims are those who are the least economically privileged.[12] Clearly, such economic disparities, when it comes to the affordability of abortion, remain contemporary in both France and the United States.

As spectators of the film, however, we are made to feel at least some complicity with the judges and their reprehensible, outrageous position: up until her arrest, we have been witnesses to Marie Latour's less than perfect conduct during the war, and are implicitly called upon to judge her moral shortcomings—shortcomings that play into Vichy propaganda condemning individualism, materialism, and immorality, *especially* in women. Ultimately, one comes to wonder if Marie is not condemned for these faults as much as for being an abortionist. In Chabrol's film, it is Marie's own husband who turns her in to the authorities, and his reasons have more to do with the fact that he is being shamelessly cuckolded than with Marie's abortion activities.[13] Chabrol makes his viewers recognize the workings of collaboration by placing us in the compromising position of judges. The spectators, sitting in neat rows of armchairs facing the screen, constitute the contemporary jury that is to pass sentence on Marie's actions.

There are two sides of this issue that I would like to emphasize: first, I am concerned with the final image left for us to ponder, that is, the victimized woman's destruction as it plays into national politics, with woman becoming national symbol, albeit an ambivalent one. How do a government *and* a filmmaker use women's issues to raise questions of collaboration and patriotism during the war? In a sense, we are being asked to judge France, via Marie, as a national symbol. Although Chabrol is certainly not known as a feminist filmmaker, his construction of an effective, mythic version of the Szpiner account enacts, through the individual woman's life story, the socio-political ambiguities and harsh difficulties of survival in France in 1942–43, at a time when much of the population began shifting alliances from Pétain to the resistance. In a second section, I explore the ways the final scenes require a rereading of the film as a whole— a rereading that reveals to us how complicity takes place, as we are called upon to pass *our* judgment on Marie Latour, not just as abortionist but also as woman. In a final note, we will look into the family secret of the real life Marie-Louise Giraud.

WOMAN AS NATIONAL SYMBOL

What is conspicuous to me, in the image of this woman about to be executed, are her associations with Joan of Arc and Marie-Antoinette, and the paradoxes that arise from the expressly visual ties to Joan the Patron Saint of France (the nation's savior-victim), Marie-Antoinette (the traitor to the Republic), and Vichy's "National Revolution." The guillotine symbolically conflates opposing "revolutions"—that of 1789 and of Vichy's anti-democratic, anti-republican cause—making us contemplate Marie Latour's ties to France's tradition of turning its female victims into national symbols (principally Joan, but to a lesser degree, Marie-Antoinette as well). The indirect references to Joan of Arc also bring together, in one figure, patriotic appeals of the Left and the Right: on the Right, we find the frequent propaganda links to Joan during the Occupation, which helped to legitimate Marshal Pétain's role as savior of the French people.[14] In Jean Marboeuf's 1993 film, *Pétain*, the comparison between Pétain and Joan of Arc is made explicit. Also, of more recent date, Jean-Marie Le Pen's far Right party, Le Front National, appropriated Joan of Arc for its racist, xenophobic brand of nationalism.[15] Although the Left has resorted less to this kind of ploy (of reviving past national symbols for contemporary political gain), during the war, the peasant girl from Domrémy *was* adopted by that other liberator, General de Gaulle. De Gaulle, who hailed from the province of Lorraine, as did Joan, ardently cultivated the comparison between himself and Joan, making the cross of Lorraine the very symbol of French independence and resistance against the Germans and the Vichy government.[16] Pierre Laborie has also shown how Joan of Arc was made "a symbol of unity and rallying in the Catholic southwest press during the war."[17]

The links to Joan of Arc and Marie-Antoinette in Chabrol's film are numerous, even if they go unspoken. The first markers that associate them lie in Marie's preparation for her beheading: the nuns, who are her jailers, have her hair cut off before the fateful morning, almost as if to prefigure the actual beheading. Marie's hair is left in a crude, blunt cut, with her neck exposed. On the day of her death, she wears a dark dress made of coarse material and dark socks that hang around her ankles. Her worn, simple shoes complete a look that makes her seem almost childlike, although she is forty years old. Finally, the small stature of Chabrol's Marie, played by Isabelle Huppert, makes the character seem all the more vulnerable at the end. In the procession led by the priest and attended by policemen, lawyers, and Vichy officials (all symbols of the powers bringing about her death), Marie is more or less dragged toward the guillotine with her hands bound behind her back. In this final instant, her appearance strikingly resembles portraits of Joan of Arc and Marie-Antoinette (see Figure 5.1). It is not, of course, the warrior Joan of Arc clad in armor that we recall, and it is not to the actual history of Joan's death that we are led. (Joan's head was reportedly shaved before her burning.) The cropping of Marie's hair and her subsequent beheading are obviously reminiscent of Marie-Antoinette's end. Marie

Figure 5.1. *Story of Women*, Claude Chabrol, 1987. Marie Latour about to be guillotined.

Latour—in the final scenes—does, in fact, bear a resemblance to Jacques-Louis David's famous pen sketch of the queen en route to her death. But Chabrol's protagonist *also* reminds us of the representations of Joan of Arc as poor peasant girl and martyred victim. In the film, the haircut and drab peasant clothing are all the more conspicuous because, as was the case for Marie-Antoinette, we have witnessed Marie's increasing attention to her appearance—hairstyle, makeup, clothing—up to the point when she is arrested (see Figure 5.2). Like the haircut, the stripping of Marie's outward beauty and sensuality presages the beheading, and takes on the function of a female castration. Concurrently, both Marie and Marie-Antoinette are also turned into quasi-monsters in order to merit fully their punishment: Marie is accused of depriving the country of its children; Marie-Antoinette was accused of sexually abusing her son.

Marina Warner's work on Joan of Arc provides several examples of artistic images of Joan that intersect with her political significance, and that are pertinent to our discussion of Chabrol's Marie Latour.[18] Of particular interest are two visual portrayals that show Joan's recuperation by Vichy and by the Gaullists. The 1943 Vichy propaganda poster, "Assassins Always Return to the Scenes of Their Crime," evokes Joan burning at the stake in Rouen, and clearly suggests that the English (rather than the Germans) are once again the enemies of

Figure 5.2. *Story of Women*, Claude Chabrol, 1987. Marie Latour just before her arrest.

France. Joan looms larger than life in the background, against a red sky full of black smoke, as the Allied bombings, portrayed in the foreground, cause Rouen to go up in flames. Joan herself, like Marie, is dressed simply: she wears robes reminiscent of a choirgirl's, and has her hands manacled. Her eyes are closed, as if she were in prayer, and her haircut is reminiscent of Marie Latour's.[19] Like Chabrol's protagonist, this Joan also has a childlike quality. It should be noted, however, that everything about Vichy's Joan is carefully staged, the perfect icon, whereas Marie's blank look and ill-kept appearance are devoid of the calm assurance visible in Joan's demeanor. Marie leaves us, instead, with an unsettled and unsettling image, seemingly combining martyr and betrayer, Joan *and* Marie-Antoinette.

The picture of the Gaullist Joan is even more stylized: enclosed in a frame within the picture, Joan is an elongate figure, dressed in a flowing white robe (and in an almost sensual pose, revealing bare feet and a bare shoulder), tied to the stake, with her smiling head raised to the burning sky, while what is perhaps a spiritual mother (a nun or the Virgin Mary?) looms protectively over her. At the very bottom of the print we see knights with drawn swords, and to each side of the scene is the Cross of Lorraine, as if the Gaullist symbol were meant to enshrine Joan. In contrast to this Gaullist Joan, it is interesting to note that Marie, like the Vichy Joan, is not represented as a sexual being when she is executed: in Chabrol's film, Vichy makes sure that Marie is stripped of the exuberant sensuality she has unabashedly displayed up to the end. Vichy's Joan wears robes that camouflage her to the point that it could just as easily be a boy as a girl. In this context, Joan's famous androgyny is merely an absence of sexuality rather than an ambivalence. The same goes for Marie, whose sexuality, as we shall see later, is ambivalently represented in the earlier parts of the film, and then denied totally at the end. At Marie's death, we could not be further from France's sensual feminine symbols, such as Delacroix's 1830 "Liberty Guiding the People," with bare breast and barefoot, or as Marianne, symbol of the republic. The sensual portrayal of the Gaullist Joan, on the other hand, reminds us of the frequent references by de Gaulle to a feminine France that he felt destined to save.

Like these predecessors, Marie Latour becomes a symbol to be manipulated.[20] The similarities with Joan's story are, in fact, striking. Both Joan and Marie undergo trumped-up trials in which the state and the church align themselves against an uneducated woman who is actually betrayed by her own people: the initiative against Joan is led by Frenchmen (Pierre Cauchon under the auspices of Jean de Bourgogne) who sympathize with the English cause rather than with Charles VII; Chabrol's Marie is denounced anonymously by her husband, and then prosecuted by representatives of the French government of Vichy.[21] It is no doubt one of the fascinating and horrifying ironies of these histories, that it is certain traitorous Frenchmen who help to crush the person who then becomes the very symbol of their patriotism. The presence of the nuns as prison guards, and of the priest who officiates at her death, underscores in Marie's case the complicity between church and state. Collaboration with foreign powers and complex national politics also inflect the two cases. In both, the steamrolling procedures by which the accused are tried are too complex or hermetic for either Marie or Joan to be able to understand completely just what they are supposed to have done. In the heresy trial of Joan by the Inquisition (composed primarily of French Inquisitors), Joan is never informed of what her crimes might have been. Warner explains: "The Inquisition did not bring formal charges against a suspect; but its duty was the diagnosis and eradication of heresy. The plaintiffs could never be defended against specific accusations, because the actions that had brought them under suspicion were never set forth clearly by the accusers, but appeared only under the veils of their questions. Joan's trial has the nightmarish ambiguity, formlessness, confusing menace of *The Trial* or *The Castle*: she has no means of knowing where the interrogation is driving, what the concealed charge is."[22] Marie's difficulty at grasping what is happening to her is a similar nightmare. She has erroneously assumed that Vichy's state tribunal only tries communists, and is thus confused about her own trial when she learns that it is a state matter. Under normal circumstances, the abortions she admits to having performed would have led at most to a prison term, but certainly not to a death sentence for what had been considered a minor crime under the Third Republic. Marie's understanding is at the level of standard judiciary practices: she does not realize that the government is making of her a diabolic symbol that it will then consider its obligation to crush. She is told to sign a document by a justice ministry official, without understanding just what she is signing. And, when a cellmate asks what she is being tried for, her response is both comical and tragic, revealing the extent to which the process has overwhelmed her: she tells her cellmate that she did not really understand (or trust) her lawyer's description of her case, that he told her she had assassinated the president of the republic. By this, she refers to the accusations against her for crimes against the state. Although Chabrol's spectator may not realize it, the metaphor also reflects the actual phrasing of Vichy's law of February 15, 1942, stating that abortionists are assassins of their country.[23] Clearly, the accusations against Marie are much more severe than she has ever dreamed of. Her tragic-comical remark is all the more ironic because it shows that Marie has not fully realized what it means for France to no longer be a republic during the Occupation. That there is only a "French State" with a "Chief" is, in fact, crucial to the way her case is being treated.[24] When her lawyer explains to Marie that the State prosecution plans to make an example of her, she naively repeats: "An example of what?" The outcome of her case depends less on evidence and jurisprudence than on the Vichy government's vengeful sadism and vacuous discourse on morality. Miranda Pollard pointedly notes another agenda underlying the eradication of abortionists: "Uncovering abortion made female sexuality manifest and inescapable. Feminine desire—feminine excess—were summoned up by the disclosure of abortion. So it was not the literal phenomenon of abortion that Vichy had to suppress most urgently . . . The very acts (adultery, infidelity to a POW husband, sleeping with German soldiers, 'living it up' under the Occupation), the activities that might be 'hidden' by abortion had to be attacked."[25] Sexual treason is what lurks dangerously behind abortions for Vichy.

In the film, the melodramatic 1808 painting by Pierre Prudhon, "Justice and Divine Vengeance Pursuing Crime," hangs above the presiding magistrate of Marie's trial.[26] The camera silently zooms in on this icon as another ironic, mythic reminder of the overblown rhetoric used to condemn Marie, a rhetoric that, like the painting, unites the powers of law and religion to carry out the pursuit of this woman. When Marie stands in court to have her sentence read to her by the magistrate, the camera shot cuts off her head as we glimpse her lawyer seated in front of her. Then, as if this were not enough, the camera returns to the judge who, at the moment he pronounces her guilty, covers his own head with his official hat. The visual decapitation, like the painting, belongs to an elaborate network of images that appear to confirm the inevitability of Marie's execution.

In the discourse of Chabrol's judge, Marie's crime as abortionist is rendered a capital offense because it involves accepting money for her actions (the abortions and renting rooms to prostitutes). The fact that Marie performs the first abortion just to help out a friend in need and then, later, is able to give her two children and husband a degree of security and material comfort, is irrelevant to the self-righteous magistrate.[27] Vichy's moralizing discourse affirms Marie's culpability for hiding dangerous female desires via the abortions. But it also has to cover up the hypocrisy of its attacks on Marie's materialism: Vichy's police officials and thugs were known to abscond with the belongings of Jews and others they were tracking down.[28]

Another similarity between Joan and Marie that underscores the ambivalent quality of the icon conjoining woman and national symbol lies in their abjurations. Joan's abjuration, Warner tells us, has often been overlooked when her story is retold.[29] It is perhaps not featured because Joan later says she was tricked into signing her recantation. But it is also probable that the episode is underplayed because it does not fit well into the tidy (pure) image that a patron saint must provide. In Marie's case, the equivalent of an abjuration would be her acceptance of guilt in the terms that Vichy's ideology advocated. Whereas Joan's death is triumphant, Marie's only confirms her victimization.

Marie's disavowal of her own actions unfolds in two steps and remains much more ambivalent than Joan's. After a certain vacillation on her part about the nature of her deeds, the forces of state and church eventually triumph over her. Following her trial, she is placed in a freezing cell, and sitting alone with tears in her eyes, she begins to recite a "Hail Mary." But her vehement words betray the contrite figure she *appears* to be: "Hail Mary, full of shit. The fruit of thy womb is rotten." Marie repudiates her namesake, the Virgin Mary, and then angrily rips off a religious medallion, in (implicit) recognition of the church's role in condemning her.[30] Were the film to stop here, spectators might be able to appropriate Marie either as a symbol of feminist strength (on the Left), resisting all too powerful forces, or as a symbol of blasphemy (on the Right), deserving of God's wrath. Chabrol would have reproduced a more standard symbol within the field of nationalist iconography. The penultimate scene undercuts such unequivocal interpretations of Marie, however. After going to confession, Marie articulates a certain repentance for her actions in a most revealing way: "Marshall Pétain was right," she says to the young intern lawyer sent to see to her needs before the execution. Paradoxically, it is the victim who now espouses the condemnation as she seeks forgiveness, whereas Vichy's representative sees through the falseness of the "family values" that Pétain was advocating: the legal intern (sent by Marie's lawyer, who is too much of a coward to face her himself), almost tells Marie not to believe in the validity of the judgment, but checks his remark, no doubt realizing that it will do Marie no good to know she has been tricked by the Pétainist ideology. The unsettling visual image of Marie we noted earlier is perfectly consonant with this painful image of the woman's defeat and the state's treachery.

The end of *Story of Women* leaves us with no doubt about the caricatured, hypocritical nature of the switch from the Revolution of 1789's secular trinity, "Liberty, Equality, Fraternity" to the "New Order's" hollow equivalent, "Work, Family, Homeland." In a park where "good" mothers stroll with their babies in carriages, Marie's lawyer expresses his disgust with his own and general French complicity with Vichy, but it is described in terms of male mutilation and castration: "They're cutting off our balls. They're carving up our flesh." Ultimately, however, as the blade drops, it is *Marie's head* that will fall. There is a repeated impression that the woman's head must be cut off in order to avoid a masculine castration. Superimposed on the final image of the guillotine is a biblical-style injunction that belies Vichy's treachery: "Take pity on the children of those who are condemned." The individual case of Marie ultimately supposes many more victims than just Marie: stigmatized, unwanted children born from "illicit encounters" or those (like Marie's) who lose their mother; women who have no choice to decide their own fate (to become mothers or not); mothers, some of whom will have their heads shaven at the end of the war as the sign of their truck with the Occupant; and women having been accused of aborting or helping others to abort. But all this is lost under the layers of propaganda, with the state machine harming women and children in the name of family and country. As Chabrol's symbol, Marie Latour embodies, to the end, the paradoxical, double icon of victimization and betrayal under Vichy's policies.

Given my description thus far, someone who had never seen *Story of Women* would undoubtedly wonder how on earth the spectator could possibly feel any complicity at all with sadistic justice officials who speak of amputating the gangrened limbs of society, when referring to Marie, or even with cowardly lawyers who do their jobs with a bad conscience. I am not trying to suggest, in fact, that spectators identify with these characters. Our early negative evaluations of Marie are, of course, incommensurate with the subsequent treatment she receives. It is rather an issue of perspective: I am concerned with who is looking at Marie's life. What position does the spectator occupy when watching the depiction of Marie before and during her trial? What kind of visual rhetoric has created the negative viewpoint, and what allows the spectator to shift to a sympathetic one?

Throughout most of the film, the audience does not really have a clear idea of who is telling this story, of whose eye the camera might embody. It is not until the final scenes that we have the sense of a definable perspective, thanks to a voice-over in the seconds before the execution. The last voice we hear, the one that gives a retrospective meaning to the film we have just witnessed, is, in fact, the voice of Marie's little boy, Pierrot—now a grown man—who describes having learned about the execution as we watch his mother approaching the scaffold: "The weather must have been very fine on that morning, July 30, 1943. The neighborhood children told me about it. Your mother was guillotined. It's hard to believe, even when you're seven years old. It's like a big black hole inside you. She was sometimes so cheerful and she loved to sing so much." Although it is an adult who utters these words, we acknowledge in them the child mourning his mother's death, a child who (in the last scene in which he appears) beats his head against the wall as a reaction to that death. Thus, when we thought we had been watching a factual unrolling of events, we were instead witnessing the construction of memory along skewed lines—a lens of a male desire for a lost mother. This final scene makes us aware of history and personal story as versions, as perspective, rather than as unequivocal truth. There may also be an autobiographical dimension to this scene, for we remember that Chabrol was a child during the war, and that his mother was involved in *hidden* activities involving the resistance, activities that deprived the young Claude of her presence.

If we approach the first parts of the film through the little boy's perspective on his mother, and on the past we have just seen, this rereading makes clearer the mark of a male viewpoint that feeds into Vichy's patriarchal discourse condemning Marie at the end. It will confirm the complicity between the two parts of the film (before and after Marie's arrest).[31]

Rereading Motherhood

There are several early episodes in the film where the gaze of the young son Pierrot colors the way we evaluate Marie, particularly as a "bad" or unfit mother.[32] Before Marie ever thinks of helping out her neighbor, who wishes to end an unwanted pregnancy, she is viewed with a certain suspicion by the spectator. In the opening scene of 1942, Marie, whose husband has been a prisoner of war for some time, scrounges for food along the bleak, if beautiful, cliffs outside Cherbourg with her son, Pierrot, and baby daughter, Mouche. Although the spectator may not notice it the first time around, Pierrot's voice is the first (as well as the last) we hear in the film, as if to confirm the importance of his point of view as frame for the story. Before we see any of the characters, the audience hears Pierrot crying, and then the camera focuses briefly on his face. Then we see Marie chide Pierrot and lightly swat his cheek when he begins to cry that the nettles are stinging him as they collect food. Eventually we will understand that impatience and frustration, in the context of a poverty stricken life, ignite this impulsive act, but there is no visual justification to soften our negative impression at the very beginning. It is a sort of defining act that will be confirmed in the next scene, when Pierrot gazes at his mother's tender care of Mouche, while Marie says to neighbors that having Mouche was her one success. The camera emphasizes Pierrot's silent, watchful presence in this scene, and his feelings of being neglected are rendered explicit when he later asks his mother: "And me, when I was born, were you happy then, too?" Marie explains to him that boys are automatically considered a success. The spectator infers that she is commenting on the gender hierarchies of society (that is, it is traditionally "better" to produce a boy than a girl), but Pierrot's sense of unfair exclusion stays with the spectator nevertheless.

These first episodes (and subsequent negative ones) are balanced by many others where Marie shows love and caring for both her children, but because of the ordering of events (with the negative sequences establishing a framework), Marie appears very early on to be biased against her son (in favor of her daughter) and ultimately is portrayed as self-centered and hard. When we later see Marie dancing with her friend Rachel in the local café (rather than with the men there),[33] or when she shows that she is not in love with her husband who returns from a prisoner of war camp, or when she befriends the prostitute Lulu (after Rachel is deported because she is Jewish), Marie's frequent preference for the company of women seems relatively well established, and it is not entirely in a sympathetic light that her friendships are viewed. What also seems clear, however, is that if we are aware of the way Pierrot's perspective on his mother's life shapes our attitudes (in the rereading of the film), the negativity is easily explained as a function of the subject (Pierrot) as much as of the object (Marie). It is certainly not unusual for a child to selectively remember key moments of hurt or neglect by the most important person in his life, Mother. Pierrot's love for his mother is insatiable, and her attention to girls and women leaves him an outsider gazing in, even when that attention is not a denial of Marie's maternal love for Pierrot. His father, upon returning to the family, is portrayed similarly as an unwanted intruder in Marie's life. This difficulty in adjusting to the husband's return has been documented historically. With women having taken on more responsibilities and having acquired a certain independence, the idea of serving the ex-POW husband was not always welcomed.[34]

It should be noted here that in the subsequent trial, Chabrol's Marie is not accused of maternal negligence. Szpiner's account, on the other hand, stresses the thousands of anonymous accusations and denunciations that Vichy and the Germans received during the Occupation, and states that many of Marie-Louise Giraud's female neighbors actually did accuse her (in either anonymous or signed letters) of being a bad mother. Thus, Chabrol greatly downplays women's roles in these kinds of pernicious actions, since the only anonymous letter (of denunciation) that is sent in the film is from Marie's husband. In terms of the actual Giraud trial, Szpiner tells us that Marie-Louise Giraud successfully defended herself against the accusations of maternal neglect. Chabrol, instead of making Marie's care of her children an explicit topic of accusation in the trial, has the silent camera eye present the case to the spectators, leaving us to ask uneasily: which of us (viewers) might have written accusatory letters concerning Marie's childrearing the way Marie-Louise's neighbors did during the Occupation?

Pierrot's role as visual filter for our understanding of Marie is actually thematized in the film as he (retrospectively) comes to embody the voyeuristic properties of film-viewing: the camera repeatedly fixes on Pierrot as a voyeur, surreptitiously spying on his mother through the kitchen keyhole. Pierrot is curious about his mother's concealed actions, and senses something is going on in secret that involves taboo issues concerning sex and women's bodies, even if he doesn't understand exactly what he is spying—how babies are (not) made. Laura Mulvey compares prototypical cinematic scopophilia to "the voyeuristic activities of children, their desire to see and make sure of the private and the forbidden curiosity about other people's genital and bodily functions, about the presence or absence of the penis and, retrospectively, about the primal scene."[35] Pierrot's desire to see (the woman's missing phallus—in this instance, the aborted fetus) is structurally analogous to the spectator's hidden, anonymous pleasures in watching the screen that does not return the gaze.

Pierrot's father, Paul, uses the boy as his private informant to try to find out with whom Marie spends her time, and how she acquires more and more money to support the family. Pierrot and his father both unwittingly embody a certain logic of the Vichy collaborator. In a café scene, where the father orders plenty of wine for Pierrot (no doubt to loosen his tongue about his mother's activities), the father-son conversation is interrupted when the boy rushes to pick up and return a coin to a German soldier who has dropped it. Pierrot even knows enough German to respond to the soldier's thanks in German. The boy has unquestionably learned his civics lesson well: the scene symbolically enacts Vichy propaganda fostering Franco-German cooperation. The complicity with the German cause enacted by this little boy (whose family listens faithfully to Pétain's radio speeches) seems all the more natural, or at least understandable, given the context: this is a scene in which the father asks his unsuspecting son to betray his mother's secrets. Again, the ordering of events is significant: after Pierrot has rendered service to the German, his father Paul then remarks that he doesn't really care after all about how Marie gets her money, as long as they get a better apartment. It may be that when Paul realizes, through Pierrot's responses, that Marie spends most of her time with women rather than men, he stops worrying about the personal threat to his "manhood." Pierrot's public action (assisting the German soldier) is consonant with his father's willingness to look the other way when his wife's potentially objectionable actions benefit him. Paul's private betrayal of Marie to the Vichy police merely uses Vichy's public rhetoric concerning the sanctity of the family to exact a personal revenge on a wife who has ignored his feelings and bristled at his advances.

And, although the spectator feels a certain sympathy for him in the middle parts of the film (when, jobless, he cares for the children or is neglected by Marie), his anonymous accusation makes him fully a partner in the hypocrisy and deception of the state discourse and actions in Marie's case. This scenario of weak, excluded men—feeling castration anxiety and taking vengeance—plays on a variation of the Burch/Sellier Occupation scenario in which a strong woman overshadows a weak man.

The symbolism of Pierrot's voyeuristic treachery is most poignantly brought to our attention in a wish he makes when blowing out a candle at a family celebration. He matter-of-factly tells his family that he has made a wish to become an executioner ("un bourreau"). As we reread the film, this startling, horrifying remark from a seven-year-old suggests complicity in his mother's future execution (perhaps feelings of guilt on the adult Pierrot's part), and also links him again to us as anonymous spectators who judge Marie without being seen (with impunity), similar to the henchman whose identity is hidden by a hood.

Pierrot's betrayal also links him to the handsome Vichy thug, Lucien, who first captures Marie's fancy by winning a town competition set up by the German authorities.[36] This contest consists of trying to lop off the head of a goose with a sword while the contestant's head is covered by a huge mask (reminiscent of the cowl worn by an executioner) in the shape of the head of Mother Goose. The winner, and eventual lover of Marie, presents to her his prize, the headless goose, a gift symbolically presaging Marie's own beheading, but also materially valuable at a time when severe food shortages and deprivation are part of daily existence.[37] The official contest is an execution of sorts, and one that plays into the local politics of collaboration between Vichy and Germans as they control the French population by trying to placate them with a rare food stuff that, says the German official, is not from the black market. (It is thus a legitimate, legal slaughter.) Marie's lover, husband, and son thus enter into the network of Vichy's legalities, its collaborations and executions, symbolic and real. Marie's own role remains ambivalent, in that she is both a passive adherent of the Vichy regime and victimized by it.

THE POLITICS OF GENDER AND COLLABORATION

Given that Marie's activities and political affinities exceed the com-
prehension of her young son, this last section will explore, in addition to, or beyond, the "bad mother" image, Marie's relationship to
Vichy before her arrest. We have already seen that one of the key perspectives on Marie can be defined as male and collaborationist.
Although this viewpoint is an important frame for the negative judgment of Marie, the spectator need not identify solely with it. Because
the gaze is rendered so visible to the spectator *within* the film, we are
more apt to take it as just one possible attitude toward Marie. Let us
consider how politics and gender interact where Marie and the other
female characters are concerned.

The women in *Story of Women* are involved in cooperative efforts
for survival, both emotional and physical. Marie's friendships and
associations with other women suggest a loose, informal solidarity
across certain boundaries. Marie does not judge the women who
come to her for abortions: what does it matter that their pregnancies
are the result of relations with a husband who then leaves for the
forced labor camps, with a German soldier, or a French lover, if in
each case there is no way to provide for the child (made all the more
difficult when the encounter is outside marriage)? Loneliness,
poverty, and a stifling, repetitive daily life are things Marie understands well. The women are forced to rely exclusively on one
another, because, ultimately, Vichy's "New Order"—and to a lesser
extent our own society—consider such problems to be women's
business ("une affaire de femmes"), even if officials mouth a rhetoric of caring, concern, and protection of women and children.[38]

Marie is also (unconsciously) attracted to women relegated to the
margins of French society during the Occupation. Her friendship
with Rachel is on an individual level that does not take into account
the kinds of markings that racist public policies and socio-political
divisions emphasize: before her friend's disappearance, Marie does
not have a clue that Rachel is Jewish and does not have a clear idea
of what the implications of this fact might be. "Rachel has never
been Jewish," says Marie (when she learns Rachel has been taken
away), as if one could choose and cast off origins like clothing or
political beliefs. Being Jewish is like being a communist: Marie is
aware that both are hunted down by the government, but never
stops to ask why. All that is evident to her is the immense grief she

feels at the loss of her friend. The spectator (especially in the film's rereading) wonders whether Rachel is turned in by one of the men in the café who watch the two women dance. This conjecture would confirm the pattern of vengeance against women by men who feel excluded. The spectator occupies a similar position to these male characters who spy on Marie and condemn her for their own exclusion.

Marie's friendship with the prostitute Lulu flows smoothly from a pleasure they derive in each others looks and company, to a commercial association that mutually benefits them: Marie rents out bedrooms to Lulu.[39] (The same pattern is suggested by the smooth shift from neighborly assistance in an abortion to financial gain by performing abortions.) Lulu's politics are particularly revelatory in the context of the Occupation: she tells Marie that contrary to popular thinking, the Germans are no more brutal toward prostitutes than the French. Although the patriotic spectator might be offended by Lulu's steadfast treatment of German soldiers as individuals rather than as a national group of invaders, in her own small way Lulu is a resister to the German occupation, because, as she tells Marie, as a matter of principle, she fleeces them whenever she gets a chance. (This contrasts with Pierrot's returning the coin to the German soldier.) Lulu's gesture is reminiscent of the small acts of defiance that the French began to make after the 1940 defeat.[40]

As for Marie's conscious ties to national politics before her arrest, we may note that her patriotism is full of the paradoxes and contradictions of the times: like substantial numbers of French in 1942–43, she remains faithful to Pétain, but also declares herself for the resistance, while continuing to take advantage of her ties to her collaborating lover, Lucien. She acts according to personal dictates of pragmatism (survival), self-gratification (a certain greediness), but also of caring and friendship. Her strong ties to her own working class, especially to poor women for whom an unwanted pregnancy intensified the deep personal distress and financial hardships that the war had already imposed, make of Marie a resister of sorts. Critics and historians have come, more and more, to realize the importance of survival as a major form of resistance during the war. Marie's help to the women who seek her out benefits them and her as they attempt to persevere in difficult times. Chabrol seems to make a symbolic connection between Marie and the resistance when a resister who has just been shot by the authorities dies looking intently into Marie's face. Marie is haunted by the man's gaze: "It is as if he knew me," she says, symbolically suggesting the recognition between kindred souls who die for their actions under Vichy. An autobiographical connection also seems likely: Chabrol implicitly links Marie's hidden activities to the clandestine activities of the resistance. The latter are precisely what kept his own mother away in Paris during the war, while he remained in the village of Sardent.

What is perhaps most remarkable about the solidarity among women in Chabrol's film is that even Vichy's staunchest, most vivid female representative does not betray Marie to the authorities after her sister-in-law has died following an abortion (that may or may not have caused her death). When this woman shows up with two of her dead sister-in-law's six children, her disapproval of Marie is unwavering. Her Catholic beliefs match Vichy's image of women as childbearers ready to sacrifice themselves for the family. She explains that she is going to raise the children herself because the children's father has committed suicide following his wife's death.

The surviving sister-in-law's choice of self-abnegation and self-righteousness contrasts with an earlier scene in which the mother of the six children had begged for an abortion after a thoroughly moving description of painful pregnancies, and of raising unwanted children in an impoverished household with no control over her own body's reproductive system. Both sisters-in-law are victims of social pressures that church doctrine and state policy promote. Chabrol's film presents both sides of the abortion issue—for and against—through women characters who live the problem in a concrete historical framework that shows Vichy's inflated pronouncements to be hollow and beside the point. Although the woman who takes on the task of raising her sister-in law's children moralizes about abortion in a discourse consonant with Vichy's pro-family policy, *she nevertheless pays Marie for her sister-in-law's abortion and does not tell the police about the incident.*[41] The Catholic woman's overriding concern for the wellbeing of her orphaned nieces and nephews foreshadows the final words written across the screen: "Take pity on the children of those who are condemned." This is one of the crucial issues that Vichy consistently neglects in its "family" policies. Both Marie and the sister-in-law attend to the necessities of survival (of women, of children). Their forbearance contrasts sharply with the dead husband's suicide: his death reveals weakness, and an inability to face up to a difficult life of childcare and economic hardship.

Chabrol has made of Marie Latour an icon around which swirl the complex interactions among gender, class, and politics during the Occupation. In the process of mythmaking, Chabrol alters Szpiner's account in significant ways. The film strategically concentrates on an imperfect *individual* victim to suggest the connections among Vichy politics, the difficulties of women's lives during the period, and the general issue of French collaboration during the war. Francis Szpiner's account, on the other hand, underscores more the generalized discrimination against women, particularly poor women (without neglecting the moments when women denounce women). Chabrol only hints at the female networks of mutual support that Szpiner had emphasized. Although we are certainly aware in the film of other women's predicaments, Chabrol concentrates on Marie as *the* victim of Vichy, the symbol of State treachery. Szpiner emphasizes the fact that all the women involved in Marie-Louise Giraud's abortion case—from her clients to her assistants—were tried with her and punished, and that her husband, who was involved in the abortions (having disposed of a fetus by burying it), went scot-free.[42] In Chabrol's version, Marie alone is on trial and her husband is more obviously associated with Vichy's bogus justice than with his wife's actions, since he is the author of the unsigned accusation against Marie. (According to Szpiner, Marie-Louise Giraud's accuser was never named.) Thus, Chabrol more clearly identifies the private male resentments and biases toward women with Vichy's hypocritical public policies. It would seem that, in his wish for a sympathetic, although ambiguous portrayal of the abortionist, Chabrol sacrifices the extremes that often become the clichés of womanhood (women's "natural" perfidy and victimization), while simultaneously polarizing the gender divisions.

Chabrol's transformation of Marie-Louise Giraud into the national symbol of Marie Latour involves, no doubt, a certain amount of Hollywood-style idealizing to make us more sympathetic to Marie Latour's story than a large public might have been to Marie-Louise Giraud's[43]: Isabelle Huppert is beautiful, whereas Giraud was homely, according to Szpiner, and had a criminal record before the abortions began. Marie is thus morally more palatable and esthetically more seductive to the film viewer than Giraud would have been. The female neighbors and maid of Giraud denounced her at will, whereas Marie Latour's female entourage shows solidarity for the most part. The only women who are sympathetic to her undoing

are the representatives of the church and state (the jailer-nuns, for
example), and certain inmates. These anonymous characters are
associated more with socio-political groups than recognized as individuals. Latour is also at least symbolically associated with the resistance, whereas Giraud was not. Finally, Chabrol gives Marie Latour a
Jewish friend, whereas this was never an issue in Giraud's story, as
told by Szpiner. Critics have complained that Marie's and Rachel's
association was unlikely because Marie didn't know Rachel was Jewish. Chabrol is criticized for failing to make the public anti-Semitism
of the period more visible. And yet, given that the friendship is itself
a fictive embellishment and that Marie's friendships consistently
depend less on recognized ethnic origins and political awareness
than on other, personal affinities, the friendship with Rachel is not so
incongruous. It certainly seems credible that Marie would not think
of associating her best friend with the hateful, anti-Semitic propaganda and laws initiated by Vichy, particularly if that friend were trying to conceal her origins to keep out of harm's way.[44] Chabrol's
addition of the Jewish friend does, on the other hand, appear to
reflect what Henry Rousso calls our contemporary obsession with
the Holocaust and France's responsibility in the deportations.

Although Chabrol's embellishments on events act to counterbalance the patriarchal viewpoint promoted by Vichy, to which Marie is
subject in the film, Marie's transformation into pure heroine (or
saintly victim) is far from complete. Chabrol's ambivalent Marie, in
fact, most resembles another Joan of Arc whom we have not yet
mentioned—that of filmmaker Robert Bresson in his 1962 film
Procès de Jeanne d'Arc ("*The Trial of Joan of Arc*"). Historian Robert
Gildea paraphrases Bresson: "Joan was neither a naive peasant girl
nor a pure and obedient saint, but a young woman of 'magnificent
insolence,' who loved royal finery and powerful horses."[45] Chabrol,
like Bresson, refuses to deliver an unequivocal portrait of the female
icon. Our ability to evaluate Marie's actions and character is precisely
what is at stake in Chabrol's version of Giraud's story: is she merely
an opportunistic, calculating, callous, and shallow woman, as viewed
through the lens of an excluded male gaze, or is she a courageous,
gutsy, resourceful woman who falls prey to Vichy? Clearly, neither
description fully does her justice. By retaining a certain opacity to
her character—we glimpse her through the filmic peep-hole just as
Pierrot spies on her through the kitchen keyhole—Chabrol leaves it
up to us to think through the value of her actions, tending to nudge

us alternately toward and away from Marie: yes, she helps out her neighbor for free, but later, she revels too much in the material success of her enterprises.

If we grant that Chabrol's Marie is indeed self-centered, tough, and manipulative,[46] the director makes us wonder, nevertheless, to what extent this is negative *because* she is a woman. Do a man's "enterprising, resourceful" talents become "calculating and callous" when enacted by a woman? Chabrol's gender polarization in the story (whether intentional or not) intensifies the question. As one film reviewer put it: "The case for a 'selfish' women is still a tough one to make, demanding that filmmakers overcome the knee-jerk assumption—held by women as well as men—that women justify their actions by what is good for others."[47] Both the Vichy magistrate and the Vichy mother wholly subscribe to such an assumption. In the first part of the film, Chabrol attenuates the case against Marie's self-interest by first emphasizing her poverty and desperation (the early scenes are bleak, dark, depressing), and then by showing her sharing her new monetary gains with her children and husband. But, little by little, Chabrol seamlessly leads us through the network of gazes toward disapproval of Marie, making *us* take on the negative view. These gazes, whether male (the boy's, the father's, the magistrate's) or female (Lulu's, the Vichy mother's, the neighbors') all condemn the "selfish" woman. Because Chabrol does not make us privy to Marie's unspoken thoughts, motivations, and intentions, we have no privileged position through which to understand her point of view. Whereas Szpiner's account constantly rushes to Marie-Louise Giraud's defense, Chabrol places the responsibility for evaluating Marie Latour squarely on our shoulders. It is up to the viewer to determine the nature and value of her actions. And while most could probably agree that Marie is a pragmatic, immoral woman who increases her own and her family's wealth and comfort beyond the point of good taste or social acceptability, we must ask to what extent our negative attitude toward her remains a function of gender expectations.

Were it not for Chabrol's embellishments on Giraud's story, how many more spectators would be tempted to don the Vichy judge's hat and pronounce her guilty for the "sin" of self-interest, as well as immorality? At issue is the danger of sliding from these moral judgments concerning Marie's character flaws to fatal juridical pronouncements: it is as if the filmmaker temporarily lured us into watching Marie through a progression of collaborationists' eyes— her son's, her husband's, the judge's. In significant ways, Marie Latour is the predecessor of the women whose heads were shaved at the time of the liberation for having sexual relations with Germans. Alain Brossat has effectively shown how France, during the postwar purges, tried to free itself of the humiliating, emasculating memory of national defeat and collaboration, by taking revenge on French women through the head shaving.[48] At the end of the war, famous film stars like Arletty (*Children of Paradise*), Mireille Balin (*Pépé le Moko*), and Ginette Leclerc (*The Raven*) were imprisoned for their sexual relations with Germans or for collaboration, while women from the lower classes who were (often quite summarily) condemned for "horizontal collaboration" had their heads shaved.[49] Marie Latour, hair cropped, imprisoned, and then guillotined, represents Vichy's biggest scapegoat and victim.

Chabrol's feat is to have made visible the collaborationist gaze of Vichy (in its private and public dimensions) through our own eyes, while also filling us with outrage toward that gaze's injustice. *Story of Women* invites the conflation of moral and juridical judgments in order to then make us all the more aware of the danger of slipping too easily from one to the other. To appreciate Marie's self-interest as a sign of survival (*and* pleasure), one need not make of her a saint or a demon. She is at once the unique symbol of women's difficult survival during the war, the victim of Vichy's duplicitous treatment of women, especially in reproductive issues, and the unsettling national symbol of a French public whose daily survival choices and self-interest often made it at least passively complicit with Pétain and Vichy. For those who yearn for a position of purity, Marie cannot fail to elicit strong reactions: Chabrol calls upon us to rethink our assumptions about this woman who becomes the icon of France's ambivalence toward its own past, representing all at once complicity, survival, victimization, heroism, and opportunism. Marie's multifaceted portrait defies a simple appropriation by the Left or the Right: on the Left, she is unsuitable as an idealized heroine because she falls sway to the bogus rhetoric of church and state, and cares nothing about making a conscious political choice to resist; on the Right, because she is the victim of supposedly Christian, French, national values, it would be hard to make her a "proper" representative (not to mention that the fact her marital infidelity, blasphemy, and willingness to perform abortions would disqualify her). Chabrol's film makes us more fully aware of the difficult negotiations the French have continued to make with their nation's collaborationist past. Unlike France's patron saint, Chabrol's protagonist is more a symbol for reflection than for celebration.

I would also argue that this tribute to the mother-victim-betrayer is also Chabrol's unconscious working through of his role as a postwar filmmaker: could we not think of his own rejection of postwar moralizing as a certain parental betrayal? Chabrol's implicit dismissal of his parents' resistance activities in his early films (such as in *Les Cousins* where he toys with images of fascism rather than featuring French wartime heroism) resembles little Pierrot's betrayal of his mother. In this autobiographical scenario, *Story of Women*'s first person narration of a son betraying his mother becomes a self-accusation bound to national guilt.

AN ADDED TWIST: TRUTHFUL FICTIONS AND FRAUDULENT REALITIES

I have been stressing throughout this book how the films in question both represent and produce perspectives on France's past. In the case of *Story of Women*, the effects of Szpiner's historical research and Chabrol's fiction spill over into the present, with the final chapter on Marie-Louise Giraud becoming even more poignant than one might have thought. Although Szpiner and Chabrol were not able to locate Giraud's family to ask about Marie-Louise, a *Paris Match* journalist tracked down Giraud's daughter two years after Szpiner's book was published. In a short, rather sensationalized piece, journalist Guillaume Clavières describes finding Paulette Barjavel, Giraud's daughter, in an "HLM" (a low-income housing project) in the ex-mining town of Alès in the south of France. The journalist underscores the family's and Paulette's poverty: a cleaning lady at city hall and mother of four grown children, Marie-Louise Giraud's daughter at age fifty-one did not escape her family's class background.

What is most amazing about this story, however, is that the daughter is completely unaware of how her mother died when the journalist calls at her door. She had not seen Chabrol's film, had never read Szpiner's book, and was told by her father (now dead) that her mother had died in a German camp! Her brother, who had died some fifteen years earlier, never learned the truth. The mother goes from being a shadowy memory of resistance to one involved in crime. With the rug pulled out from under her, Paulette's reactions are quite understandable: first, there is anger at her father's lying, then, she tries to make this new information mesh with her child-hood recollections of her mother. One is reminded of the surprise that Chabrol's Marie Latour expresses at learning that her friend Rachel has been taken away because she is Jewish. Finally, uncon-sciously aligning herself with Chabrol's female characters, Paulette Barjavel evaluates her mother's actions: "I excuse my mother and what she may have done. Helping women to abort isn't criminal, even during that somber period. I am a believer and I think that there's only one who can judge: that's God. Unfortunately, things happened differently. Men condemned her. I have the sense of an immense mess. Despite our situation, I was happy in my family. Today, I can only think about this story, day and night. I am haunted." [50] With no desire to see the film or read the book, the daughter searches instead through the scraps of her own distant memory. The article concludes melodramatically: "A woman mourns the second death of her mother," thus indirectly pointing to the wrenching interweaving of past and present.[51]

CHAPTER 6

———·✹◈✹·———

LOVE STORIES, REAL/CINEMATIC
HEROINES, THE POSTMODERNS:
THE 1980S AND BEYOND

ROMEO AND JULIET FILMS—
MALLE'S AND TRUFFAUT'S PALE LEGACY

If the public is not by nature as stupid as too many producers
imagine, it does particularly dislike having its habits disturbed.
Those who are among the first to upset it, run the risk of paying heavily, to the benefit of competitors who then safely pass
through the breech opened in the wall of conventionalism.
—*André Bazin (October 1943)*

Toward the end of her 1993 book, *French National Cinema*,
Susan Hayward speculates about why there was an increased prominence of women characters in 1980s and 1990s films on the Occupation in World War II France. "Why," she asks, "in the postmodern
era when history is being rejected," do we begin to see more women
portrayed in historical film? The possible responses she imagines
mostly offer up cynical commentary on postmodernism: "Because
history no longer exists, it is timely to represent woman"; "It is now
all right to talk about courageous women because feminism is dead
(in France, that is)." Her third explanation posits that cinema
"delud[es] itself that it is making an historical film historically," and

"because there is no history, it can also be made up."[1] These answers reveal Hayward's pessimism about the ability of the (French) postmodern and its films to take history—and women—into account in any serious way. Let us look at some of the prominent female icons of the 1980s and 1990s as they articulate French identity and the Occupation. To what extent do they correspond to Hayward's assessment?

One might initially ask whether the last decades of the twentieth century are really as postmodern as Hayward assumes, and whether portraying courageous women is a function of feminism's demise. Many of the films on the Occupation in the 1980s and 1990s tend, in fact, *not* to be terribly postmodern, if by that we mean playful, self-conscious, open-ended, polyvalent, citing the past in order to re-form it in the present, freely mixing history and fiction to the point of dissolution, challenging standard interpretations of events, as well as standard narrative choices. More numerous in France in the 1980s and 1990s were feature films that no longer challenged the public's understanding of Occupation events. Although Hayward's comments about the disappearance of history and feminism's demise in France are no doubt exaggerated, there does seem to be a loosening of connections between specific historical events and the films on the Occupation, and the viewing public is less personally challenged by the cinematic renderings of the period. The anger that raged over *Lacombe Lucien* turned into praise for a more "comfortable" representation, like Malle's *Goodbye, Children* (1987). Films focusing on women's stories, like *Stella* (1983, Laurent Heynemann), *Blanche et Marie* (1984, Jacques Renard), *De Guerre lasse* (1987, Robert Enrico), and *L'Accompagnatrice* (1992, Claude Miller) offer up the Occupation in relatively predictable stories that milk its clichés (fashions, cars, conventional portrayals of Germans, Nazis, resisters), without strong ties to precise historical events. They are the kind of films that air comfortably as reruns on French TV. One might well argue that the true *mode rétro* is principally found in the films that take up *Lacombe Lucien*'s themes and images in the 1980s and 1990s.

In the case of *Stella* and *De Guerre lasse* (loosely translated: "Weary of Fighting"), the filmmakers offer variations on the Romeo and Juliet model, with star-crossed lovers separated by the political divide between resistance and collaboration. The Jewish Stella (Nicole Garcia)[2] is freed from a French internment camp by her lover, the handsome Yvon (Thierry Lhermitte). Yvon has turned to collaboration in order to obtain the connections necessary to get Stella out of the camp. In *De Guerre lasse* (based on Françoise Sagan's popular novel of the same name), Alice must choose between her resister soul mate Jérôme, whom she cherishes but does not love passionately, and his uncommitted friend, Charles the shoe company owner, whom she does. Both films seem like bland replications of *Lacombe Lucien*. The female protagonists are pale, blond beauties who favor resistance against the occupier, but who are attracted to men tied to collaboration. Although many viewers were surprised by *Lacombe Lucien*'s brightness in the scenes of southern France, Heynemann's and Enrico's films go much further in defying the description of the Occupation as the "dark years" by infusing many of their scenes, both indoors and out, with radiant light. Stella's and Alice's clothing are frequently white, as if to emphasize the light and their purity, offsetting, perhaps, the fact that both characters have previously been in "mixed marriages" between Jew and Gentile: Stella is Jewish, whereas her ex-husband was not. Alice is not Jewish, but her husband was. Although in Sagan's novel (*De Guerre lasse*), Alice's Jewish husband has already fled for America when the story opens, filmmaker Enrico has the Jewish husband commit suicide instead, in a flashback to Nazi-ridden Austria. Again, we are reminded of the Jewish father in *Lacombe Lucien* who lets himself be caught by collaborationist authorities in a quasi suicide. But Malle's Jewish character, Horn, seems courageous when he confronts the Nazi authorities, whereas Alice's Jewish husband in Enrico's film seems weak as he jumps out of window when no one is pursuing him.

In *Stella* and *De Guerre lasse*, the lovers' idyll in nature (again the unoccupied zone in southern France) acts as a counterbalance to the threats and dangers of occupied Paris. But just as we saw that the idyll in *Lacombe Lucien* risked crumbling from within because of its own potential violence, both *Stella* and *De Guerre lasse* portray physical violence that undercuts our assumptions about relationships: the supposedly gentle lover, Yvon, smacks Stella when she irritates him; the supposedly gentle resister Jérôme, in *De Guerre lasse*, slaps Alice when it becomes clear she will never return his love. The misogyny in these two films is independent of political positions.

While *Stella* and *De Guerre lasse* both feature the ambiguous heroine who is a victim and a resister, but who is also attracted to a collaborator, the female icon seems to obscure our understanding of motivations rather than clarify it. Whereas *Lacombe Lucien* made us understand the process by which an ignorant boy might become a collaborator, *Stella* and *De Guerre lasse* skirt the issue. This is particularly the case in *Stella*, where Yvon's decision to collaborate out of passion for Stella has already taken place before the story begins, so that the spectator does not witness this key choice. Whereas Malle and Modiano's script was anchored in history, Heynemann's and Enrico's are more embedded in clichés and fictions not sustained by historical accounts. And, yet, the films' redemptive finales tend to confirm the model that we have been following throughout this book: Stella chooses *not* to flee with Yvon to Spain; Alice leaves Charles (whom she loves) to save resister Jérôme, who has been arrested.[3] Political commitment prevails over physical attraction. Still, there is a differential twist to the model that makes these films of the 1980s more interesting: because the romantic relationships are not portrayed as the best life-choice for the women characters, their personal interest and the public good of resistance are aligned. The women do not have to forsake their desire to be able to commit their energies to the just cause. Rather, they choose *themselves* and political commitment in the same gesture. While this ending implicitly harbors a feminist turn of female self-affirmation, it is only realized in stories that have little anchoring in *history*. Susan Hayward's link between female protagonists and a detachment from history is confirmed here.

Jacques Renard's *Blanche et Marie* is perhaps the film that most forcefully supports an unambiguous portrayal of heroic women in the underground resistance. Basing his script on the personal accounts of poor working class women in the northeast of France who were friends of his mother, the filmmaker sets out to pay homage to their unassuming courage. To be sure, there are female (and male) characters who collaborate with the occupiers in this film in pernicious ways, but the focus is on true heroines, from a grandmother, to a mother, to an adolescent girl. Romance is neither obstacle to, nor facilitator for, political commitment. This film brings into view typical female roles in the resistance that, as Paula Schwartz has shown, were often neglected in postwar accounts. Schwartz notes women's non-combatant activities, often initiated through family contacts rather than formal prewar political party affiliation, too often went unnoticed in official portrayals of the resistance. Their subaltern roles and non-flashy participation also reduced their recognition, with their work going unidentified in archives.[4] Renard sets out to remedy this lacuna, although he does not entirely succeed in fully engaging the spectator in this representation. Part of the reason that this film fails to stir viewers more—in anger, admiration or something subtler—is that the conflicts in the story are always external to the female protagonists. At peace with themselves, the resisters are women of action who battle quietly behind the scenes against collaborators, Germans, and sexist resisters. Their psychological life seems relatively unproblematic; external forces are what dictate their actions. Renard chose big name stars Miou-Miou and Sandrine Bonnaire to embody these heroines. The pregnant Blanche (Miou-Miou) is ready to undergo torture by the Nazis if necessary; Marie (Sandrine Bonnaire) risks her life daily as a liaison agent without flinching. Renard underscores the necessity of hiding one's identity, of changing names and eschewing family ties for the sake of political action—to the point that spouses sometimes do not know that their companion (wife or husband) is a resister. The Occupation, with its secrets and dangers, is literally dark: the characters emerge from the greenish, murky light of the Occupation scenes into the dazzling sunlight of the liberation in the final scenes. Again, the contrast tends to remain external to any personal dilemmas the characters might have suffered. This film's iconography offers a reaffirmation of French heroism and the resistance, in contrast to the 1970s' *mode rétro* (focusing on collaboration). *Blanche et Marie* hearkens more back to the heroic period of the early postwar years, but with a feminist, collective twist, for these heroines belong to a *movement* rather than standing out as *individuals*. Renard's Marianne is doubled and then multiplied, in contrast to Chabrol's Marie in *Story of Women*, who remains a singular figure and an ambiguous heroine. Renard's Leftist political inclinations help make Blanche and Marie the symbols of collective political action in a relatively straightforward way. I would add that there is slippage between the representations of the specific heroines and a more generalized representation of France: the nation's good elements triumph over the bad. *Blanche et Marie* often seems akin to a photographic negative of *Lacombe Lucien*.[5]

IDENTITY WARS IN "L'AFFAIRE (LUCIE) AUBRAC": HISTORY, FICTION, FILM

Susan Hayward's assessments of 1980s and 1990s films offer sweeping generalizations that are confirmed in a good number of the films just discussed; for the most part, these films lack the historical anchorings or innovative visions of Malle's and Truffaut's Occupation films. There are, however, important counter examples from the period that stand out: a film such as Chabrol's *Story of Women* underscores the precise historical victimization of an unheroic woman while raising feminist issues. Hayward's analysis also cannot account for the later, passionate controversies swirling around *Lucie Aubrac* (1997), directed by Claude Berri, with the collaboration of Lucie Aubrac herself. This film, the third historical film Berri made in the 1990s, recounts how Lucie Aubrac and her resistance group twice rescued her husband and resistance leader Raymond Aubrac from the hands of the Gestapo in 1943 (once in May, once in October), and was part of an ongoing battle over the meaning of wartime events.[6] Although no one would accuse Berri's film of being postmodern—it tells a relatively unreflective, unselfconscious narrative of heroism—the larger context of its production in the France of the 1990s embroils it in questions about the nature and proportions of memory, history, fiction, and myth in the mix of historical film. It belongs to the genre of "heritage films" that feature France's past as part of a national heritage to be commemorated and treasured, and as such, quickly becomes another arena for competing interpretations of French identity. As for Hayward's suggestion that feminism's demise in France has enabled visions of heroic women, presumably because they are no longer a threat, Lucie Aubrac as historical personage, historical witness, and film object, was involved in too many polemics to be comfortably dismissed as safe (and hence not debatable), even if that is precisely what Berri, historians, feminists, and former resisters might have wished "Lucie Aubrac"—the film and the person—to be. Brash and outspoken, she was never afraid to speak her mind even when it got her into trouble, sometimes justifiably so.[7]

As Occupation accounts and documents have poured forth and continue to be reviewed, questioned, and contested, France has experienced, all the more fully, the need to construct an ultimate version of this past. And the debates have not been restricted to reevaluating and trying such collaborators as Maurice Papon. Scandals also swirled around resistance leaders like Jean Moulin (falsely accused of being a Soviet agent), and in the 1990s, Raymond and Lucie Aubrac. These newer debates connote another anxiety attack for France about its past and current identity. In what follows, I explore how the "Aubrac Affair," in personal account, film, and history, reveals France's attempt to shape an image of itself that would not make it wince. Although I focus on the female icon in the articulation of French identity, it will not be a question of wholly endorsing or defending Lucie Aubrac's own treatment of historical remembrance, nor of falling sway to the hypercritical position taken by some historians on hers and Raymond's "case."

As I have noted throughout this book, the material details of *daily* Occupation existence have often been articulated through women's experiences. For Lucie Aubrac, and many like her, daily routines during the war came to signify forms of survival and resistance. (Naomi Schor's description of everyday "prosiness" accounts for this connotation of the detail, but without any negativity.)[8] On the other hand, the precision of historical detail—or rather its lack—is exactly what also will get Lucie Aubrac into deep trouble with historians, when fictive embellishments sacrifice, or at least obscure, facts. Schor's "ornamental" or esthetic detail is functional in this example, and it retains its negativity. Details in this context splinter into a scientific, "objective" domain of rigor and accuracy, and one of fiction or effective storytelling.[9] The "Aubrac Affair," as we shall see, involves the connections between individual action and historical events, but also a whole set of premises concerning the ways one tells a story.

How do the details of domestic existence articulate heroic *or* nefarious public action? One thinks here of a character like Madame Lafarge in Dickens's *Tale of Two Cities*, who quietly inscribes secret revolutionary information (the names of those to be executed) in her knitting. In French terms, the connections between "la petite histoire"—little (hi)stories, associated with behind-the-scenes individual experience—and "Histoire" (grand scale events), are often seen most acutely through women's lives. While a few years ago, as Hayward suggested, it may have *looked* as if women's participation in the war was beginning to receive attention *only because* most issues had been "settled," with minutia being heeded after the "important" issues had been resolved, more recent developments have challenged this opinion. As France struggles to define itself through positive values from the past, the assertion of heroic resistance in the war is all the more pressing as it is assailed from several sides. Is it possible to avoid the kind of mythification of the resistance that took place under de Gaulle without becoming vulnerable to accusations against resisters by a Nazi like Klaus Barbie? Can—and should—the actions of one woman like Lucie Aubrac be used to represent those of countless (anonymous) others? Are verisimilitude and fact compatible when some notion of "historical truth" is at stake? What is the heuristic value of these stories, and is it opposed to their historical worth?

Although many have thought that the continued obsession with the events of the Occupation is primarily a cover-up of France's other guilty, hidden memories (such as the Algerian war), I would argue that the renewed fixation on the facts of the resistance is more. First, contemporary historians in the late 1990s were intent upon unearthing the "true" story of the Occupation as accurately as possible, without mythification, while there were still some surviving participants. Second, there has remained an anxious desire to rescue some idea of honor and morality that the fascination with collaboration memories had obscured. In a France contending with racism, immigration, high unemployment, globalization, and its postcolonial position in the world, positive anchorings (role models from the French past) are still sought out by an older generation eager to leave an ethical legacy. As we map out the large cast of characters, events, and issues in the "Aubrac Affair," it will be necessary to keep in mind the "identity stakes" involved in the search for "the truth."

ACT ONE: FROM EVENT TO MEMOIRS

In many ways, Lucie Aubrac was the kind of woman Simone de Beauvoir often wished to be: rather than staying at the margins of social and political events in the shadow of "her man," Lucie was a co-actor in the first and last hour with her husband.[10] Very early in the war, when most were still confused about what course to follow, Raymond and Lucie Aubrac became resistance fighters; in post-war years, they remained politically active: promoting peace in Vietnam, publicly opposing the war in Algeria, and speaking out for immigrants' rights in France.[11] In general, they espoused causes of the disenfranchised throughout their lives and were occasionally described as "compagnons de route" (fellow travelers) of the Communist Party, without actually being members. Ho Chi Minh was, in fact, a close friend and the godfather to their daughter. Although Raymond was no doubt more directly involved in international diplomacy over the years, Lucie, with an advanced degree in history (she is an "agrégée")[12], actively engaged in teaching history and its civic lessons in the classroom and in the media. In 2000, Lucie Aubrac published a short text with the Editions du Seuil entitled *La Résistance expliquée à mes petits enfants* ("The Resistance Explained to My Grandchildren"). This work is part of an educational series in which well-known authors explain key concepts and events such as racism, the republic, love, Auschwitz, and nonviolence to their children and grandchildren. Many French intellectuals of today are intent on providing some kind of clear legacy of values to future generations who undergo the onslaught of media versions of French identity. That is one of the reasons why the stakes of French film are especially high.

Rather paradoxically, had it not been for the innuendoes and accusations of Jacques Vergès, the lawyer for ex-Nazi official Klaus Barbie, the "Butcher of Lyon" who was captured in the 1970s, Lucie Aubrac's particular story might have remained buried in the annals of resistance history as an interesting, although minor, footnote. But when Barbie began making claims of treason against the resistance of Lyon upon his capture, Lucie was persuaded by her friend and ex-student, actress Simone Signoret (ex Simone Kaminker), to tell her story of the period, which Lucie Aubrac published as *Ils partiront dans l'ivresse* (*Outwitting the Gestapo*) in 1984. These memoirs may not read as great literature, but they do present a gripping life story of suspense, and provide Lucie's personal window on the historical events surrounding the famous Caluire meeting of resistance leaders in 1943, when the Gestapo arrested all but one. The memoirs, in turn, inspire two films during the 1990s: Josée Yanne's *Boulevard des Hirondelles* in 1993, and Claude Berri's 1997 *Lucie Aubrac*. Yanne's film received rather scant attention, and was deemed by one critic to belong to the (mercifully) dying genre of simplistic, edifying films on the resistance.[13] What marks this film as a *woman* filmmaker's creation is less a matter of style or narrative technique than the fact that the camera focuses on the character Lucie, neglecting the portrayal of Raymond's actions and historical events, unlike either the memoirs or Berri's film. The wooden dialogue, visually dull decors, and lack of concrete historical details leave Lucie's portrayal stilted rather than moving or even problematic.

Berri's *Lucie Aubrac*, which, with its big budget, well-known stars (Carole Bouquet, Daniel Auteuil, and Patrice Chéreau), and ample publicity, received much more attention, and somewhat more critical praise, than the earlier film.[14] But, when wild applause rang out after an initial showing of the film in Berlin in 1997, it was just as much a tribute to the eponymous heroine who was present for the showing as for Berri's work. A look at differences between written and visual versions of events will help us to discern their sociopolitical agendas as they define a sense of national identity through history.

Lucie Aubrac's book, *Outwitting the Gestapo*, tells at least three stories: first is the personal account of a female resister's daily actions, as they might be capable of representing the typical actions of untold others; second is the love story between a husband and wife in dangerous times; third is the precise, dated series of events emphasizing the two rescues of resistance leader Raymond Aubrac by Lucie and her group, as well as other covert actions by the resistance. The book opens with a foreword highlighting key dates of Lucie Aubrac's life and explaining that the French title was the BBC coded radio message confirming the Aubracs' departure for England: "Ils partiront dans l'ivresse," that is, "they will leave with joy." To this generalized frame that situates the book as a work of *memory* (rather than an actual or imagined present), she then adds another: the first scenes portray Lucie giving birth in a London hospital in February 1944, to her second child, Catherine, just after she and Raymond have successfully escaped the Nazis in France. This opening again stresses that the accounts of resistance adventures Lucie is about to tell are part of a more distant past, but more importantly, Lucie portrays herself giving birth in the most unheroic terms, as if to underscore the fallible, rather ordinary human quality of her persona. When she screams from the pain, the British midwife tells her to "shut up, we're at war."[15] Both the size of the baby girl—a healthy, strapping ten pounds—and the English requisite of a stiff upper lip in wartime, implicitly underscore British hardships while making Lucie's plight seem rather trifling.

By downplaying her own courage at the beginning of the book, Lucie Aubrac emphasizes the lack of singularity of many of her wartime actions. In later sections, she convincingly makes one appreciate that scrubbing filthy clothes can be resistance work, as is the daily search for food and heating material, or teaching history in the classroom. A lesson on the scarcity of workers and resources becomes an indictment of the occupiers and forced labor.[16] A required celebration of Pétain, as Joan of Arc's inheritor, turns into a sly game of derision of the marshal.[17] As history teacher, she protests taking her students to see Vichy's 1941 anti-Semitic exhibition on racial traits.[18] But she also takes stock of her own rash actions and occasional fits of bad temper, thereby showing that it is fallible human beings (like herself) who make up the resistance, not perfect ideologues.[19] She also portrays the difficulties of Raymond's prison routine: how, for example, to manage in collective life with one slop-bucket for five. These are the gritty details of daily existence that help us imagine the resistance in its less glorious aspects. And, while Lucie includes in her account both details about people faithful to Vichy as well as resistance members, her narrative's didactic bent aligns resistance with survival in a forceful way.

Although the opening de-emphasizes the heroine's flashiness, these memoirs are nevertheless an inspiring tale of bravery. Lucie Aubrac, in fact, links in intimate ways female heroism and bearing a child: her memoirs' subtitle—*Lyon, mai 43, Londres, février 44*—perfectly matches the nine months it took to conceive and deliver her child, as well as to rescue her husband and escape to London. *Outwitting the Gestapo* is unabashedly a pedagogical work that offers civic lessons, historical accounts, and an example of "typical" female valor. This defense of her actions is not so surprising, given that the work is a response to Barbie's attacks.

While Jean Genet complained that the "wrong" kind of people ended up in prison during World War II (that is, resisters and good guys), Lucie Aubrac's memoirs seem to revel in the topsy-turvy conditions of the war that make necessities of disguise, play-acting, shrewd lies, and new identities. It is as if the pleasures of fiction ("make believe") become permissible when danger is at hand, because the disguises are politically expedient. She even calls this pleasure a "strange addiction."[20] Curiously reminiscent of Marguerite Duras's characters, Lucie Aubrac ingeniously adopts traditional female roles as both masquerade and accepted choice in a brand of pragmatic, but also playful, feminism. To look more "feminine" and alluring to a German official who can help her get to Raymond before he is executed, Lucie dresses up in fancy clothes and

makeup and takes on the aristocratic name of Ghislaine de Barbentane. (In her interviews with Corinne Bouchoux, she adds that
assuming the name of this countess for whom her father had worked
as gardener was a form of social revenge.)[21] Claiming to be unwed
and pregnant with the child of François Vallet (Raymond's pseudonym at the time), Lucie uses "family values" and traditional attributes of women—needful of protection and respectability when
dishonored by a man—to convince the official to let her marry her
condemned fiancé (in actuality her husband, Raymond). The marriage meeting will provide the occasion for helping Raymond to
escape. Combining swashbuckling romance and political efficacy,
the memoirs emphasize stereotypical feminine guile (the disguise of
the vamp-gentlewoman ingeniously combined with Lucie's very real
pregnancy) in the freeing of the husband/resistance leader. Lucie
revels in the performative aspects of her roles and shows us how she
gleefully mixes truth (e.g., her pregnancy) and falsehood (she is *not*
an unwed mother). Public and private personae appear intertwined
for her in the play-acting of real life.[22] Lucie, in fact, extends the performative qualities of her activities to all resisters: "engineers, drafts-
men, teachers, middle-class or workers, every one of us entered the
world of cheating and lies with the utmost serenity."[23]

ACT TWO: FILM VS. MEMOIRS?

The films *Boulevard des hirondelles* and *Lucie Aubrac* not surprisingly
follow the more dramatic aspects of the Aubrac story and are devoid
of much of the reflective side of Lucie's memoirs. The films emphasize the love story between Lucie and Raymond, with the wife rescuing her husband from death. It is simplified heroic action
comfortably combining romantic love, glamour, and duty against
the evil Gestapo. *Boulevard des hirondelles* particularly lacks an integral frame that would underscore the larger act of remembering.
Although at the beginning of the credits there is an on screen reference to Lucie Aubrac's memoirs, there is no other historical preparation, so an uninformed viewer would barely realize that the film
contains real, major figures from the war. It is not until the final
credits that Yanne juxtaposes actors' photos with those of the actual
people portrayed. In Berri's film, there *is* a historical text on the
screen in the very beginning to situate the story as the portrayal of

"real life" events from the past, but it is careful to insist that while the events are "authentic," the filmmaker had to take certain "liberties" with characters and the unfolding of events. Lucie Aubrac herself appears briefly on screen at the end of the film, thereby tying the actions viewed with a living person.[24] Berri is clearly concerned with providing a careful treatment of Lucie Aubrac's book. (Both Yanne and Berri credit Lucie's memoirs at the beginning of the films as their inspiration.) But once the actors come on the scene, we are thrust into a lived present, and all actions are absolute, as the camera plunges into a reenactment that makes no reference to the act of remembering. Admittedly, Lucie's memoirs welcome such treatment, in that they are presented in an open diary form with dates, direct dialogue, and the present tense, despite the fact that the book was constructed some forty years after the events. Not once does the author express doubts about the accuracy of her memory.[25] But where the memoirs can and do take stock of the intricacies of many events, with ample commentary and explanation, the films adopt the glossier, quick-cut adventure format to actualize the past in a simpler dimension. In both film and memoirs, the internecine battles involving the various resistance groups vying for power are downplayed. Lucie's perspective emphasizes the coming together of resistance leaders rather than their struggles for power. On the whole, the understanding of action remains more personal than political, with the result that heroism remains relatively unproblematic.

Berri has, in fact, said: "The important thing was not to make a chronicle of the Occupation, but rather a tense dramatic narrative."[26] Such statements confirm the priority of fictive drama over the facts: although Raymond never blew up munitions trains, Berri explains that he does so in the film in order to establish quickly his work in the resistance. It would also seem to be an implicit homage to René Clément's early 1946 heroic saga, *La Bataille du rail,* which features resistance railroad workers (often actual railroad workers playing themselves) against the Germans. Like Clément, Berri opts for an action-filled, suspenseful drama, but Berri's film does not possess the documentary allure of Clément's film (which includes film footage from 1944).

Berri acknowledges that his film concentrates only on Lucie's saving Raymond, thus narrowing the scale of her resistance work. Also absent from the films is Lucie's emphasis on the typicality of her life for many French women. The details of her daily existence as a resisting, surviving homemaker are underplayed in favor of the plot-advancing action sequences and conventional, rather plodding love scenes. But Berri *does* include a scene of Lucie teaching her young pupils about the importance of memory and history for the present, a scarcely veiled lesson for the film's spectators, on Occupation events and the necessity of remembering them. On the whole, however, Berri and Yanne both showcase the extraordinary individual and event over the typical, whereas Lucie Aubrac was equally concerned with her own ability to represent countless unnamed women and men. She, in fact, fought Berri's wish to give the film her name for fear that she steal the limelight from other resistance fighters, several of whom paid with their lives. She only accepted to have the film bear her name on the condition that Berri make a substantial gift to the resistance memorial fund.

All this is clearly not to say that Berri's film turns away from the way Lucie recounted the events. Both she and Raymond endorsed and promoted the film, while acknowledging the alterations inevitable in a quick paced film drama. And Berri, following in Lucie's steps, declared his interest to lie in the alternation of heroism and daily life.[27] In the issues of names, false identities, and life experiences, Berri's own past in the war, and that of the Aubracs, actually hold points of convergence. Doctor Dugoujon, whose office was to be the site of the resistance leaders' meeting in Caluire in 1943, happened to have been the family physician for Berri's family (Berri was then known as Claude Langmann). Berri also reports having been hidden as a boy in the countryside under a false name (to hide his Jewish origins), just as the Aubracs' son was hidden. His autobiographical film *Le Vieil Homme et l'enfant* (*The Two of Us*) from 1966 dramatizes his hiding with an elderly farm couple during the war.[28] Raymond and Lucie's married name, Samuel, had to be discarded, not only to protect their resistance identities, but also to conceal Raymond's Jewish origins. (Both his parents were, in fact, deported in 1943, after refusing to believe their Jewish name and identity would cause them harm). Aubrac is but one of the numerous names Lucie and Raymond sported during the war, and then later decided to keep.

Although Berri's historical films are neither esthetically nor historically exceptional (tending toward stereotypes, simplified/altered versions of history, conventional film *topoi*), a film like *Lucie Aubrac* is nevertheless of interest, for it can carry considerable weight and power in the battle over Occupation memories. With the facts of the war in dispute, film has the ability to mold the general public's understanding of a past that new generations did not live through, and that the old may have forgotten or remember differently. Because Berri's is an action film (with the complexities of the political action remaining sketchy), some see it as a convenient, alluring way to teach to the young the civic lessons that Lucie herself was interested in conveying (and that her character teaches in the film). Although Berri's film does not try to take the place of the history lesson, it could make a claim for awakening the curiosity of the general public—a first step toward exploring complex issues.

Berri is not the only one to have altered historical fact for the sake of a good story. Lucie was made to understand the price of fictive embellishments in delicate historical issues when the editor of the memoirs had her change the date of Raymond's first escape from May 10 to May 14, 1943, in order to match their anniversary date.[29] This change was meant to intensify the romantic drama because the couple had sworn to each other always to be together on that date. (Berri's and Yanne's films follow Lucie's change of date.) Convinced that such a change in "detail" did not vitiate the overall picture, Lucie nevertheless found herself embroiled later on in controversies concerning the truth of her memoirs. Barbie, in fact, used the gap between May 10 (the actual release of Raymond) and May 14 (the date given by Lucie in her memoirs) as the moment when Raymond had become an agent for the Nazis. And although scarcely anyone took Barbie's accusations very seriously, the shadowy areas of this period, the pieces of the puzzle of past events that did not seem to fit together very well, cast doubts about the truth of the Aubracs' version of events.

In this context, Berri's film, in addition to being a pedagogical tool, becomes another arm of defense for the Aubracs, a way to clear their good name. When Jacques Vergès composed "Barbie's Testament" in 1990, a document (supposedly written by Barbie, but undoubtedly coming from lawyer Vergès) that claimed Barbie had released Aubrac in 1943 in order to use him as his agent against the resistance, the Aubracs were intent upon defending themselves. Whereas Barbie claimed that Aubrac revealed the location of the Caluire meeting (June 21, 1943), Berri's film suggests that another man, René Hardy, was the traitor, even though Hardy was later tried and twice acquitted of the crime. A more recent book, *La Diabolique de Caluire* ("The Diabolical Woman of Caluire") by historian Pierre Péan, convincingly argues that Hardy was actually protecting the real culprit, his beautiful, diabolical mistress, Lydie Bastien, an evil counter version of heroine Lucie Aubrac.[30]

Clearly espousing the Aubracs' understanding of the mystery concerning who revealed the Caluire address to the Gestapo, Berri gives the public a plausible version of events (the Aubracs'), but it is crucial to note that he *also* allows room for questioning this version by having other resister characters suggest other possibilities. Additionally, a mysterious woman in a red blouse is shown to be following Jean Moulin and Raymond Aubrac on the way to the meeting, and we never find out what her connection is to the betrayal. (This may well be the mysterious Lydie Bastien.) The riddle is never solved—in the film *or* reality—but the film is unambiguous about the Aubracs' heroism. And for all its publicity and hype, there is some truth to Lucie's claim that the film helped to kindle serious discussion about the period despite historians' assertions to the contrary.

ACT THREE: HISTORIANS AND ACTORS, VERISIMILITUDE, AND TRUTHS

In 1996–97, the Aubrac affair came to a boil. The 1996 publication of Raymond Aubrac's memoirs, *Où la mémoire s'attarde* ("Where Memory Dwells"), and the February 1997 opening of Berri's film caused a renewed public and professional interest in the events of 1943. Then in April, 1997, Albin Michel published a highly controversial book, *Aubrac, Lyon 1943*, by historian Gérard Chauvy. Using German police reports from the time, Chauvy not only questioned the Aubracs' versions of the two rescues of Raymond in May and October 1943, but also seemed to point to possible treachery on their part. The story of heroism began to look seriously tainted in Chauvy's account. Included at the end of Chauvy's book is the infamous "Testament de Barbie" ("Barbie's Testament"). Nineteen ex-resistance leaders publicly rose up to defend the honor of the resistance against Chauvy, and the publication of his book was actually delayed several weeks because of the intense debates surrounding its content. Finally, in May 1997, after repeated requests by the

Aubracs, a round table discussion was organized by the newspaper *Libération* to allow the Aubracs to respond to historians' questions.[31] In attendance were the Aubracs, their friends—historian Maurice Agulhon and ex-resister Jean-Pierre Vernant (well-known scholar of Greek antiquity)—as well as several other renowned resistance historians: Henry Rousso, Daniel Cordier (Jean Moulin's ex-secretary and biographer), Jean-Pierre Azéma, Dominique Veillon, Laurent Douzou, and veteran historian François Bédarida.

Although this encounter of historians and witnesses failed to achieve the goals of those involved, the dossier, "Les Aubrac et les historiens,"—including *Libération*'s preparatory introduction, the round table, and final comments by participants—is a fascinating document that allows the public to witness a real history lesson on the difficult, myriad negotiations between fiction and history, the constructions of multiple truths through memory, and the kind of lesson that literary critics often relish, but that historians sometimes underestimate.

DIFFERENT AGENDAS

> The good historian is not from any one period or country: although he loves his country, he does not flatter it in any way.
>
> *Fénelon (my translation)*

While Raymond and Lucie Aubrac come to the discussion to have their names cleared from any accusations of treason that Barbie, Vergès, and Chauvy may have made or implied, none of the historians at the round table really believes they are guilty of treachery against the resistance. The historians are, however, understandably troubled by inconsistencies in the Aubracs' version of the past, as revealed by Chauvy's work. At issue for the historians are such questions as to whether the Germans arrested Aubrac the first time in March 1943 for small time black marketeering (what he told the authorities) or for resistance liaison work (what the German authorities wrote in their report); whether Lucie's admittedly rash act of threatening the life of the prosecuting attorney in order to free Raymond had any effect on Raymond's actual release; whether Lucie could have really entered with her disguise as Ghislaine de Barbentane into Gestapo headquarters in Lyon to see Raymond without having to show her identity papers; and why Raymond's different postwar accounts varied so much about whether the Germans knew his "true identity" of Aubrac, an important resistance figure.[32] As the minutes tick by in the round table sessions, the incongruities, inconsistencies, and implausibilities pile up for the historians in alarming fashion. The reassurances at the beginning of the discussions tend to disappear as the historians search for an unequivocal truth. The sessions then veer uncomfortably into an inquisition-style interrogation, or at least resemble the grilling one undergoes at a doctorate oral defense. (This is Jean-Pierre Vernant's description of the event.)[33] The Aubracs look more and more like worn-out, sometimes angry, victims on trial, repeating either "I don't remember" or "I don't know why it happened that way, or why the Germans thought that." The intricacies of the historical interrogation are dizzying, as the historians weave through competing versions of what might have happened, proposing scenarios, rejecting faulty memories of the Aubracs, settling disputes over authoritative accounts in the effort to establish a truth that would disentangle the resistance (and the Aubracs) from any suspicion of wrong-doing.[34]

Clearly, everybody is uncomfortable and unsatisfied in this particular history lesson. François Bédarida invokes optimistically at the opening, the historians' "scientific responsibility" to cut through the "legend" of the resistance, and, with scrupulous decrypting, to unearth the "positive knowledge" of what really happened. No "half-truths" can be permitted. While the ideal may be admirable, the naiveté of the equation "history = hard science" can hardly go unnoticed, especially in an encounter where the historians sometimes end up in the awkward position of using Nazi reports to challenge the surviving resisters' version of events. Bédarida remembers the clearing of Moulin's name and expects the same will occur in the new context. His rhetoric is worth quoting: "When we had to deal with false allegations made against Jean Moulin, the simple application of the historian's method in all its rigor was enough to pulverize the groundless accusations."[35] But what the "simple application" of the historian's method unveils here instead is his curious over-reliance on notions usually associated with literary properties. Plausibility and consistency, for example, are frequently used to challenge the truth-value of the Aubracs' accounts, as if reality actually adhered to the dictates of realist fiction.[36] It is a rather disquieting scenario when the historians adopt the Germans' point of view as the basis upon which to judge what is plausible. The German occupiers' penchant for precise records places the notion of "detail" on the side of scientific accuracy, to which the historians seem to adhere. And while the historians are themselves careful to acknowledge that mistakes were made in the Germans' written reports—ones that, in fact, get perpetuated—the professionals tend to privilege the written over the oral, the official document over the private memory.

Although the historians claim precision and accuracy on their side, the discussions also reveal their own faulty memories. Jean-Pierre Azéma argues with Raymond Aubrac about what he said in his memoirs. The historian is convinced that the memoirs show Aubrac's concern for revealing his "true role" in the resistance when arrested at Caluire, whereas Aubrac maintains he referred to his "true identity." A quick check in the memoirs reveals that Raymond is right.[37] And if such a distinction between "identity" and "role" might at first seem minor, in the context of clearing up who knew what, and when, about Raymond Aubrac in the resistance, such a detail turns out to be relatively important. I am not trying here to challenge the historians in their desire to understand what happened in 1943, but rather to show that their privileged position is also subject to errors in memory.

The high moral tone of a Bédarida or a Cordier is not always absent from the younger historians. Laurent Douzou, while quite sympathetic toward the Aubracs, is skeptical of the general public's ability to grasp the complexities of the events, and declares at one point that he has no desire to see the Berri film: for him it is clearly not a legitimate source.[38] Douzou also questions the possibility of getting at a "naked truth" some fifty years after the fact, in fiction or in witnesses' accounts. I would add that the notion of a "naked truth" is problematic right from the start, not just in the postwar memories. But what all the historians anxiously recognize is that the ideological stakes at play in the discussion are too high to be dealt with lightly. A deeply troubled Daniel Cordier soundly upbraids Lucie for her loose handling of historical events. Lucie, for her part, rather unsuccessfully tries to duck this accusation, by distinguishing the professional research historian from the popularizing pedagogue that she sees in herself.

Some of these supposedly disinterested professional historians appear to be on a mission: to recover the honor of the resistance, and hence France, since the resistance is deemed a key component to the

"the national patrimony," as Bédarida puts it. The round table is thus French identity in the making: to rescue the resistance's memory is to deliver France at least partially from the sullying effects of Barbie and collaboration. But, as it turns out, the identity constructed is not the homogeneous entity desired. Somewhat paradoxically, the tensions between the historian's desire for scientific objectivity, and the desire to portray a wholly intelligible, transparent, and honorable resistance, push him into challenging actual resisters. And while the Aubracs also want to consecrate the resistance, their memories do not allow the historians to construct an unequivocal, coherent picture of events. At the end of the discussion, Henry Rousso, seemingly aware of the historical debacle they have just gone through, turns the tables around and desperately asks the Aubracs what they think the historian is supposed to do when the facts do not mesh. What distinguishes the "good historian" from the bad one? My own answer would be that the one who asks such a question is precisely on the right track. The historian who recognizes the need to review his or her own position critically is all the stronger for it. Cordier, however, winds up so disillusioned that he tells the Aubracs that he will ignore their own testimonies and use his documents to prove their innocence. By the end of the encounters, he sounds ready to plunge into deep depression because the historical research involving witnesses will not provide an indisputable truth.

The resistance historian who seems most attuned to the difficulties of incorporating actual participants' memories into the fabric of historical account is Dominique Veillon: she recognizes the delicate problem of investigating the resistance *critically* when national identity is at stake. She notes the dangers of automatically privileging written over oral accounts, or official documents over personal memoirs. But she also gently points out to Lucie Aubrac that much controversy could have been avoided if Lucie had clearly marked her memoirs as a loose, romanticized personal account of events that does not adhere strictly to historical facts, and sometimes favors plausibility and coherence over historical accuracy. Whereas Berri is careful to acknowledge the fictionalization of his treatment of Lucie's memoirs, the author herself neglects to point out her own conscious alterations of facts. Interestingly enough, what was effective for her in Raymond's second rescue (the donning of disguise, deception, a fictive identity) is precisely the kind of fabrication that becomes problematic in the remembered account. But Veillon also recognizes that the historians were too quick to take Lucie's memoirs for historical document. Henry Rousso, however, refuses to be labeled Lucie's dupe: he is especially unhappy with her, *not* because historians believed her memoirs, but because she first maintained their truth and then acknowledged their fictive aspects.[39]

The fallout from this encounter at the round table was certainly more disastrous for the historians than for the Aubracs. In *The Haunting Past: History, Memory, and Justice in Contemporary France*, Henry Rousso describes a relatively ferocious backlash against the historians who participated in the round table.[40] Obviously feeling quite bruised by the whole affair, Rousso blames the Aubracs for having tried to manipulate the historians into providing a simple vindication of their version of events, and although he found it regrettable, the outcome was deserved (in short, "they asked for it"). In an unexpected twist, he also sets the "legitimate" historians (professional researchers like himself) apart from the ex-resisters/historians (i.e., non-academics), like Daniel Cordier.[41] This is an understandable (if problematic) move, given that it was Cordier who wondered aloud if the Aubracs had been at least indirectly responsible for the deportation of Raymond's parents! The most intriguing aspect of this episode arose when it came time to publish the round table's proceedings: Rousso and others wanted to censure Cordier's outrageous question (Cordier goes along with this), but *it is Lucie Aubrac who refuses to have the passage dropped from the minutes.* It is as if the tables had been turned on the historians, who now become the object of scrutiny and responsible for the "whole truth" before the public. If historians like Rousso are right to insist on historical accuracy, lending a critical eye to legends and myths of the resistance, they must also remain mindful of the difficulties of being a participating witness in an event. At the very least, the strong reaction to the round table provides the occasion for a serious, critical reflection about the production of historical discourse.

The historians longed for a "clean" version of events that the witnesses simply could not supply. One wonders what kind of film could ever have been made to portray the jumble of conflicting versions. Perhaps only a postmodern rendering—whether film or text—could have taken into account the multiplicity of competing scenarios, contradictory facts. But could such an experimental form still make some versions more compelling than others? Could it be intelligible for a general public, for students unfamiliar with the basics of the story? Berri's film, for all its shortcomings, does not pretend to be more than it is: as a fictionalized adventure drama about the Aubracs, it makes sense of a whole array of events and facts, and presents one reading of the times.

Some historians have long claimed, rightfully so, I think, that the courts are not the best place to settle issues concerning the meanings of historical events. What the controversy surrounding the Aubrac case forcefully brings out is that history even resists *historians'* best attempts to get at the events, and steadfastly holds its share of shadows. What could be more befitting for "the army of shadows," as the resistance was called, than this history of obscure figures and multiple, conflicting accounts? It would seem that *all* these materials play their part in the (re)reading of history: memoirs, films, historical essays, and public discussion, however flawed, partial, or biased, must be weighed and compared against one another: accuracy does matter, but so does public accessibility. Ultimately, this history lesson involves the recognition that with all the good will (or bad) of witnesses, our accounts do not deliver a single final version. Questions remain.[42] The overlapping of versions—from straightforward memoirs and film to complex historical debate—allows a unique public airing of how the resistance figures in France's identity crisis.

THE POSTMODERN HISTORY FILM:
A CONTRADICTION IN TERMS?

Given that we have just hinted that a postmodern film might allow for multiple, competing versions of events to render adequately the messy complexities of the Occupation past, I would like to focus on a film that could be described as postmodern. Jacques Audiard's *Un Héros très discret* (*A Self-Made Hero*, 1995) approaches the Occupation through self-conscious explorations that are playful, stylized, and parodic.[43] It stages the act of representation, and denaturalizes the narrative forms one chooses to signify a past.[44] Audiard's film is postmodernist in the ways it is "suspicious of authoritative definitions and singular narratives of any trajectory of events."[45] What kind of truth or value claims can be made in this way? What is the position of the viewer for such a film? Is history forsaken?

A Self-Made Hero's postmodernist esthetic self-consciously displays its own cinematic contrivances, with its parodies articulated through an acute awareness of the *topoi* of the historical film, especially documentary and biography. Although *A Self-Made Hero* centers on a male hero, we will be looking at the ways the quintessentially ambiguous protagonist, Albert Dehousse, is a befitting companion of an ambiguous Marianne ("le *mari* de *Mari*anne," the husband of Marianne) that we have been discussing throughout this book.[46]

A Self-Made Hero is adapted from a 1989 novel by Jean-François Deniau. In one sense, the novel is a sort of twisted *Bildungsroman* about a young man who learns to get along in life through imitation and lying, with his most successful moment coming at the time of the liberation in 1944–45, when providing the right past credentials as a resister became crucial to socio-political advancement. Audiard's peripatetic hero recalls both Sacha Guitry's autobiographical protagonist in *Story of a Cheat*, and Truffaut's character Antoine Doinel in *The Four Hundred Blows*.[47] And like the characters in *The Last Metro*, Dehousse represents a generation of people with things to hide.[48] Audiard's story is not overflowing with the historical details often used to authenticate film representations of the war period. This is more a fiction about remembering, about lying about memories, about creating a past out of whole cloth, with the requisite researched details. It is an emblematic tale of the collective lies, deceits, embellishments, strategic acts of forgetfulness, and shifts of alliance that many French indulged in after the war. One critic aptly called it a "troubling parable of the still-unresolved French guilt about its wartime and immediate post-war record, a guilt that came into sharp focus around the time of François Mitterrand's death [in 1996]."[49] President Mitterrand's political itinerary contained the same sorts of twists and reversals as Audiard's (and Deniau's) story. As we noted earlier, Mitterrand moved from ties to the conservative right in the 1930s and to Vichy during the early Occupation, turned to resistance work near the end of the war, followed by a career on the Left, culminating in his presidency in the 1980s.[50] Audiard's fiction is indeed emblematic of the postwar era's (re)creations of palatable pasts, particularly for those who came to assume power.

A Self-Made Hero is particularly successful at showing the powers of fiction that deconstruct the realist narrative so often used to represent truth about the past. Audiard's spectator is invited to be witness, voyeur, and companion in the process of making the story. Similar to *Citizen Kane*, the film sets out early on to multiply the frames through which the character Albert Dehousse's life will be evaluated, and continually goes back and forth between time periods. The actions of the past are connected to the film's present; clearly, Audiard wishes to implicate the present in recalling/creating the past.

A *Self-Made Hero* opens with the well-known French actor Jean-Louis Trintignant talking to the camera in the present (not in a recreated past), as in an interview. Given that we do not yet know who the character is (an aging Albert Dehousse), we listen initially to his anecdote about the war, and are uncertain whether the film icon Trintignant is playing himself or someone else. The choice of Trintignant is triply ludic: first, this new role as interviewee talking about his past during the Occupation echoes his role in Michel Drach's 1974 *Les Violons du bal*, in which he played the filmmaker himself talking about his wartime childhood. In both films, the spectator is witness to a present that frames a recreated past (with the difference being that Drach's film keeps the distinction between past and present relatively clear). Second, if we continue to explore the self-conscious references that crisscross cinematic insides and outs, we note that in *A Self-Made Hero* Trintignant plays the aging Dehousse, whose younger version is played by actor/film director Mathieu Kassovitz. Trintignant again seems to be filling the same role of "standing in" for a filmmaker, but the realistic illusion is broken in both instances because he bears very little resemblance at all to either Michel Drach or Mathieu Kassovitz. These are films that repeatedly point to their own representational status.

Interspersed among the recreated scenes of Dehousse's wartime life are the requisite clips from wartime newsreels, as well as mock interviews with actors playing historians, biographers, and editors who provide disparate details about Dehousse's life. Again, the spectator is at first uncertain as to whether these interviews might be "real"—they have the aura of the documentary to which we have grown accustomed: the images appear somewhat grainy, the camera moves shakily about as the voice of the interviewee quickly recounts minutia that the spectators have trouble digesting because what they see (e.g., a middle-aged character-historian riding a bus, talking to the camera, with villages streaming by) does not coincide with what they hear (about Dehousse). The (fake) interviews, supposedly designed to shed light on Dehousse's life, instead tend to make the story seem more muddled. When two aging "eye-witness" resisters are sequentially interviewed (with each one's name printed at the

bottom of the screen to guarantee their authenticity), we are troubled by their contradictory statements: although the diegesis shows
that Dehousse was never in London, one eyewitness claims to
remember him there. Is this all a commentary on messy lives, on the
way we tell them, or on faulty memories? Probably all of the above.
At any rate, the plot twists and self-reflexive allusions in Albert's
complex story pile up at a dizzying speed.

Early on, the fictitious documentary within the film self-consciously parodies a passage from *The Sorrow and the Pity*. A woman
is interviewed (in the present) about what happened to Albert
Dehousse's Pétainist mother at the end of the war. The woman's
physical resemblance with *The Sorrow and the Pity*'s Pétainist
Madame Solange (hair, glasses, age, drawn features), and her reti-
cence to talk about what was done to Mrs. Dehousse, are hard to
miss. We sense, in both instances, that a shameful truth is being hidden. What is particularly ironic about this reference to *The Sorrow
and the Pity* is that the scene from Ophüls's film is one of the rare
passages featuring a woman, and it seems clear that the camera is
intent on making Madame Solange look guilty (whether she is or
not) by focusing on her nervous hands wringing a handkerchief.
Audiard's fictitious interviewer (who is not on camera) actually comments on *his* interviewee's nervousness in front of the camera, as if
the younger filmmaker Audiard were making a commentary on the
older one's manipulation of the female interviewee—and on the supposed "objectivity" of documentaries in general.

Audiard's film juxtaposes the trappings of realism (documentary
appearance, reconstruction of a life through interviews, research,
archives) with the fantastic and the hyper-real: young Dehousse's
first discovery of lying—he learns his father died an alcoholic rather
than a hero of World War I—is accompanied by a surreal scene in
which his father's portrait on the wall comes to life and cries out "Vive
la France!" At another moment, when Dehousse has succeeded in getting a high rank in the resistance, thanks to his fabrications, his interior
joy is rendered visually by a younger Dehousse jumping around in his
underwear (doing calisthenics, flapping his arms, as if to fly) in
speeded-up time against a black backdrop. This exuberant image
recalls nineteenth century experiments in film, such as Jules-Etienne
Marey's series of "chronophotographies" (1882–1895) that research
the movement of men and horses.[51] At the opposite edge of the
realist spectrum is the instance where Audiard's camera moves

seamlessly from a fictive scene of the character Dehousse jumping on a train, to the room where a real string quartet is performing the music that we have been hearing as background. The film straddles, often comically, the line between illusion and reality, commenting on it inside the plot, as well as making it tangible in the self-conscious visibility of the illusion's accessories (such as the musical score's performance on screen). Cinematic form and thematic content are particularly well suited, as the two show how "reality," "history," "events," and "identity" are constructed in their telling. At the end of the film, the aging Dehousse (Trintignant) looks directly at the camera and asks: "Do you think I look natural?" We are invited to take part in a fanciful parsing of verisimilitude.

Whereas realist fiction might equate research with finding the facts (and thus the truth) about the past, research for Albert Dehousse becomes a way to lie, by carefully constructing a persona, an identity that will appear plausible to others and will allow him access to positions of power and authority. In one way, at least, the film's emphasis on Albert's meticulous research of the roles he assumes makes a mockery of the claims of an historian like François Bédarida to get at the truth about the past through rigorous investigation.[52] In order to play an ex-resister during the liberation, Dehousse peruses new and old newspapers, studies the demeanor, gestures, and linguistic quirks of well-known resisters, and even memorizes London's subway lines to feign experience with de Gaulle's operation in England. He is very convincing and quickly rises in the resistance ranks: because nobody's position seems entirely safe in the postwar era—can one ever be an entirely "pure" or untainted resister in a world of ambiguous, underground politics?—Dehousse is rarely challenged, as he plays one group off another. As one critic wrote: "[Dehousse] soon learns that people will believe what they want to hear regarding a period they would rather forget."[53] When he does get into trouble, that is, when someone recognizes his name and tries to link him to his real past (a drunken dead father, a pro-Vichy mother), Dehousse wriggles out of the problem by (falsely) claiming the name Dehousse is a pseudonym and that his name is actually Rozinsky (a Polish Jewish name), thereby completely silencing the man who questions his identity. Audiard shows that to be a Jewish resister in postwar France constitutes effective credentials that few would dare to challenge. Given that the role of Dehousse is played by actor-filmmaker

Mathieu Kassovitz, who actually is Jewish, the boundaries between reality and fiction again prove to be permeable, keeping us thinking about the film's implications for contemporary France, and perhaps drawing our attention to Rousso's "obsessive period" when France's involvement in the Holocaust is recalled at every turn.

Dehousse's very name points to his chameleon-like identity, since "housse" in French means a slipcover. With the "de" connoting nobility, his name crowns him a prince of disguises that he slips in and out of with more or less success. He takes on the role of novelist, hotel doorman, patriotic resister, and eventually his con games get him promoted to the rank of lieutenant colonel in charge of psychological and propaganda operations in postwar Germany. As knowledgeable spectators of Dehousse's various performances, we watch the preparations that allow him to dupe his interlocutors; we occupy less the position of judge than of accomplice. Like him, we are voyeurs. Our awareness of the protagonist's deceptions implicates us in his increasingly risky performances because we are implicitly invited to root for his success: his charades seem for a while to carry little weight, as if constructing roles were the same as living, as if—to return to the postmodern question—the differences between fiction and reality were of little consequence.

But, ultimately, the difference does count for Dehousse and for us, too. At the end of the war when Dehousse assumes his new position as Lieutenant Colonel in the French army, a voice-over comments on the ruins of Germany in 1945, whose representations we watch on screen (old clips of bombs falling, of destroyed cities viewed from the air). For Dehousse, this is where the real war was, "with real armies, real ruins, a real debacle, and sometimes real deaths, which Dehousse couldn't help but find exciting" (my translation). This reality impinges upon his consciousness and his conscience when he must figure out what to do with some French soldiers who had fought for the Wehrmacht, and who are now desperately fleeing across the German countryside. The real/fake lieutenant colonel holds the life of these ragtag French soldiers in his hands. Dehousse quickly decides that they will be shot, but that their families will be told they died in combat. Dehousse thus prefers to create dead heroes of the men rather than to acknowledge them as guilty, misguided traitors to France. Similarly, shortly after proffering the soldiers' death sentence, when Dehousse's deceptions have begun to unravel, he admits his own elaborate fraud as a resister and is sentenced to jail. The film offers no "explanations," as such, for his decision: has his feigned role become too real for him as he has soldiers put to death? Does he turn himself in because his new love, Servane, an intelligence officer herself, reveals that she has guessed his trickery from the start (and is fascinated by it), or is it because he wants to be honest with her and is tired of pretending to be what he is not? The film elides the reasons, whether private (the love story) or public (the moral dilemma), but it does offer a parallel between Dehousse's condemnation of the soldiers and the way his own criminal case is handled. Rather than being tried for his military fraud, which would be too embarrassing for the army that he has successfully duped, he is charged with the lesser transgression of bigamy (he has never bothered to divorce his wife Yvette before hooking up with Servane). In both cases, one deception covers over another. This is a portrayal of a public and a private France, for whom expediency and decorum are much more important than truth or justice.

Were it not for the comical quality of many of Albert's antics, this exploration of French duplicity might have appeared sinister. The tone is lightened by speeded-up action, quick juxtapositions, and, in general, by anti-realist visual devices that tend to underplay the severity of any judgment we might have been inclined to formulate about Dehousse's travesties. In addition, the complex interweaving of different narrative versions keeps us continually off-balance, so that we are virtually "too busy" trying to construct a coherent story of Dehousse's life. The aging Dehousse appears on screen at three different moments among segments of the recreated past, the newsreel clips, and the fake documentary interviews. Finally, Dehousse's double-dealing and play-acting seem less outrageous because they are echoed by all the other major characters. Young Dehousse's wife Yvette initially demonstrates her ability to simulate when she hides from him the fact that she is engaged in resistance activity during the first years of their marriage. The mysterious Monsieur Jo, for whom Albert works for a time, enters into shady deals with the Nazis as well as the communists.[54] The gay resistance hero, Captain Dionnet, who befriends Dehousse in Paris, is a double agent and his friendship with Dehousse retains sexual undertones. Dehousse's own sexuality remains ill-defined: as a mediocre heterosexual lover, he gets practice with a friendly prostitute in order to improve. When later stationed in postwar Germany, his relationship with his German manservant appears unclear. There is an erotic charge in the scene where the elderly (perhaps fatherly?) butler teaches Albert to waltz. In *A Self-Made Hero*, characters' duplicity is echoed in an ambiguous sexuality, as if collective, political deceptions were echoed in the individual's private sexual mores (see Figure 6.1).

We noted at the beginning of this reading of *A Self-Made Hero* that Albert Dehousse is the befitting partner of our ambiguous Marianne. This is born out within the film's plot. Near the end of the story, when Albert is finally jailed, we learn that both his wife, Yvette, and his new love, Servane, wait for him during his imprisonment. The voice-over implicitly confirms what the smiling female duo visually hints at: Yvette and Servane *also* become a couple as they wait for Albert's release. Bisexuality evokes here the crossing from one "side" to another (and back)—metamorphoses of identity; it also evokes the complicated shifts of alliance and attraction that the film renders so brilliantly in the political arena. The film's last images suggest that once out of prison, Albert will continue to lead a life of convenient lies to advance his career, just as so many ex-Vichy supporters-turned-resisters managed to become prominent, powerful players in

Figure 6.1. *A Self-Made Hero*, Jacques Audiard, 1995. Albert learns to dance with his German butler (Bernard Bloch).

France's postwar politics, with François Mitterrand and Maurice Papon supplying some of the most notable examples.[55]

A more recent, explicit, questioning of Mitterrand's problematic role in the war can be found in Robert Guédiguian's 2004 film, *Le Promeneur du Champ-de-Mars* (*The Last Mitterrand*), which is a fictional rendering of Mitterrand's last days in office. The script was written by Georges-Marc Benamou, who was Mitterrand's biographer, so this story of journalist/biographer Antoine Moreau is informed by a lived experience. The film is also a work that emphasizes the act of remembering and uncovering a suspicious past, but the latter is only allusively recollected, never represented to the viewer other than through dialogue or visuals of the 1990s (Mitterrand died in 1996). As the ailing President Mitterrand eloquently, slyly, and engagingly talks of his past to Antoine Moreau (played by Jalil Lespert), he steadfastly skirts issues that might allow the journalist (and spectator) to settle the question, in some definitive way, of Mitterrand's historical culpability in the war, and its implications for his political legacy. The journalist wants to know if Mitterrand switched from his role as Vichy bureaucrat to resistance fighter in 1942 (as Mitterrand maintains) or in 1943 (as others claim), because the later date would make him unequivocally guilty of collaborating with Vichy with full knowledge of its anti-Semitic policies and atrocities committed. The "truth" hinges on a photo of Mitterrand and other resisters, which Mitterrand claims was taken in 1942. But the supposedly factual evidence cannot be delivered through this representation without agreement on the date. The photographic image is no more a guarantee of an unequivocal truth than the stories Mitterrand tells, or the film we are watching.

In an emblematic way, the journalist's fascination with the great public figure's past interferes with, and gets woven into, his own private life in the present, just as France's reckoning with Occupation memories has sometimes colored or even clouded its understanding of subsequent events.[56] The journalist's obsession with Mitterrand's occupation past also keeps him from assessing more fully Mitterrand's terms in office. But heeding the recommendations and tastes of the women-loving president, the journalist chooses a new girlfriend (the older generation still affects the young). While not as esthetically zany as *A Self-Made Hero*, Guédiguian's portrait of Mitterrand is self-conscious and complex: the national past is ultimately made up of words, and the witty, intellectual Mitterrand makes us laugh, wince, and wonder about how to evaluate this past—of a rightist, collabora-tor, resister, socialist—with all its political and moral implications for the present. Actor Michel Bouquet powerfully embodies Mitterrand in every elegant turn of phrase, literary reference, and gesture, as well as in the material decline of his failing body.

Given many of the featured backgrounds for Mitterrand's interviews—the Chartres Cathedral (viewed from a plane and from inside), a run-down factory, and Parisian neighborhoods—one critic maintained that "the film's most vivid presence is France itself . . . Guédiguian reveals a society burdened by its vast history, stretched on the rack of conscience over its wartime responsibility and mourn-ing its dreams of a brighter future"[57] (see Figure 6.2). I would add that Mitterrand's elegant speech, his clever repartee, his attachment to France's landscapes and old monuments (sepulchres of the great, including himself!) make of him a symbol of France's past much more than of its future. Although, in real life, Mitterrand was also concerned with building a French national identity of the future through his huge architectural projects that Panivong Norindr has described "as a complex extension of political reality, as cultural cap-ital,"[58] this monumental aspect of his legacy is not emphasized in the film. Nevertheless, the fictional character's self-conscious care of his own image and that of France is in tune with the real Mitterrand's strong endorsement and protection of cinema as a form of national cultural expression. In his 1993 Gdansk speech during the heated

Figure 6.2. *The Last Mitterrand*, Robert Guédiguian, 2004. President Mitterrand speaks to working-class supporters in front of an abandoned factory.

GATT exchanges, Mitterrand argued (against the United States) that "creations of the mind" are not "merchandise," and went on to declare: "To defend the pluralism of works and the public's freedom to choose is a duty. What is at stake is the cultural identity of our nations, it is the right of each country to its own culture, it is the freedom to create and to choose our images."[59] In Guédiguian's film, Mitterrand simultaneously cultivates his own image and that of France, but he remains principally an ambiguous symbol of the past, whereas the young journalist, with his doubts and anxiety about the guilty national past, and his messy, disoriented life, appears to embody France's uncertain present.

The Last Mitterrand remains steadfastly in the period of the 1990s, with no flashbacks or recreations of the war, no archival materials or old film clips. In 2004, of course, the early 1990s already compose another segment of postwar past. With its numerous allusions to an insider's knowledge of France's political and literary cultures, the film maintains a resolutely ironic attitude about "remembering" the past. We seem cut off from anything as solid as a "fact." When the Mitterrand character invokes his resistance work (rescuing Marguerite Duras's husband, Robert Antelme, from Dachau) by reading out loud a passage from Marguerite Duras's literary account, *La Douleur* (*The War: A Memoir*), in which Mitterrand is mentioned, there is little doubt that history has become hopelessly embroiled in a labyrinth of literary allusions that have shaped "the past" as Mitterrand sees it. To complicate matters, the real-life Mitterrand did, in fact, grant an interview with Duras for the review *L'Autre Journal*, about the resistance experiences recounted in Duras's *War: A Memoir*.[60] For the uninitiated, however, many of the literary and political references can remain mysterious, potentially producing two very different results: either the spectators decide that the questions of moral responsibility about the past cannot be answered, and leave the issue open-ended, or they plunge into the history books, literature, and archives of France's past to try to find out for themselves. Guédiguian's treatment of Mitterrand's past resembles the Aubrac's round table experience: definitive answers elude the participants/spectators, but the experience of the search is enthralling (and frustrating).

I would like to return briefly now to our initial question concerning the aptness of postmodern film to render the multiplicity and complexity of the Occupation. Clearly, *A Self-Made Hero* tells us a lot about how we have come to remember the Occupation and how our versions are constructed. It proclaims itself as fiction and shows how much the "truth" owes to conventions and fictive structures. Neither it nor *The Last Mitterrand* attempts, however, to "set the record straight" about specific facts of the Occupation by choosing, for example, one version of a specific event over another. *A Self-Made Hero* does not, in fact, concentrate on detailed allusions to actual events of the Occupation. In *The Last Mitterrand*, there *are* precise questions about Mitterrand's actions during the Occupation—he was, after all, a prominent figure during and after the war, but the film's narrative seems to slide off the most slippery issues: Guédiguian never provides enough information to settle the issue of culpability. For some critics who expected the film to deliver the goods on Mitterrand, with precise, historical details (dates, places, events, participants) to support either a justifying or accusatory argument, *The Last Mitterrand* was a disappointment because its treatment of the past remained resolutely vague. Ultimately, *A Self-Made Hero* and *The Last Mitterrand* are most interested in the Occupation's postwar incarnations, making them important contributions to the understanding of the war's aftereffects in France. Their postmodern bent does not allow for any resolution to the issues they raise: rather than putting things to rest, they simply air the problems in sometimes disconcertingly indirect ways.

Albert Dehousse's machinations to establish a heroic persona (like those of Guédiguian's Mitterrand) rely on a complicated mix in which memory and history are sometimes deliberately confused, sometimes held in opposition. Pierre Nora distinguishes between memory and history thus:

> Memory is life, always embodied in living societies and as such in permanent evolution, subject to the dialectic of remembering and forgetting, unconscious of the distortions to which it is subject, vulnerable in various ways to appropriation and manipulation and capable of lying dormant for long periods only to be suddenly reawakened. History, on the other hand, is the reconstruction, always problematic and incomplete, of what is no longer. Memory is always a phenomenon of the present, a bond tying us to the eternal present; history is a representation of the past. Memory, being a phenomenon of emotion and magic, accommodates only those facts that suit it. It thrives on vague, telescoping reminiscences, on hazy general impressions or specific symbolic details.[61]

Albert Dehousse uses the tools of history (books, newspaper archives, "scientific" observation) to create a "lived memory" in the present, using "vague, telescoping reminiscences" and "hazy general impressions or specific symbolic details" to appropriate a past. Similarly, the film itself presents the fiction of a lived memory constructed via history's resources ("on location" interviews, archival film clips). Audiard seems to be arguing that history has become the means by which the French have fabricated the "authentic" memories they would like to hold. Guédiguian tends, instead, to underscore that the past is buried in a weave of shadowy literary and political allusions that contemporary journalism cannot make its way through.

Although neither *A Self-Made Hero* nor *The Last Mitterrand* focuses on a central woman character to articulate a performance of the Occupation, the former does bring us back to certain issues involving France's Marianne that recall the much earlier comedy, *Babette s'en va-t-en Guerre* (1959). Just as Babette was the symbolic partner of de Gaulle in restoring France, so, too, are Yvette and Servane the doubled partners of Albert in representing the "other," more devious side of France's liberation and postwar years. The blond Babette, we remember, already had her brunette double, the politically comprised girl friend of the German Von Arenberg. Similarly, in Audiard's film, Yvette the blond and Servane the brunette are capable of duplicity *and* heroism. Both are adept at hiding their game, at handling a memory of conflicting interpretations, and are witty, nimble matches for Albert Dehousse. In fact, all the principal female characters appear much stronger and active than Albert, who never seems able to take initiative in relationships. We once again see the schema of weak man/strong women of the Burch/Sellier Occupation model. In Audiard's (post)modern twist, the issue of the symbolic couple's identity is left unresolved, as the combinations veer into a trio, opening up multiple combinations (Albert-Yvette, Albert-Servane, Servane-Yvette) for sketching the psycho-social dimensions of France's ethical implications in the Occupation and its aftermath. We are no longer dealing so much with history as with the ways we self-consciously produce memory as story, myth, and allegory.

In *The Last Mitterrand*, the women characters offer important counterweights to a male preoccupation with the past. Madame Picard, the one person with the credentials to challenge Mitterrand's claim about entering the resistance in 1942 (she, too, was in the resistance during the Occupation), urges the young journalist not to pursue this line of questioning, insisting that Mitterrand's larger political legacy is what matters. In the journalist's private sphere, his pregnant wife leaves him as he becomes increasingly obsessed with Mitterrand's past. And if she and their baby represent symbols of France's present and future that are a bit too pat, the complications of modern conjugal life—with a new boyfriend for the wife, a new girlfriend for the husband, and the journalist's on-going attachment to his ex-wife and child—underscore a chaotic scenario of the contemporary French family. Here, again, there is no "resolution"; life just bumps along. Its lack of definitive answers, like the film's, leaves us wishing for more.

CHAPTER 7

―――――❧◆❧―――――

IN LIEU OF A CONCLUSION

What seems particularly painful for many about the modern evolution of the nation (whether it be France or any other Western country) is the recognition that we so often must live without consensus, that unresolved conflict and dissent are at the heart of democracy. Without some consensus about our collective past, postmodernism's open-ended account of history may well be what we get stuck with—multiple versions with no controlling origin. In the array of films made about the Occupation, we find a constellation of overlapping, but also competing renditions of France's negotiations with its past. This is no doubt what the Vichy Syndrome is finally about: an impossible search for an explanation or representation that is both specific and general, one that can hold contradictions together. Despite its wish to proclaim itself as a unified republic, France has increasingly had to recognize that its peculiar claim to a "French universal" ill withstands the realities of a multivalent past and a multicultural, diverse population in the present.

Our cinematic Marianne has tended to be a national symbol of "crisis and conflict, of resistance and negotiation" rather than an icon of unity, coherence, and stable identity, and her moral quandaries eat at the definition of France from within.[1] To a certain extent, our concentration on dramatic genres has emphasized Marianne's controversial quality, although one need only look at early postwar dramas to witness the homogenizing, mythologizing efforts involved in the (re)construction of French identity after 1945. Comedies also tend to offer up an unwavering, unassailable identity rather than challenge spectators to rethink positions. Their reliance on commonplaces and national stereotypes provides a reassuring collective image. *La Grande Vadrouille* (1966), the biggest box-office hit in France for thirty years (as well as a success abroad), is a reminder of the enduring leitmotif of the war in French consciousness. Its stereotypes of British, Germans, and French are designed to produce laughter that gently underwrites easy, naturalized differences between self and other at the collective level. The film pokes fun at foreigners' accents (as well as the French speaking other languages), at linguistic misunderstandings, and uses popular music to identify nationality. It is hard not to smile at British bombardiers whistling "Tea for Two" in their plane, or at the use of accordion music—French *musette*—to accompany a panorama of Paris replete with the Eiffel Tower, or at French actors Bourvil and de Funès singing the same song (in accented English) in a Turkish bath as a secret code to locate the downed British pilots.[2] The madcap comedy delights in clichés and typical disguises that cross national boundaries: one British pilot must cut his handlebar mustache to look more French; another must dress as a German woman (a Bavarian *Fraülein* in a dirndl); the Frenchmen, as just mentioned, must pretend to be English, or disguise themselves in ill-fitting Nazi uniforms (too big, too small). The stereotypes, without ever being seriously challenged, make us laugh the most when they are poorly mimicked. There are no Jews here, no French collaborators, and the term "horrors of war" becomes a joke when Augustin (Bourvil) applies it to men having to sleep in the same bed because there are not enough to go around. Male bonding and homosocial desire are a constant comedic leitmotif that transcends interactions between the sexes, national identities, or different social classes. What is intriguing in this patriarchal, Gaullist comedy is that the French women characters, from a puppeteer to nuns, are real agents of effective rescue and resistance, while occupying secondary roles. Ultimately, it is male sexual identity and the ambivalence surrounding it that lie at the center of *La Grande Vadrouille*, rather than a question of national identity: Germans soldiers side with Frenchmen Bourvil and de Funès when it is a matter of showing who is boss in the household. Similar to Renoir's *Le Caporal épinglé* from the early 1960s, *La Grande Vadrouille* thematizes the unspoken threat to masculinity that the rise in women's rights and their new social roles in postwar years would appear to instigate.

The twenty-first century already covers a range of established film genres that channel socio-political views of occupied France through a particular lens, from the exceptional to the typical, from the parodic to the (auto)biographical. Whereas *The Last Mitterrand* features the exceptional as emblematic (a president as representative of the entire nation's past), Gérard Jugnot's *Monsieur Batignole* (2002) banks, instead, on a wholly fictional male character to embody the (stereo)typical: "a mediocre Frenchman, with a good heart, limited intelligence, and unwittingly funny."[3] Although the typical is embodied by a man rather than a woman, it is noteworthy that this petit bourgeois pork butcher, played by actor/director Gérard Jugnot, rises out of his collaboration with the Germans and his anti-Semitism by taking on a characteristically *female* role: the caring of young children. As he reluctantly decides to help three Jewish children flee to Switzerland, we witness the transformation of a mediocre man into an emblem of French heroism. When Jugnot's film was shown on French television in 2004, it broke records with the size of its viewing audience (12.5 million): *Monsieur Batignole* quickly managed to become a French heritage film that could be added to the collection of stock images.

Jean-Paul Rappeneau's complicated fast-paced farce/melodrama *Bon Voyage* (2002) brings us back to Marianne in the form of caricature and parody. *Bon Voyage* puts the spotlight on a female icon, Viviane, who is a self-absorbed, manipulative *femme fatale*, a starlette of comedic films, played with melodramatic flair by Isabelle Adjani, who, we remember, also embodied Marianne for the French Republic. Looking a little like Cleopatra, with black hair and heavy bangs, Viviane uses each one of her suitors to further her own interests and career, remaining steadfastly egocentric and oblivious to political and moral implications of the public events swirling around her. *Bon Voyage* is also a self-conscious reprise of the cinematic connections between filmmaking and the Occupation, with Patrick Modiano, the novelist/scriptwriter of wartime obsession and scandal (*Lacombe Lucien*) now co-writing the scenario for this caricatural Occupation thriller-comedy whose hero is a writer composing a manuscript about a lying, deceptive woman. We are soundly enclosed in the funhouse of cinematic mirrors, of playful self-references. The film's opening scene of a film premiere (starring Viviane) showcases the interior of a breathtaking, gilded movie theater, where a well-dressed audience, including Viviane and a government minister

(Gérard Depardieu), watch the actress's new comedy on the screen. The idea of national icons—of self-conscious fabrications of collective identity based on an individual—is continually thematized through Viviane. The self-conscious mockery of cinematic celebrities is playfully embodied by Adjani and Depardieu. *Bon Voyage* looks like a heritage film making fun of itself; it can no longer take the national-cinematic symbolism seriously even though it continues to spin out the connection.

A popular parallel medium for working through the Occupation for the French public over the last several years has been the made-for-TV film. This fictional genre often addresses contemporary issues via the *topoi* of the Occupation: in the 2005 airing of *Un Amour à taire* ("A Love to Keep Quiet," directed by Christian Faure), author Pascal Fontanille dramatizes the deportation of homosexuals through a moving depiction of one family's trauma. The film notes at the end that between ten and fifteen thousand homosexuals died in camps, and that Vichy's law criminalizing homosexuality was not repealed until 1981. Official recognition of homosexual deportations by the state was not granted until 2001, so the issue is anchored in the wartime past but with much more recent echoes.

It is worthy of note that the *téléfilm* is a particularly female domain: the majority of viewers are female, the lead characters are frequently female, and women directors are entering the scene, as witnessed by the 2000 téléfilm, *Deux Femmes à Paris* ("Two Women in Paris"), directed by Caroline Huppert (Isabelle Huppert's daughter), with Romane Bohringer and Julie Depardieu (daughter of Gérard) in the leading roles. Based on a novel by Nine Moati, *Deux Femmes à Paris* quite effectively exposes the ambiguities and moral dilemmas of Occupation survival through women's friendships: Maya, a Tunisian Jew recently arrived in France befriends Maud, a milliner running her own shop of female employees. Whereas Maya is politically committed (on the Left), helping foreign workers and families fleeing Nazism, Maud is apolitical, generous and fun-loving, with a lover whose extreme Right pro-fascist politics become increasingly unbearable. Both women are forced into difficult moral choices and compromises as the period blackens and the Occupation begins, and although the friendship endures with the two helping each other, it does not keep Maya from eventually being arrested as a Jew. Rather than turning into a mythic tale of redemption or of ultimate reconciliation and moral triumph, *Deux Femmes à Paris*

refuses the easy (happy) way out of the predicaments it has dramatized. Although it may not be terribly creative in terms of cinematic
convention, this film successfully captures wartime ambiguities and
compromises without losing its moral compass. Interestingly
enough, *Deux femmes à Paris* resembles *Army of Shadows* in that the
price of the central character's heroic symbolism is death.

* * *

As France's identity crisis has heightened recently to the point of
explosion in its disenfranchised suburbs, and in the rhetoric of the
egalitarian republic, it seems befitting that one of the newest incarnations of the country's wartime past reveals its colonial, racial
twists: director Rachid Bouchareb's *Indigènes* (*Days of Glory*),
released in 2006, dramatizes the fate of North African soldiers who
fought for France against the Germans. France's colonial past opens
up the newest avenue for exploring the national crisis of the Occupation beyond France's borders, and seems to dovetail with its ongoing issues of French identity in the postcolonial era.[4] If the spate of
books published on Vichy in 2006 and the production of new films
on the period is any indication, the fascination with the period continues to haunt French consciousness.

NOTES

NOTES TO CHAPTER 1

1. A. S. Byatt, "What is a European" *New York Times*, October 13, 2002, 50.
2. Chantal Ackerman, "The Filmmakers' Panel," in *Screening Europe: Images and Identities in Contemporary European Cinema*, ed. Duncan Petrie (London: British Film Institute, 1992), 67.
3. James E. Young has changed this formulation from "collective memory" to "collected memories," given that "we don't share memory but rather forms of memory." While this alteration is warranted, it may risk underestimating a shared desire for a public understanding of historical events. See *The Texture of Memory: Holocaust Memorials and Meaning* (New Haven: Yale University Press, 1993), xi.
4. Tony Judt, *Postwar: A History of Europe Since 1945* (New York: Penguin Books, 2005), 41.
5. Judt, 39.
6. Judt, 815.
7. Judt, 46.
8. Claudio Fogu and Wulf Kansteiner, "The Politics of Memory and the Poetics of History," in *The Politics of Memory in Postwar Europe*, ed. Richard Ned Lebow, Wulf Kansteiner, and Claudio Fogu (Durham, NC: Duke University Press, 2006), 296.
9. Judt, 808.
10. Robert O. Paxton, *Vichy France: Old Guard and New Order, 1940–1944* (New York: Columbia University Press, 1972).
11. Henry Rousso, *Le Syndrome de Vichy de 1944 à nos jours* (Paris: Seuil, 1987); *The Vichy Syndrome: History and Memory in France since 1944*, trans. Arthur Goldhammer (Cambridge, MA: Harvard University Press, 1991).
12. Richard J. Golsan, "The Legacy of World War II in France: Mapping the Discourses of History," in *The Politics of Memory in Postwar Europe*, 75.
13. In their work, *Vichy: An Ever-Present Past*, Eric Conan and Henry Rousso argue for a consensus on Vichy, but as Nathan Bracher has adroitly shown, in their desire to foster a national unity, to get beyond Vichy and a supposedly exaggerated "judeo-centric" view of the Occupation, Rousso and Conan themselves "articulate highly questionable positions more on the

basis of their own political and moral priorities/exigencies than on the basis of historical fact." Similar to de Gaulle, says Bracher, the historians wish to rescue France from a murky past that they think is keeping it from confronting the real issues of the present. See Henry Rousso and Eric Conan, *Vichy: An Ever-Present Past*, trans. Nathan Bracher (Hanover, NH: University Press of New England, 1998); and Nathan Bracher, "Timely Predications: The Use and Abuse of History in Contemporary France," *Soundings* 81, no. 1–2 (Spring–Summer 1998): 235–56.

14. See Moses I. Finley, *The Use and Abuse of History* (London: Chatto and Windus, 1975); Stanley Hoffmann, "Regards d'outre-Hexagone," *Vingtième siècle, revue d'histoire* 5 (January–March 1985): 142; In her book *Les Ecrans de l'ombre: La Seconde Guerre mondiale dans le cinéma français* ("Screens in the Dark: The Second World War in French Film," Paris: CNRS Editions, 1997), 7–8, Sylvie Lindeperg chooses Finley's formulation over Hoffmann's, emphasizing the ways the past is used in the present over the return of an "indigestible past." For my purposes, both metaphors are useful, as I will be exploring how the wartime past haunts filmmakers and how it comes to symbolize France's identity crisis.

15. Jacques Revel uses the term "éclatement de l'histoire" in his essay "Histoire vs Mémoire en France aujourd'hui," ("History vs Memory in France Today") *French Politics, Culture & Society*, 18, no.1 (Spring 2000): 1–11. See also Marc Ferro, *The Use and Abuse of History or How the Past is Taught* (Boston: Routledge & Kegan Paul, 1981); Régis Debray, *La République expliquée à ma fille* ("The Republic Explained to My Daughter," Paris: Seuil, 1998); Max Gallo, *L'Amour de la France expliqué à mon fils* ("The Love of France Explained to My Son," Paris: Seuil, 1998).

16. See Revel, 3 (my translation).

17. Susan Rubin Suleiman, *Crises of Memory and the Second World War* (Cambridge, MA: Harvard University Press, 2006), 8.

18. Henri Rousso, *La Hantise du passé: Entretien avec Philippe Petit* (Paris: Editions Textuel,1998). *The Haunting Past: History, Memory, and Justice in Contemporary France*, trans. Ralph Schoolcraft (Philadelphia: University of Pennsylvania Press), 2002.

19. Pascal Ory, "Why Be So Cruel? Some Modest Proposals to Cure the Vichy Syndrome," in *France at War: Vichy and the Historians*, eds. Sarah Fishman et al., trans. David Lake (New York: Berg, 2000), 278 (my emphasis).

20. Iain Chambers, "Citizenship, Language, and Modernity," *PMLA*, 117, no. 1 (January 2002): 25.

21. See: *The Papon Affair: Memory and Justice on Trial*, ed. Richard J. Golsan (New York: Routledge, 2000).

22. Devaivre wanted—and received—in the film credits, more formal recognition of his memoirs as a source of Tavernier's story. It was even reported that Devaivre sent out his spies to provincial theaters to ensure that the film credits did indeed include a specific reference to his memoirs.

23. Jean-Benoit Lévy, *Les Grandes Missions du cinéma* (Montreal: Lucien Parizeau & Compagnie, 1994), 11 (my translation).

24. Benedict Anderson, *Imagined Communities: Reflections on the Origin and Spread of Nationalism* (London: Verso Editions, 1983), 40, cited in Allen Carey-Webb, *Making Subject(s): Literature and the Emergence of National Identity* (New York: Garland, 1998), 4.

25. Jean-Paul Sartre, *The Words*, trans. Bernard Frechtman (New York: George Braziller, 1964), 122.

26. Sartre, 118.

27. For professional critics, this sort of emotional, unreflective response to film is no doubt frowned upon. Nevertheless, it *is* a group reaction in which the audience recognizes itself as a community with a shared experience.

28. Jean-Michel Frodon, *La Projection nationale: Cinéma et nation* (Paris: Ed. Odile Jacob, 1998), 19 (my translation).

29. Jill Forbes has shown that, in fact, the time limit coincided more or less with the actual production capacity of the French, but that perception was different. See: "The French Nouvelle Vague," in *World Cinema: Critical Approaches*, ed. John Hill and Pamela Church Gibson (Oxford: Oxford University Press, 2000), 77.

30. Jean-Pierre Jeancolas, "The Reconstruction of French Cinema," in *France in Focus: Film and National Identity*, ed. Elizabeth Ezra and Sue Harris (New York: Berg, 2000), 16.

31. Forbes, 77–78.

32. Sue Harris and Elizabeth Ezra, "Introduction: The French Exception," in *France in Focus*, 2–3. The term "French Cultural Exception" became particularly in vogue during talks on the General Agreement on Tariffs and Trade (GATT) in 1993.

33. See Suleiman's analysis of how Sartre implicitly exonerates the French in *Crises of Memory and the Second World War*, 13–35.

34. André Bazin, *French Cinema of the Occupation and Resistance: The Birth of a Critical Esthetic*, intro. François Truffaut, trans. Stanley Hochman (New York: Frederick Ungar Publishing Co., 1981), 33.

35. In his famous article "The Birth of a New Avant-Garde: La Caméra-Stylo," published in English in *The New Wave*, ed. Peter Graham (Garden City, NY: Doubleday, 1968), 17–23, Alexandre Astruc envisions the postwar cinema as a medium equivalent to the novel or essay, as a fully expressive language with the camera functioning like a pen, the famous "caméra-stylo." Truffaut's equally famous piece of 1954, "A Certain Tendency in French Cinema," taking issue with the "The Tradition of Quality" of the war years, adds the notion of the cinematic *auteur* who is the *artistic creator* of the film, writing the script, controlling its vision, again expressing the filmmaker's personality. Truffaut's essay appeared in English in *Movies and Methods*, vol. 1, ed. Bill Nichols (Berkeley: University of California Press, 1985), 224–37. Although the films we will be considering are not autobiographies

in any formal sense, they do present personal or "signed" responses to the lived experience of the war period. It is thus at the juncture of film and memory that we can explore the intersections of private and collective experience.

36. Timothy Murray, *PMLA* 3 (March 1999): 280. This quotation is drawn from a forum on interdisciplinarity.

37. Carey-Webb, 4.

38. Ernest Renan, "Qu'est-ce qu'une nation?" ("What Is a Nation?") in *Oeuvres complètes*, vol. 1 (Paris: Calman-Lévy, 1947–1961), 892. This is, no doubt, an exaggeration, for it is quite clear from Rousso's analysis of the postwar years that the Occupation was, in fact, not forgotten, that references to it in contemporary political struggles abounded as the past was used to support contemporary arguments. My point here is that a direct review of France's wartime responsibilities would not come about until much later.

39. Michael Kelly, "The Historical Emergence of Everyday Life," *Sites: The Journal of 20th Century/Contemporary French Studies* 1, no. 1 (Spring 1997): 77.

40. Kelly, 77–78.

41. Jacques Le Goff, "Mentalities: A History of Ambiguities," in *Constructing the Past: Essays in Historical Methodology*, ed. Jacques Le Goff and Pierre Nora, intro. Colin Lucas (New York: Cambridge University Press, 1985), 169.

42. Naomi Schor, *Reading in Detail: Aesthetics and the Feminine* (New York: Methuen, 1987), 4.

43. See Maurice Agulhon, *Les Métamorphoses de Marianne: L'Imagerie et la symbolique républicaines de 1914 à nos jours* ("The Metamorphoses of Marianne: Republican Imagery and Symbolism from 1914 to our Time," Paris: Flammarion, 2001), 111. Agulhon says the resistance was reinventing the "living allegory" through this type of action. All translations from this book are my own.

44. Dominique Veillon, *Vivre et Survivre en France 1939–1947* ("Life and Survival in France 1939–1947," Paris: Payot, 1995), jacket cover.

45. Hannah Arendt, *The Human Condition* (Chicago: University of Chicago Press, 1958), 33–35. Quoted in *Nation and Narration*, Homi K. Bhabha (New York: Routledge, 1990), 2.

46. Noël Burch and Geneviève Sellier, "Evil Women in the Post-war French Cinema," in *Heroines with Heroes: Reconstructing Female and National Identities in European Cinema 1945–51*, ed. Ulrike Sieglohr (New York: Cassell, 2000), 61.

47. Henri Lefebvre, *Everyday Life in the Modern World*, trans. Sacha Rabinovitch (New York: Harper and Row, 1971), 35.

48. Although in hindsight it is quite easy to dismiss Vichy as an unacceptable choice, in 1940, the signing of the armistice appeared to many as the only viable option for France.

49. Michèle Sarde, *Regard sur les Françaises* (Paris: Editions Stock, 1983), 612.
50. Paula Synder, *The European Women's Almanac* (New York: Columbia University Press, 1992), 125.
51. Albert and Nicole du Roy, *Citoyennes! Il y a cinquante ans, le vote des femmes* ("Women Citizens! The Women's Vote Was 50 Years Ago," Paris: Flammarion, 1994), 220 (my translation). The du Roys are quoting from Florence Montreynaud's *Le XXe Siècle des femmes* ("The Twentieth Century of Women," Paris: Nathan, 1992), 305.
52. Quoted in *Citoyennes!*, 220 (my translation).
53. Sarde, 612.
54. Montreynaud, 304 (my translation).
55. Although the Assembly voted in favor of granting women the vote, the Senate was opposed. Blum appointed as ministerial undersecretaries, Irène Joliot in Scientific Research, Suzanne Lacore in Public Health, and Cécile Brunschvicg in National Education. See Laure Adler, *Les Femmes politiques* ("Political Women," Paris: Seuil, 1993), 120–28.
56. See, for example, Margaret L. Rossiter, *Women in Resistance* (New York: Praeger, 1986).
57. Adler, 131.
58. Paula Schwartz,"Redefining Resistance: Women's Activism in Wartime France," In *Behind the Lines: Gender and the Two World Wars*, ed. Margaret Randolph Higonnet, Jane Jenson, Sonya Michel, Margaret Collins Weitz (New Haven: Yale University Press, 1987), 142.
59. Prior to the war, de Gaulle's family had been associated with ultra-conservative, anti-republican monarchist, Charles Maurras.
60. Sarah Fishman, *We Will Wait: Wives of French Prisoners of War, 1940–1945* (New Haven: Yale University Press, 1991), 169.
61. Paula Schwartz, "Precedents for Politics: Pre-War Activism in Women of the French Resistance," (master's thesis, Columbia University, 1981), quoted in Fishman, 169.
62. Adler, 133. "Already in June 1942, General de Gaulle had announced women's right to vote, which is adopted by the consultative Assembly of Algiers on March 23, 1944" (my translation). With a good dose of skepticism, Adler wonders whether this granting of the vote was merely a useful political ploy or a genuine recognition of women's heroic accomplishments during the war.
63. Montreynaud, 305 (my translation).
64. Robert Gildea reports that Pierre Laval actually remarked that Pétain wielded more power than Louis XIV. See *The Past in French History* (New Haven: Yale University Press, 1994), 25.
65. Robert O. Paxton, *Vichy France*, 189 (Paxton's translation). I'd like to thank Ethan Katz for drawing this quotation to my attention.
66. Montreynaud, 305 (my translation).

67. Charles de Gaulle, *The Complete Memoirs of Charles de Gaulle 1940–1946*, vol. 1, *The Call to Honour*, trans. Jonathan Griffin (New York: Da Capo Press, 1984), 3.

68. Agulhon points out that this change in symbols may also suggest the desire to take distance from the bad reputation that the parliamentary republican regimes had acquired during the Fourth Republic. The "V" could stand for the *Fifth* (Republic) as well. It is worth noting that all the presidents after de Gaulle chose not to use Marianne on their presidential medals.

69. The Phrygian cap is a tradition dating back to Roman times, when it was a sign that an ex-slave had been granted his or her freedom.

70. Although recognizing that the choice of a *woman* to represent the Republic seems particularly French (a part of "French traditions and the French mentality"), Agulhon does not hazard an explanation of the gendered symbolism. See Maurice Agulhon, *Marianne into Battle: Republican Imagery and Symbolism in France, 1989–1880*, trans. Janet Lloyd (New York: Cambridge University Press, 1981), 9.

71. Agulhon, *Marianne into Battle*, 9.

72. Agulhon, *Les Métamorphoses*, 187-88.

73. Agulhon, *Les Métamorphoses*, 189.

74. Agulhon, *Les Métamorphoses*, 188.

75. Agulhon, *Les Métamorphoses*, 189.

76. Agulhon, *Les Métamorphoses*, 190.

77. André Bazin, *What is Cinema?* vol. 2, trans. Hugh Gray (Berkeley: University of California Press, 1967), 170.

78. Antoine de Baecque, *La Cinéphilie: Invention d'un regard, histoire d'une culture 1944–1968* ("Cinephilia: Invention of a Gaze, History of a Culture 1944–1968," Paris: Fayard, 2003).

79. Ginette Vincendeau, "Brigitte Bardot," in *World Cinema: Critical Approaches*, ed. John Hill and Pamela Church Gibson (Oxford: Oxford University Press, 2000), 112.

80. The government's censors reduced de Gaulle's lines to a bare minimum—one word, in fact: "impossible." His more chatty response seemed "inappropriate" for the Leader of the Republic. See Lindeperg, 367–68.

81. Lindeperg, 362. Lindeperg also notes that it is the first film about the war in color and cinemascope.

82. Lindeperg plays upon the title of Molière's play, *Le Médecin malgré lui* ("The Doctor in Spite of Himself"), and calls Babette the "hero despite herself," 362.

83. Again, due to the absence of many French men (imprisoned, dead, or exiled), women took on new social and professional roles and responsibilities.

84. Noël Burch and Geneviève Sellier, *La Drôle de Guerre des sexes du cinéma français: 1930–1956* (Paris: Nathan, 1996).

85. Burch and Sellier, 26 (my translation).

86. François Garçon, "Ce Curieux Age d'or des cineastes français" ("This Curious Golden Age of French Filmmakers"), *La Vie culturelle sous Vichy*, ed. Jean-Pierre Rioux (Brussels: Editions Complexe, 1990), 293–313.

87. Censorship by the Vichy government, as well as by the Germans, obviously put any direct treatment of the war off limits.

88. This quick overview does not pretend to account for the subtlety and breadth of Burch and Sellier's analysis. I merely wish to provide some insight into the gender patterns of Occupation films, patterns that will make their mark on future filmmakers.

89. Burch and Sellier, 172.

90. Burch and Sellier, 174 (my translation).

91. Claude Berri's autobiographical film, *The Two of Us* (*Le Vieillard et l'enfant*), is an exception, given that it came out in 1966, thus well before Robert Paxton's work and *The Sorrow and the Pity* in the 1970s. Born in 1934 of Jewish Polish-Romanian parents, Berri (b. Claude Langmann) was one of the younger filmmakers of the group considered here who probably did not feel the burden of national guilt, because his family was a victim of Vichy's racism.

92. Jean Douchet and Cédric Anger, *French New Wave*, trans. Robert Bonnano (New York: Distributed Art Publishers and Editions Hazan/Cinématique Française, 1999), 11–12.

93. Christian Metz, *The Imaginary Signifier: Psychoanalysis and the Cinema*, trans. Celia Britton, Annwyl Williams, Ben Brewster, and Alfred Guzzetti (Bloomington, IN: Indiana University Press, 1982), 63.

94. See Maurice Halbwachs, *La Mémoire collective* (Paris: Presses Universitaires, 1950).

95. Lynn A. Higgins, "Two Women Filmmakers Remember the Dark Years," *Modern and Contemporary France* 7, no. 1 (1999): 60.

96. Marc Ferro, *Cinema and History*, trans. Naomi Greene (Detroit, MI: Wayne State University Press, 1988), 81-82, cited in Naomi Greene, *Landscapes of Loss: The National Past of Postwar French Cinema* (Princeton, NJ: Princeton UP, 1999), 12.

97. Lynn A. Higgins, *New Novel, New Wave, New Politics* (Lincoln, NE: University of Nebraska Press, 1996), 22.

NOTES TO CHAPTER 2

1. Jean-Pierre Jeancolas, "The Reconstruction of French Cinema," in *France in Focus: Film and National Identity*, ed. Elizabeth Ezra and Sue Harris (New York: Berg, 2000), 13.

2. Women were either portrayed negatively, as in Duvivier's *Panique* (1946) or Clouzot's *Manon* (1949), or are virtually absent, as in Clément's popular *La*

Bataille du rail of 1946. Sylvie Lindeperg does note, however, that the eminently patriotic *Le Bataillon du ciel* ("The Battalion of the sky," directed by Alexandre Esway and based on a fiction by Joseph Kessel) contains one heroine presented briefly, the wife of a Breton Resistance fighter. This "modern Marianne," as Sylvie Lindeperg calls her, remains faithful to her husband and becomes "queen of the Resistance." See Lindeperg, 141.

3. See Rousso, *The Vichy Syndrome*, 229.

4. See Lindeperg, 426–29.

5. See Joseph Daniel, *Guerre et cinéma: Grandes Illusions et petits soldats 1895–1971* (Paris: Armand Colin, 1972), 304.

6. See Rousso, 229. Rousso rightly notes that in the Fourth Republic "although collaboration, Vichy, and fascism still have no political status and are rarely mentioned except by allusion, the collabo has become a familiar, even commonplace, figure." We will see that this distinction between portraying the individual "collabo" and dramatizing collaboration as a general phenomenon is crucial when considering whether a story engages its public or keeps it at arm's length.

7. Julien Duvivier's film *Marie Octobre*, also from 1959, concentrates on the construction of war as a memory in the present, and refuses a one-dimensional understanding of the protagonists' political and social positions. Duvivier focuses on a group of resisters reuniting in the 1950s and features a woman, Marie Octobre, at its center.

8. As Geneviève Sellier has pointed out, even the collaboration between the male director and female scriptwriter challenges the singular (male) subjectivity that New Wave "auteurism" promoted. See Geneviève Sellier, *La Nouvelle Vague: Un Cinéma au masculin singulier* ("The New Wave: A Cinema in the Masculine Singular," Paris: Centre Nationale de la Recherche Scientifique, 2005), 186.

9. James Monaco, *Alain Resnais* (New York: Oxford University Press, 1979), 34.

10. Nancy Lane, "The Subject in/of History: *Hiroshima mon amour*," in *Literature and Film in the Historical Dimension*, ed. John D. Simons (Gainesville: University Press of Florida, 1994), 96. Lane also very rightly points out that Hiroshima's identity as *Japanese* has also been effaced by postwar internationalism, and especially by the U.S. economic and cultural influence. Neon signs in English abound; the café in one of the last scenes is named *Casablanca*—most assuredly a conscious play on the most famous American romance film about the war.

11. Both the French woman and the Japanese man are married and neither seems inclined to leave what seem to be relatively happy, stable relationships.

12. Higgins, *New Novel, New Wave, New Politics*, 32.

13. "Elle," meaning "she" or "her" in French, is how the French actress is referred to in Duras's script. See Marguerite Duras, *Hiroshima mon amour: Scénario et dialogues* (Paris: Gallimard, 1960).

14. Lane, 94. But as Gilles Deleuze noted, a global apprehension of time and memory is also implied in *Hiroshima mon amour*'s decentered cinematic universe: its two narratives are "like two incommensurable regions of past, Hiroshima and Nevers [France]. And while the Japanese refuses the woman entry into his own region . . . the woman draws the Japanese into hers, willingly and with his consent up to a certain point. Is this not a way for each of them to forget his or her own memory, and make a memory for two, as if memory was now becoming world, detaching itself from their persons?" See Gilles Deleuze, *Cinema 2: The Time-Image*, trans. Hugh Tomlinson and Robert Galeta (Minneapolis: University of Minnesota Press, 1989) 118.

15. Higgins, 49.

16. This characterization recalls the misogyny that Burch and Sellier have identified in films from the liberation. *Hiroshima mon amour* offers a fictional dramatization of this filmic trend at war's end. See Burch and Sellier in *Heroines with Heroes*, 47–62.

17. My quotation marks here denote, of course, the irony that Duras continually points out in her novels. The commonly accepted notion of health covers over, even embodies, a form of madness. "Forgetting" is not an act of will; it is a form of unconscious repression.

18. Rousso, 80. Anne Donadey has convincingly argued that discussion of World War II frequently acted as a screen to obscure the events of the Algerian War. See "Une Certaine Idée de la France: The Algeria Syndrome and Struggles over "French Identity," in *Identity Papers: Contested Nationhood in Twentieth Century France*, ed. Steven Ungar and Tom Conley (Minneapolis: University of Minnesota Press, 1996), 215–32. See also Benjamin Stora's *La Gangrène et l'oubli: La Mémoire de la Guerre d'Algérie* ("Gangrene and Forgetfulness: Memory in the Algerian War," Paris: La Découverte, 1992).

19. Alain Finkielkraut, quoted in *The Vichy Syndrome*, 162.

20. Significantly, in *Hiroshima mon amour*, it is through the introduction of a third term that the specular oppositions are undone, and the impasse to community and memory overcome: by displacing the love relationship, repeating it (with an "enemy"), jumping (again) across national boundaries, the traumatic is worked through once more, and allows the airing of the initial violence carried out against the young French girl. This repetition in difference signals the symptomatic return of the repressed—both the love affair and the public punishment. The return is symptomatic in the sense that the actress's choice of a Japanese man from *Hiroshima* as a lover is not arbitrary. Rather, it is a symptom of the repressed memory.

21. Higgins, 38.

22. Monaco, 37.

23. Higgins, 42.

24. As Joseph Daniel has pointed out (305–6), this film could not have been made right after the war: the connections it makes are too controversial, and the political ambiguities too scandalous.

25. Interview with Alain Resnais in *Tu n'as rien vu à Hiroshima!*, ed. Rayond Ravar (Brussels: Editions de l'Institut de Sociologie, 1962), 216.

26. See Daniel, 307. Bardèche's evaluation originally appeared in his critical work on cinema with Robert Brasillach, *Histoire du cinéma* (Paris: Les Sept couleurs, 1964), 459.

27. We will see the same move to emphasize chance over choice in Louis Malle's work in the 1970s.

28. Duras, 7 (my translation).

29. Geneviève Sellier, "Masculinity and Politics in New Wave Cinema," *Sites: The Journal of 20th-Century/Contemporary French Studies* 4, no. 2 (Fall 2000): 486.

30. A French prisoner also notes that a non-commissioned German officer is "just like the ones at home," again emphasizing the similarities with the enemy rather than the differences. Renoir's de-centered, de-nationalized point of view was no doubt enhanced by the fact that he spent the war years in Hollywood. Renoir's attempt to make a film for Americans about France at war (*This Land is Mine*) was a failure, pleasing neither public. See Bergstrom, 86–103.

31. In his 1937 masterpiece, *The Grand Illusion*, Renoir had already sketched out cross-national affinities between German and French soldiers. In this World War I story, class associations supersede national ties. Sylvie Lindeperg (209) has eloquently shown how the immediate postwar French public in the mid- to late 1940s was unprepared for a revival of *The Grand Illusion*. The film's sympathetic German officers were anathema to a public having just gone through the horrors of a war with Nazi Germany. By 1958, however, the French public welcomed the re-release of *The Grand Illusion*. Clearly, its Franco-German ties were approved by the end of the 1950s, although the issue of German soldiers being portrayed too sympathetically resurfaced with Jean Dewever's *Les Honneurs de la guerre* (begun in 1960, aired in 1962), which the filmmaker had a hard time getting produced. See also Daniel, 314.

32. In *The Grand Illusion*, Renoir had already depicted Franco-German complicity against the war via cross-national gender relations: a German peasant woman hides French officers in her home.

33. Whereas at the time of the liberation many were convinced a true revolution in French society was in the making, the Renoir of 1962 realizes that a classless society, with true equality among citizens, has not materialized. The fact that the women have been empowered as French citizens, however partially, does not figure into Renoir's androcentric vision.

34. Filmmakers such as Claude Autant-Lara, Pierre Bost, and Jean Aurenche are part of this group whom Truffaut ferociously attacked in his critical essays.

35. In this sense, he is closer to Resnais (born 1922), although their political positions were quite different (with Resnais much more on the Left and critical toward the Gaullist regime).

36. Jacques Zimmer and Chantal de Béchade point out that the Centre National de Cinéma was highly politicized in the early postwar years (heavily populated by the Left, particularly by the communists), and persistently countered Melville's efforts to make *The Silence of the Sea*. Melville's staunch Gaullism didn't make it any easier for him. See *Jean-Pierre Melville* (Paris: Edilig, 1983), 12.

37. Ex-Resister Emmanuel d'Astier, who appears in *The Sorrow and the Pity*, was staying at Vercors' house when Melville came to film. See Rui Nogueira, *Melville on Melville* (New York: Viking Press, 1971), 25.

38. The New Wave favored natural light, bustling sidewalks of the city on location, and often encouraged actors to ad-lib.

39. Jean-Michel Frodon, *L'Age moderne du cinéma français: De la nouvelle vague à nos jours* (Paris: Flammarion, 1995), 98. It was not uncommon in the Jewish (Resistance) community to keep one's *nom de guerre* in the postwar years. Resistance fighters Raymond and Lucie Aubrac did not return to Raymond's family name, Samuel, after the war. Filmmaker Claude Berri (born Langmann) also chose to keep his pseudonym.

40. See Lindeperg, 262. Stéphane's comments are from an interview with Lindeperg.

41. Lindeperg, 262 (my translation).

42. Nogueira, 28.

43. Nogueira, 27.

44. Duras's "Elle" in *Hiroshima mon amour* will provide the counter image to the niece, as the desiring female who gives full expression to her passion.

45. See Anne Simonin, *Les Editions de Minuit 1942–1955: Le devoir d'insoumission* (Paris: Institut Mémoires de l'Edition Contemporaine, 1994), 263.

46. If Brigitte Bardot could be named the official comedic icon of Gaullist Resistance in *Babette Goes to War*, Emmanuelle Riva embodies the victim/survivor of the war with her leading roles in both *Hiroshima* and *Leon Morin, Priest*. In the battle of the stars, however, it is the sexy BB who triumphs. As we saw in Chapter 1, Bardot was unthreatening to the patriarchal order, and supported a mythic, positive symbolism for France, culminating in her role as Marianne.

47. My translation.

48. See Joseph Daniel, *Guerre et cinéma: Grandes Illusions et petits soldats 1895–1971*, 305–6. Daniel quotes this passage from Melville as an example of how the spectator is made to appreciate the way one could argue for or against Vichy's principles through the prism of religious belief.

49. Béatrix Beck and Valérie Marin La Meslée, *Confidences de gargouille* ("Gargoyle Confessions," Paris: Grasset, 1998), 88.

50. Frodon has argued that Melville, over and against the psychologizing commonplaces of the story, often pays more attention to "things, acts, materials, a veritable cinematographic asceticism that works against the script and makes the hidden power of the film" (94). While I think Melville *does* highlight objects and actions not included in the dialogue, I think that the way Melville plays one off the other is what makes the film effective in representing the Occupation.

51. During the war, Beck was relieved that she had acquiesced to her husband's desire *not* to give their baby daughter a Jewish or foreign name (they named her Bernadette).

52. Daniel, 312.

53. Beck and La Meslée, 184.

54. Melville quoted by Nogueira, 141.

55. Lindeperg, 136.

56. Frodon, 95. He does not think, however, that there are very many good films on the Resistance, so the compliment is limited.

57. Frodon, 266.

58. Other clichés that Melville uses include the sharing of the prisoners' last smoke just before their execution, as well as questioning by the Nazis, torture scenes, night flights, and parachuting into occupied territory. See Lindeperg, 330.

59. Zimmer and Béchade, 28 (my translation).

60. Vichy is represented early in the film by a policeman and a prison camp official, but the Resistance network's attacks are always focused on the Germans.

61. Joseph Kessel, *L'Armée des ombres: Chronique de la Résistance* (New York: Pantheon, 1944), 174 (my translation).

62. It is worth noting that Mathilde is the *object* of our gaze whereas Gerbier is the subject of the narrative.

63. Her situation resembles more the Boss's, who hides his Resistance role from his younger brother, Jean-François.

64. In Kessel's novel, the Mathilde character is the mother of numerous children. Melville may have reduced the number to one daughter in order to intensify the potential loss for the mother.

65. Mathilde's name is suggestive of her symbolic role: its beginning "ma" evokes motherhood ("maman"), as well as Marianne.

66. Rousso, 232.

67. Mary Ann Doane, "The Close-Up: Scale and Detail in the Cinema," *Differences: A Journal of Feminist Cultural Studies* 14, no. 3 (Fall 2003): 93–94.

68. See Margaret Atack, "*L'Armée des ombres* and *Le Chagrin et le pitié*: Reconfigurations of Law, Legalities and the State in Post-1968 France," in *European Memories of the Second World War*, ed. Helmut Peitsch, Charles Burdett, and Claire Gorrara (New York: Berghahn Books, 1999), 160–74. Atack, too, takes issue with Rousso's evaluation of Melville's film. She also argues that *L'Armée des ombres* marks itself as an intertextual narrative. "*L'Armée des ombres* is guaranteed as authentic by other texts" (172). Atack points out indirect references to Clément's *La Bataille du rail*, the cast of well established stars, and more subtle markers, such as displaying the fictional Luc Jardie's books bearing the titles of works by the real philosopher and mathematician, Jean Cavaillès, who was shot in 1944. Melville's film, says Atack, continually alludes to familiar works, people, and sources to validate its version of events. As I have been arguing, these details, taken from several sources, make up composite images to figure Resistance work. The images carry in them both specifics and typicality, which makes them all the stronger. Melville's Mathilde was also reportedly inspired by resistance fighter Lucie Aubrac who is discussed in Chapter 6.

NOTES TO CHAPTER 3

1. Colin MacCabe, *Godard: Images, Sounds, Politics* (Bloomington: Indiana University Press, 1980), 19.
2. Jill Forbes, *The Cinema in France after the New Wave* (London: MacMillan, 1992), 31.
3. Forbes, 27.
4. Michel Mitrani's *Les Guichets du Louvre* (*Black Thursday*) and Joseph Losey's *Monsieur Klein* (made a year later in 1975) belong to this group of innovative films that explore cinema's narrative language, while representing the Occupation. All these films concern themselves with the issue of Jewish deportations in France.
5. See Rousso, *The Vichy Syndrome*, 274. According to Rousso's research on ticket sales, *Lacombe Lucien* had an audience of 528,373 in a 23-week run, a very respectable audience for the time. To provide a point of comparison, *The Sorrow and the Pity* was seen by 258,327 people in a 15-week run. The most successful box-office hit dealing with the Occupation between 1969 and 1986 came out much later: Jean-Marie Poiré's farce, *Papy fait de la résistance* ("Grandpa's in the Resistance," 1982) sold 927,000 tickets in just 13 weeks, with a total of four million during its showing. Clearly the nature of this film (a slap-stick satire) and the period of its airing (after the issue of collaboration had been amply treated), played a role in its box-office success.

6. Rousso, 100-103. Rousso says *The Sorrow and the Pity*'s scales tip clearly in favor of the resistance voices, but he is careful to omit from the count, on either side, those characters whose actions (or lack thereof) remain ambiguous. For example, he does not name as collaborators the two lycée teachers, Mr. Danton and Mr. Dionnet, who never protested the arrest of students and colleagues who were in the resistance. Rousso also acknowledges that Ophüls's own reading of the proportions (portraying resistance and collaboration) shows more of a balance: 20 percent resistance, 25 percent collaboration and Vichy, and 55 percent not belonging clearly to one side or the other. However one interprets the figures, there is no doubt that *Lacombe Lucien* pays more attention to the collaboration side than does *The Sorrow and the Pity*.

7. Jill Forbes notes that "in *Cahiers du cinéma*'s reassessment of Renoir's *La Vie est à nous* . . . it had been suggested that there were two ways of making a political film—either a *mise en scène* of a fictional political event, or the montage of film events that had actually taken place" (*Cinema in France*, 43). Although Malle chose the "*mise en scène*" (the staging of fictive events), he, like many other filmmakers of the same period (late 1960s, early 1970s), tends to blur the distinction between truth and fiction by supporting the latter with historical data.

8. Ferro, *Cinema and History*, 15.

9. Stanley Hoffmann, "Cinquante Ans après, quelques conclusions essentielles," *Esprit*, special issue "Que faire de Vichy?" 181 (May 1992): 38-42.

10. Rousso, 235.

11. Richard J. Golsan, "Collaboration and Context: *Lacombe Lucien*, the *Mode Rétro*, and the Vichy Syndrome," in *Identity Papers*, ed. Steven Ungar and Tom Conley (Lincoln: University of Nebraska Press, 1996), 140.

12. A more obvious example of a sympathetic view of collaboration can be found in Jean Bommart's short novel from the 1950s, *Dieu reconnaîtra les siens* ("God Will Recognize His Own").

13. In similar fashion, the name of the fascist in the story, Faure, scandalously suggests a symbol of France: Félix Faure was President of the Republic (1895-1999), and Edgar Faure was President of the National Assembly (1973-1978).

14. In Claire Denis's film *Chocolat* (1988), France is also the name of the young French heroine in colonial Africa. It is when French identity is not taken for granted, is threatened, or is established as distinct (superior) from another nationality or group that the female name seems most likely to be in vogue.

15. Malle had to do a good deal of research on the period to make *Lacombe Lucien*, which threw him back into the era that he had buried for so long.

16. Louis Malle and Philip French, *Malle on Malle* (London: Faber and Faber, 1993), 168.

17. Malle and French, 104.

18. Malle and French, 91.
19. Rousso, 118.
20. Rousso, 234.
21. Recalling his own experience of *Lacombe Lucien*, Jean-Luc Nancy wondered if the color process used in making the film was a new, improved kind, because the colors seemed so intense at its first showing.
22. See Pierre Billard, *Louis Malle: Le Rebelle solitaire* (Paris: Plon, 2003), 336.
23. It is interesting to note, however, as several critics have done, the strong physical and moral resemblance between Lucien and Robert Bresson's young collaborator, named Jost, in his 1956 film *Un Condamné à mort s'est échappé* (*A Man Escaped*). If Jost did not elicit the same strong reactions in the public as Lucien, it is no doubt because the film focuses on the escape of a resistance hero, Fontaine. In addition, the beautifully stylized work of Bresson de-emphasizes the specific political involvements, stressing the struggles of the human condition, instead.
24. Malle and French, 89.
25. Paul Jankowski, "In Defence of Fiction: Resistance, Collaboration, and *Lacombe, Lucien*," *Journal of Modern History* 63 (September 1991): 457.
26. See Jean-Paul Sartre, "Qu'est-ce qu'un collaborateur?" ("What Is a Collaborator?"), *Situations III* (Paris: Gallimard, 1949), 45-46.
27. Pascal Bonitzer and Serge Toubiana, "Anti-Rétro: Entretien avec Michel Foucault," *Cahiers du cinéma*, 251-2 (July-August 1974): 5-15.
28. During this period, the prevalence of the *Annales* school of historiography (Georges Duby, Emmanuel Le Roy Ladurie, François Furet, Maurice Agulhon), which emphasized the chronicle of daily life over event-oriented history, tended to level previous hierarchies of importance, so that what was recounted and who was recounting the past were opened up to just about everyone. This positive, equalizing move produced an unfortunate effect among non-specialists of "flattening the perception of time and [creating] a relative disorganization in historical discourse." See Jacques Revel "Histoire vs Mémoire en France aujourd'hui," *French Politics, Culture & Society* 18, no. 1 (Spring 2000): 9 (my translation). One might well argue that the leveling of meaning in *Lacombe Lucien* runs parallel to the Annales' move in historiography, and has caused the subsequent strong reactions and confusion about the film's politics.
29. Hannah Arendt, *The Human Condition* (Chicago: University of Chicago Press, 1958), 5.
30. This reading of the global nature of *Lacombe Lucien*'s collaboration is shared by some contemporary critics, including those who look upon this film with favorable eyes. See, for example, Richard J. Golsan's enlightening essay, "Collaboration, Alienation, and the Crisis of Identity in the Film and Fiction of Patrick Modiano," *Film and Literature: A Comparative*

Approach to the Adaptation, ed. Wendall Aycock and Michael Schoenecke (Lubbock: Texas Tech University Press, 1988), 107-21.

31. The final music of the scene—the first notes of the Grappelli-Reinhardt score—provides the second historical frame, a specifically French jazz connoting the late 1930s and 1940s, but without the collaborationist overtones of the war that the voice of Henriot had evoked.

32. Annette Insdorf, *Indelible Shadows: Film and the Holocaust*, 2nd ed. (Cambridge University Press, 1989), 123. Insdorf ties Lucien's violence to his survival instincts, which, in turn, are associated with his collaboration.

33. Insdorf does agree, however, that Malle avoids using the camera to provide "directorial judgments" on the actions we are viewing (123).

34. The scene's intertextual predecessor can be found in Jean Renoir's classic, *The Rules of the Game*, in which hunting animals and hunting down the socially dissident are visually equated. I am thankful to Professor Keith Reader for pointing out to me the resemblance.

35. Stanley Hoffmann, "Neither Hope nor Glory," review of *Au Revoir les enfants* (*Goodbye, Children*), *New York Review of Books*, May 12, 1988, 21.

36. See Pierre Billard, 340-41. Billard adds that novelist Jean Genet, with whom Malle had first thought of working on the script, also thought the *Milicien*'s portrait would not work.

37. This pattern recalls Burch and Sellier's description of Occupation films that thematize the absence of strong father figures.

38. The spectator infers that Lucien's turn to Peyssac may already be in imitation of the farmer Laborit's son, Joseph, who has joined the resistance (and who receives recognition from *his* father for this act).

39. In the case of Modiano's novels, the missing father's past is a mystery linked to the period of the Occupation. In *Livret de famille* (Paris: Gallimard, 1977), the father is possibly a Jew hunted by the Gestapo; in *Les Boulevards de ceinture* (Paris: Gallimard, 1972), he is a collaborator.

40. Malle and French, 94-95.

41. Malle and French, 98-91.

42. Jean de Baroncelli, "'Lacombe Lucien', un adolescent dans la Gestapo," *Le Monde* (January 31, 1974): 1.

43. See "Faut-il voir 'Lacombe Lucien'?" ("Should one see *Lacombe Lucien*?"), *Le Monde* (February 14, 1974): 13.

44. René Andrieu and Louis Malle, "*Lacombe Lucien* et l'Occupation: Louis Malle s'explique, René Andrieu conteste" ("Louis Malle Explains, René Andrieu Challenges"), *Humanité dimanche* 156 (April 3, 1974): 19-22.

45. Naomi Greene, "*La vie en rose*: Images of the Occupation in French Cinema," in *Auschwitz and After: Race, Culture, and "the Jewish Question" in France*, ed. Lawrence Kritzman (New York: Routledge, 1995), 283-98. This is an earlier version of a chapter in Greene's book, *Landscapes of Loss: The National Past in Postwar French Cinema* (Princeton: Princeton University

Press, 2000). The book's analysis of postwar films about the war is somewhat less vehement in its attacks, but Greene's unequivocal positions remain the same in both versions.

46. Greene, 289.
47. Emmanuel Le Roy Ladurie, *Paris-Montpellier: P.C.-P.S.U. 1945-1963* (Paris: Gallimard, 1982), 15.
48. Greene, 288.
49. Stanley Hoffmann, "Collaborationism in France during World War II," *Journal of Modern History*, 40 (September 1968): 375.
50. Malle and French, 92-93.
51. Hercule's physical description and situation resembles, in fact, more closely that of the character Joseph in *Goodbye, Children*, the kitchen boy who, after being fired for his black market activities in the Catholic boarding school, collaborates with the Germans.
52. Greene, 289.
53. Greene is not alone in this error. At least two other critics have mistakenly identified this quotation as coming from Lucien.
54. In Drach's film, the little boy who has not been told that he is Jewish learns it from a schoolmate. In an attempt to make the boy feel just like every other French child, his mother and grandmother reduce the importance of the family's Jewish heritage. In Malle's film, the young Julien actually uses the derogatory term "youpin" ("Yid") when asking the question, as if he wanted to know what the negative connotations were of being Jewish. Lucien asks instead, "What is a Freemason?" which seems a relatively plausible question for a peasant boy to ask, particularly given the secret nature of the group. Even supposing that Greene were right, and that Lucien had asked about the nature of being Jewish, it would still be possible to understand the question as an interrogation about ethnic identity. In Modiano's work, identity, whether collective or individual, is always shifting, problematic.
55. Greene says that it is Tonin, the ex-cop, whom Lucien is quoting, but it is in fact Faure, the ideologue, who makes the remark. It seems fitting that Faure would be the one spouting anti-Semitic rhetoric.
56. Lucien is constantly measuring new information by what he has already learned, as when he asks Albert Horn if sewing is not a woman's job. The traditions with which he is familiar do not allow sewing as a man's activity.
57. Golsan, in *Identity Papers*, has aptly spoken of Faure as the "fascist zealot of the collaborationist group" (115).
58. Michel Mohrt's review of *Lacombe Lucien* in *La Nouvelle Revue Française* 257 (May 1974): 116, calls the film unrepresentative "even if many copies of Lucien existed." What viewers of the 1970s seemed to expect was a collage of "typical" collaborator traits molded into one, the height of verisimilitude, whereas Malle and Modiano offer a portrait that relies more on

specific, extreme cases of collaboration. For example, although it was certainly not common to find blacks among the collaborators, Malle's Martinican character is based on an actual person. (See *Malle on Malle*, 100.) Malle and Modiano chose to include the character as much for the provocative effect as for actual veracity.

59. Michael R. Marrus and Robert O. Paxton, *Vichy France and the Jews* (New York: Schocken Books, 1983), 322. Such acts of resistance sabotage are dramatized in René Clément's 1946 *La Bataille du rail*.

60. Gordon, 338.

61. Gordon, 339. Paul Jankowski also confirms the criminality of collaborators: "In Marseille hunters of Jews and *réfractaires* routinely blackmailed and robbed their prey. In the Indre-et-Loire the prefect called the Milice and the PPF [Parti Populaire Français] 'veritable gangsters . . . [carrying out] veritable operations of banditry for their own profit." See Jankowski, 471.

62. See Golsan in *Film and Literature*, 112.

63. Jankowski, 473–79.

64. The influences go both ways across the Atlantic. Keith Reader has pointed out to me that Reinhardt was influenced by American jazz artists Joe Venuti and Eddie Lang.

65. Jazz was, of course, considered decadent by the Nazis.

66. For a biographical account of Reinhardt's life, see Charles Delaunay, *Django mon frère* ("Django My Brother," Paris: Le Terrain Vague, 1968). More recent biographies include: *Django: The Life and Music of a Gypsy Legend*, by Michael Dregni (New York: Oxford University Press, 2004); and *Django Reinhardt: Le génie vagabond*, by Noël Balen (Monaco: Rocher, 2003).

67. Like Pierre Blaise (and Lucien Lacombe), Django Reinhardt was hungry for fame and is said to have wanted to have the star-stature of a Cary Grant or a Tyrone Power (along with the pay). See Delaunay, 107.

68. For an overview of the "mode rétro," see Alan Morris, *Collaboration and Resistance Reviewed: Writers and the Mode Rétro in Post-Gaullist France* (New York: Saint Martin's Press, 1992).

69. I am thinking of the numerous reflections on assuming and denying Jewish identity in France, such as those found in the writings of Alain Finkielkraut. See, for example, Alain Finkielkraut's *Le Juif Imaginaire* (Paris: Seuil, 1980) and *La Mémoire vaine* (Paris: Gallimard, 1989).

70. Insdorf, 126.

71. I am not so much trying to negate Insdorf's interpretation here, as to suggest that the film's heterogeneous choices trigger uneasy critical responses that reopen the issues of ethnicity, especially when the critic yearns for more clarity to reveal the specificity of the Jewish experience. It is an interesting twist of irony that in *Les Violons du bal*, Michel Drach's Jewish mother, a blond, is consciously played as a brunette.

72. Horn's oppressive situation appears so unbearable that his search for Lucien at the Nazi headquarters looks like a suicide mission.

73. Greene, 289. Albert Horn's cosmopolitanism is in line with his multicultural background.

74. Mona Ozouf, "Sans chagrin et sans pitié" ("Without Sorrow or Pity"), *Le Nouvel Observateur*, 489 (March 1974): 56 (my translation).

75. The actor Holger Löwenadler is, in fact, Swedish.

76. As Stanley Hoffman has pointed out, Vichy patriotism remained attached to the land, with the French State being inseparable from the territory, whereas for de Gaulle, the French State was where *he* was. Malle's film seems to be implicitly raising this issue of where "true French identity" resides. See Hoffman in *Le Régime de Vichy et les Français*, ed. Jean-Pierre Azéma and François Bédarida (Paris: Fayard, 1992), 252.

77. See Christian Zimmer, "La paille dans le discours de l'ordre," *Les Temps Modernes* 336 (July 1974): 2495.

78. Colin W. Nettelbeck and Penelope A. Hueston add that the "back to nature" episode, with Lucien playing the "good savage," providing food and shelter for the "family," and France resuming her role as city girl, *looks* like a return to the way things were before the war, as if nothing had changed. But the violent undercurrents of the episode harken back to the historical reality of the war. See *Patrick Modiano: Pièces d'identité* (Paris: Lettres Modernes, 1986), 62.

79. Zimmer, 2495.

80. For a fascinating account of the film's making and reception, see Evelyn Ehrlich, "French Film during the Occupation: The Case of *Le Corbeau*," *Wide Angle* 4, no. 4 (1980): 12-17. Erlich explains that French film producers would not have been able to make the film because of Vichy censorship.

81. I am exaggerating the point somewhat, given that the grandmother does not appear to partake of "high culture."

82. The way humor undoes claims to "authentic identity" in Malle's film recalls the humor in Agnieszka Holland's *Europa Europa* (1990), about a Jew who disguises himself as a Nazi in Germany in order to survive. See Susan E. Linville, "Agnieska Holland's *Europa, Europa*: Deconstructive Humor in a Holocaust Film," *Film Criticism* 19, no. 3 (Spring 1995): 44-53. Radu Mihaileanu's 1998 hit comedy, *Train de vie*, also has Jewish characters disguised as Nazis.

83. I hope to have already shown that Malle's portrayal of *specific* aspects of collaboration under the Occupation does not impede the possibility of resonances with other events in other periods.

84. It is worth noting a switch in political positions of the *Positif* crew: in the 1950s they were lambasting Claude Chabrol for portraying a rebellious youth toying with Nazi symbolism, whereas, in the 1970s, they come to the defense of Malle.

85. H. R. Kedward, "The Anti-Carnaval of Collaboration: Louis Malle's *Lacombe Lucien* (1974)," in *French Film: Texts and Contexts*, ed. Susan Hayward and Ginette Vincendeau, 2nd ed. (New York: Routledge, 2000), 229. See also, Michel Sineux, "Le Hasard, le chagrin, la nécessité, la pitié" ("Chance, Sorrow, Necessity, Pity"), *Positif* (March 1974): 157.

86. The fact that the three boys' names all begin with "J" seems to place them in a closed triangle of victim-aggressor-witness.

87. Jacques Mallecot, *Louis Malle par Louis Malle* (Paris: Ed. de l'Althanor, 1978), 9.

88. Kedward, 232.

89. A portion of this chapter is an extensively revised, expanded version of my essay "Salubrious Scandals/Effective Provocations: Identity Politics Surrounding *Lacombe Lucien*," *South Central Review*, Special Issue: "*Cinéma Engagé*: Activist Filmmaking in French and Francophone Contexts," ed. Van Kelly and Rosemarie Scullion, 17, no. 3 (Fall 2000): 71-88.

NOTES TO CHAPTER 4

1. Truffaut's biographers note that Laubreaux actually published a play (*Les Pirates de Paris*) under the pseudonym Daxiat. See Antoine de Baecque and Serge Toubiana, *François Truffaut* (Paris: Gallimard, 1996), 618. All translations from this work are my own.

2. A direct parody of this female character from *The Sorrow and the Pity* can be found in Jacques Audiard's *A Self-Made Hero*. See my discussion in Chapter 6 in the section "The Postmodern History Film: A Contradiction in Terms?"

3. Lynn Higgins convincingly makes the argument that *The Last Metro* possesses a childlike vision. See *New Novel, New Wave, New Politics*, 157. Mirella Jona Affron also notes the childlike view: see *The Last Metro, François Truffaut, Director*, ed. Mirella Jona Affron and E. Rubenstein (New Brunswick, NJ: Rutgers University Press, 1985), 12–13.

4. The controversies surrounding a film like Jean Dewever's 1960 *Les Honneurs de la guerre* confirm our sense that it was indeed difficult to portray a "balanced" view of the Occupation without running into strong opposition. Dewever's portrayal of French villagers was not heroic enough for many French critics, and his depiction of tired German soldiers at the end of the war was considered much too sympathetic by these same critics.

5. There is, of course, a secondary character, the youngster Jacquot, who can be identified with Truffaut as a child, but he is no longer the protagonist.

6. De Baecque and Toubiana, 35. Truffaut's biographers rightly note that Truffaut was under the spell of American filmmakers after the war. It is interesting to note, however, that Truffaut wrote a positive (if sarcastic)

review of Autant-Lara's *Four Bags Full* (*La Traversée de Paris*). Autant-Lara's "truculence, tendency toward exaggeration, roughness, vulgarity, and outrage" seem to succeed in creating a comic epic of the Occupation. It is as if the murky period suited Autant-Lara's style for Truffaut. See François Truffaut, *The Films in My Life*, trans. Leonard Mayhew (New York: Simon and Schuster), 171.

7. Aline Desjardins, *Aline Desjardins s'entretient avec François Truffaut* (Paris: Ed. Ramsay, 1992), 22, 37. Quoted in Higgins, 156.

8. Mme Doinel is not, of course, Mme Truffaut, but it is clear that François did not feel wanted by his mother (he was born out of wedlock), and spent the first several years of his life being cared for by grandparents. Truffaut is relatively categorical about it: "she [his mother] couldn't stand me" (my translation). See the interviews from 1971 in *Aline Desjardins s'entretient avec François Truffaut*, 12.

9. It should be noted that in both *The Sorrow and the Pity* and *The Last Metro*, attention is also paid to gays' participation in the war.

10. Higgins, 155.

11. In the case of *To Be or Not to Be*, the issue of the lead character (Jack Benny) being made a cuckold by his wife may have been an extra source of curiosity for François: in *The 400 Blows*, Truffaut portrays Madame Doinel as unfaithful to Antoine's stepfather. The issue of infidelity is picked up in *The Last Metro*.

12. Alan Williams, *Republic of Images: A History of French Filmmaking* (Cambridge: Harvard University Press, 1992), 259.

13. While there are outdoor scenes in *The Raven*, a claustrophobic atmosphere is predominant.

14. De Baecque and Toubiana, 35.

15. Letter of October 8, 1976, Archives of the Film du Carrosse, dossier "CCH 76 (2)." Cited by de Baecque and Toubiana, 519.

16. De Baecque and Toubiana, 35–36.

17. De Baecque and Toubiana, 47.

18. De Baecque and Toubiana, 47.

19. De Baecque and Toubiana, 47–48. Truffaut's remarks were made in his preface to *Le Cinéma et moi: Sacha Guitry*, André Bernard et Claude Gauteur (Paris: Ramsay, 1977).

20. De Baecque and Toubiana, 40.

21. De Baeque and Toubiana, 41. This quotation is from an interview with Claude de Givray that took place in 1984, and is in the archives of the Films du Carrosse, 23.

22. De Baecque and Toubiana, 42.

23. De Baecque and Toubiana, 42.

24. It is no wonder that François delighted so much in Sacha Guitry's *Story of a Cheat* in 1945–46. Guitry's undermining of conventional morality, through wit and resourcefulness, perfectly matched the young François's

NOTES

skepticism about the rhetoric of heroic wartime action and justified his own questionable survival tactics (what the French call the "system D").

25. Bernard's attack on Daxiat is based on a real event: actor Jean Marais actually beat up Laubreaux during the Occupation after Laubreaux had nastily attacked Marais and his partner, writer Jean Cocteau, in the press. Laubreaux turned in Marais's name to the Nazis, but Cocteau saved him by using his own Nazi contact, sculptor Arno Breker, who was in favor with Hitler. See François Truffaut, *Le Cinéma selon François Truffaut*, ed. Anne Gillain (Paris: Flammarion, 1998), 393.

26. Tavernier's character in *Safe Conduct*, Jean Aurenche (based on the real-life scriptwriter who worked on many of Tavernier's films), bears a resemblance to Bernard: both are portrayed as womanizing resisters who make a lot of noise about not compromising but do so when necessary. For those familiar with Occupation filmmaking, Tavernier's fast-paced, dense film offers a treasure trove of authentic details and references to the period's cinematic production, film crews, and events. Tavernier's film also offers an intriguing crisscrossing of moral choices. Alternating between Jean Aurenche and Jean Devaivre, Tavernier shows the complications of Occupation politics: while Aurenche exhibits his moral resistance by refusing to compromise himself with the Continental (the German production company), director Jean Devaivre accepts to make films at the Continental while secretly conducting resistance work. Whereas Aurenche passes from one woman to the next, Devaivre is a faithful family man. Tavernier's film is a sort of latter day "film of quality": it legitimates the work of those such as Aurenche whom Truffaut attacked in the 1950s. Truffaut's and Tavernier's stories are similar, however, in that they emphasize a *collective* portrayal of artists in the period.

27. Truffaut's equalizing moves here recall those in Claude Berri's 1991 film of the Marcel Aymé novel, *Uranus*. In *Uranus* (film and novel), the abuse of power by the communists in a small postwar French village closely resembles the abuses under Vichy.

28. François Garçon was one of the few critics to complain about this when the film first opened. See: "Le Retour d'une inquiétante imposture: *Lili Marleen* et *Le Dernier Métro*," *Les Temps modernes* 422 (1981): 539–48.

29. *Le Cinéma selon François Truffaut*, 442 (my translation).

30. This is not to say that Truffaut turned on all French filmmakers of the war years. Bresson, for example, remains a favorite of Truffaut. Autant-Lara provides a gauge against which Truffaut measures the innovations of his own work: for example, *Douce* opens up with a traveling view of Paris, including construction of the Eiffel Tower (it is a period piece taking place in 1887). Truffaut's opening of *The Four Hundred Blows* thus pays a homage of sorts to *Douce* by including the Eiffel Tower in its opening, but with the big difference that Autant-Lara's tower is a model, whereas Truffaut filmed the French icon outdoors.

31. De Baecque and Toubiana, 108–9.
32. We are reminded of Julien Duvivier's dinner party of resisters in *Marie Octobre*, where each guest harbors a secret about the past. Duvivier, however, is less forgiving of the duplicities.
33. See Serge Added, *Le Théâtre dans les années Vichy, 1940–1944* (Paris: Ramsay, 1992), and de Baeque and Toubiana, 520.
34. Presented differently, the necessity of such a move could have been put into question.
35. As noted in Chapter 1, the quintessential example of selfless female devotion can be found in the role played by Gaby Morlay in the immensely popular Vichy film of 1942, *Le Voile bleu*.
36. Lynn Higgins suggests that the love scene between Marion and Bernard could well be a "play within a play," similar to the *trompe-l'oeil* of the finale; that is, it could be an imagined scene rather than one that "really" takes place in the story. While this is possible, the script neither confirms nor denies it, whereas it does show the staged fakery of the later scene between Marion and Bernard in the finale. See Higgins, 148.
37. Affron and Rubinstein, 74.
38. I have used Russell King's translation of Truffaut's comment. See Russell King, "Truffaut's Imagined Community," in *France in Focus: Film and National Identity*, 172.
39. Truffaut's biographers note that the plot resembles that of a Jean Renoir play, *Carola*, filmed by Norman Lloyd. Truffaut was reportedly miffed when it was suggested that he had not given due credit to this play as his inspiration. Here, we have the "French source" in the cellar! See De Baecque and Soubiana, 519.
40. Rappeneau's 1965 version of France's Marianne performs the postwar restoration of patriarchical attitudes toward women: Deneuve's Marie, a young free-spirit in Normandy at the time of the D-Day landing, is married to an older, apparently weak and impoverished aristocrat (Philippe Noiret). Although she is alternately courted by a French Resistance fighter and a German soldier, thus caught between the Allies and the Axis, Marie is eventually won back by her husband who almost casually saves the day (nonchalantly throwing a grenade that will destroy a German beachhead). In the happy ending, the masculine order (and virility) is restored, as the young woman submits to the authority of her husband. Marie is the object of desire, but her own desires are more for freedom than for any particular love object.
41. *Le Cinéma selon François Truffaut*, 395 (my translation).
42. Agulhon, *Les Métamorphoses de Marianne*, 198.

NOTES TO CHAPTER 5

1. Claude Chabrol, *Et pourtant je tourne* ("And Yet, I'm Still Filming," Paris: Robert Laffont, 1976), 19–20. All translations from this work are my own.
2. Chabrol, *Et pourtant je tourne*, 59.
3. Chabrol, *Et pourtant je tourne*, 59
4. Chabrol, *Et pourtant je tourne*, 80.
5. Chabrol, *Et pourtant je tourne*, 82.
6. Claude Chabrol, *Un Jardin bien à moi: Conversations avec François Guérif* ("A Garden All My Own: Conversations with François Guérif," Paris: Denoel, 1999), 172. All translations from this work are my own.
7. Claude Blanchet, *Claude Chabrol* (Paris: Rivages, 1989), 43.
8. *Un Jardin bien à* moi, 92. Chabrol did manage to leave his mark in invisible ways: when Rémy insisted on including a scene where the spectator was supposed to distinguish, in 1943 France, between good German soldiers (the *Wehrmacht*) and bad German police (the Gestapo), Chabrol bolted at the idea and pretended to film the scene to placate Rémy, but with no film in the camera. In this curious twist, Chabrol's own affinity for equivocal situations carries an ethical force that leads him to refuse Rémy's portrayal of the German occupiers.
9. Chabrol, *Un Jardin bien à moi*, 174.
10. Francis Szpiner, *Une Affaire de femmes: Paris 1943, exécution d'une avorteuse* ("A Story of Women: Paris 1943, Execution of an Abortionist," Paris: Balland, 1986). All translations from the French are my own.
11. See Eva H. Kissen's review in *Films in Review* 41 (March 1990): 172–73.
12. Abortion was legalized in France in 1975.
13. In *Reign of Virtue: Mobilizing Gender in Vichy France* (Chicago: University of Chicago Press, 1998), 192; Miranda Pollard points out that Vichy's abortion laws were applied selectively. They came down much more on poor, working class abortionists and their clients than on those from the bourgeoisie.
14. During the Occupation, there was much interest in recuperating Joan of Arc for Vichy propaganda, or, more generally, as an artistic lightning rod for patriotic values. See, for example, the work of fascist Robert Brasillach, *Domrémy*, in his *Oeuvres complètes*, vol. 4 (Paris: Club de l'Honnête Homme, 1963). This is a play written in 1933 that he reworked in 1943, adding, here and there, analogies between the occupation of France in the fifteenth century, and the Occupation by the Germans after 1940. Brasillach also wrote a theatrical adaptation for the trial proceedings of Joan of Arc, (vol. 4 of the *Oeuvres complètes*), probably some time in April of 1944. He was executed as a German collaborator in 1945.

15. Le Pen also stirred up controversy by attempting (along with Pope John Paul II) to recuperate an early sixth-century king, Clovis, as a symbol (for contemporary consumption) of French nationalism and Christianity, with numerous historians decrying the attempts as another example of revisionist history.

16. I am obviously using "Left" very loosely here for the purposes of contrasting Vichy and the Gaullists. Clearly, communists and socialists would be far to the Left of de Gaulle and his followers.

17. Burch and Sellier, 17. Burch and Sellier quote Laborie's study, "Les symboles sexués dans le système de représentation des Français, 1940–44" ("Gendered Symbols in Representational Systems of the French, 1940–44"), that was delivered as a paper at the Institut d'Histoire du Temps Présent in 1993.

18. Marina Warner, *Joan of Arc: The Image of Female Heroism* (New York: Knopf, 1981). Other useful sources on the image of Joan of Arc during the Occupation include: "The Role of Joan of Arc on the Stage of Occupied Paris," by Gabriel Jacobs in *Vichy France and the Resistance: Culture & Ideology*, ed. Roderick Kedward and Roger Austin (Totowa, NJ: Barnes and Noble, 1985), 106–22; *Histoire des droites en France*, 3 vols., ed. Jean-François Sirinelli (Paris: Gallimard, 1992). In particular, see vol. 2, "Cultures," Chapter 10, "Jeanne d'Arc dans la mémoire des droites" ("Joan of Arc in the Memory of Rightist Groups"), by Philippe Contamine, 399–435.

19. Marie's haircut also recalls the politically conservative sculpture of Joan by Maxime Réal del Sarte, whom Warner describes as "one of the most ardent adherents to the extreme right-wing movement, the Action Française" (227).

20. Although it may not be intentional on Chabrol's part, Marie's closer physical resemblance to Vichy's Joan, than to the Gaullist one, makes her all the more apt to represent the ambiguities of state betrayal, since she is both its victim and its representative.

21. In his account, Francis Szpiner does not say that it was the husband who turned in the anonymous accusation against the real Marie-Louise Giraud, so one may assume that this is Chabrol's touch. I will return to this issue later.

22. Warner, 117. It should be pointed out here that Warner's interpretation tends to make it seem as if the secrecy surrounding the accusations in Joan's case were unique to that case. Michel Foucault maintains, however, that this sort of secrecy was generalized in trial cases in France and in most European countries before the eighteenth century. According to Foucault, a presiding magistrate had every right to receive anonymous accusations, to hide from the accused the nature of the case, and at times to use insinuations against

the accused. See Michel Foucault, *Discipline and Punish*, trans. Alan Sheridan (New York: Vintage Books, 1979), 35.

23. See Szpiner, 31.

24. The French word for "chief" is "chef," but it is also an old term for "head" in French (a fact that any school child learns in France). It is because Marie threatens the head (of state) that she must lose her head (at the guillotine, the symbol of the power of the head of state, as noted earlier).

25. Pollard, 191.

26. I would like to thank Mary Hatch for having brought this painting to my attention.

27. Marie's career as an abortionist seems to happen by accident, and thus is reminiscent of the way Lucien Lacombe comes to work for the German police.

28. In 1988, the trial of Paul Touvier, who was the Milice chief for Lyons during the war, provided much evidence of such thievery.

29. Warner, 140-41.

30. This blasphemous scene got Chabrol into a fair amount of trouble with Catholics. See Blanchet, 185.

31. I am not trying to make the argument that the camera lens should be equated with the little boy's vision. There are many scenes that he does not witness himself. Rather, it is a question of understanding how his viewpoint, his particular gaze, inflects what we see, making us view Marie negatively, or at least judgmentally.

32. Rosemarie Scullion also notes this negativity, but attributes it almost exclusively to Chabrol's own sexism. While this interpretation is certainly feasible, there is another one that stresses more the film's internal dimensions: the intervention of Pierrot at the end provides a key perspective that need not be identical to Chabrol's. As an artistic device, the voice-over at the end establishes an internal male viewpoint for the film. See Rosemarie Scullion, "Family Fictions and Reproductive Realities in Vichy France: Claude Chabrol's *Une Affaire de femmes*," *Esprit Créateur* 33, no. 1 (Spring 1993): 88–89.

33. This is before the return of her husband from the prisoner of war camp.

34. Sarah Fishman, in her essay, "Waiting for the Captive Sons of France," in *Behind the Lines: Gender and the Two World Wars*, ed. Margaret Randolph Higonnet, Jane Jenson, Sonya Michel, and Margaret Collins Weitz (New Haven: Yale University Press, 1987), 193, quotes a POW wife whom Yves Durand had interviewed: "When one has lived all alone with the children, assumed alone the family responsibilities, one becomes a bit used to this independent existence." See Yves Durand, *La captivité des prisonniers de guerre français 1939–1945* (Paris: Fédération Nationale des Combattants Prisonniers de Guerre—Combattants d'Algérie, Tunisie, Maroc, 1980), 230.

35. Laura Mulvey, "Visual Pleasure and Narrative Cinema," *Screen* 16, no. 3 (Autumn 1975): 6–18.

36. In an era of proliferating denunciations and false accusations, it is also not so surprising that the boy would seek refuge in an all-powerful image of anonymity.

37. The sword itself is an explicit phallic symbol for Marie and Lucien that connotes the latter's sexual prowess, as well as his political power and athletic skills.

38. Vichy, in the early years of the war, provided subsidies to allow mothers to stay home to care for their children. The problem was that the money was insufficient to live on, so the mothers still needed to work, particularly later on, when so many men were sent to camps, leaving families with no means of support.

39. Marie is also attracted to Rachel because of her looks.

40. See H. R. Kedward, *Occupied France: Collaboration and Resistance, 1940–1944* (New York: Blackwell, 1985), 49.

41. This individual Catholic woman does, however, plant the seed of doubt in Marie (telling her babies in the womb have a soul) that in the end will help push Marie into accepting culpability, and hence, the role of Vichy's victim.

42. Szpiner, 136.

43. Chabrol could have made a film emphasizing more the collective dimensions of the story instead of featuring Latour as heroine-star.

44. New Novelist Nathalie Sarraute, herself a Jew, refused to wear the yellow star during the war and had to hide her origins in order to avoid being deported. Part of her concealment involved posing as the governess of her own children. Eventually, however, she was denounced by a local merchant and had to flee her home.

45. Gildea, 164.

46. At one point, Marie hesitantly offers to pay her maid/assistant to sleep with her husband, Paul, a situation that has the potential to please all parties, but Paul realizes that the whole thing is Marie's idea and refuses.

47. Marcia Polly, "Women's Business," *Film Comment* 25, no. 5 (1989): 16.

48. Alain Brossat, *Les Tondues: Un Carnaval moche* ("The Shorn: An Ugly Carnaval," Paris: Ed. Manya, 1992).

49. See Burch and Sellier, 218.

50. Guillaume Clavières, "La Fille de la guillotinée," ("The Daughter of the Guillotined Woman") *Paris-Match* 2054 (Oct. 6, 1988). All translations from the French in this article are my own. I would like to thank Richard Arzt for bringing this article to my attention.

51. A portion of this chapter is a revised, expanded version of my essay "Vichy's Female Icons: Chabrol's *Story of Women*," in *Gender and Fascism in Modern France*, ed. Melanie Hawthorne and Richard J. Golsan (Hanover, NH: University Press of New England, 1997), 156–74.

NOTES TO CHAPTER 6

1. Susan Hayward, *French National Cinema* (New York: Routledge, 1993), 287.
2. Stella's name evokes the Star of David that she wears on her coat at the beginning of the film.
3. Nazi anti-Semitism will ultimately push Charles to become a resister as well.
4. See Paula Schwartz, "Redefining Resistance: Women's Activism in Wartime France," in *Behind the Lines: Gender and the Two World Wars*, ed. M. Higonnet, J. Jensen, S. Michel, and M. Collins Weitz (New Haven: Yale University Press, 1987), 141–53.
5. André Téchiné's 2002 film, *Les Égarés* (*Strayed*), is a more recent example of a film that follows the model of *Lacombe Lucien*.
6. The first two were *Uranus*, based on Marcel Aymé's satire of a post World War II village, and *Germinal*, drawn from Zola's novel.
7. Claire Gorrara's feminist reading of Lucie Aubrac's work, while well grounded in the text, tends, nevertheless, to gloss over the questionable aspects of Lucie's memoirs, especially the fictional alterations of the past that caused the uproar. See Claire Gorrara, "Reviewing Gender and the Resistance: the Case of Lucie Aubrac," *The Liberation of France: Image and Event*, ed. H. R. Kedward and Nancy Wood (Washington, DC: Berg, 1995), 143–53.
8. Schor, 4.
9. Schor, 4.
10. In her 1997 book of interviews, Lucie Aubrac added that, although Raymond's resistance actions were more consequential than her own, he never begrudged the fact that she sometimes received more attention than he. See Lucie Aubrac, *Cette Exigeante Liberté: Entretiens avec Corinne Bouchoux* ("This Demanding Freedom: Conversations with Corinne Bouchoux," Paris: L'Archipel, 1997), 204.
11. See Jean Lacouture, "Lucie-la-lumière," *Le Nouvel Observateur* 1685 (Feb. 1997), 57.
12. The "agrégation" is the national competition French students must undergo in order to enter the teaching profession in higher learning.
13. Eric Conan, "D'ici Londres à ici Vichy," *L'Express* 2175 (March 18, 1993), 53.
14. I will be concentrating more on Berri's film because it has had a much wider audience, is more complex in the way it portrays historical events, and has been endorsed by the Aubracs.
15. Lucie Aubrac, *Outwitting the Gestapo*, trans. Konrad Bieber, intro. Margaret Collins Weitz (Lincoln: University of Nebraska Press, 1993), 11.

16. *Outwitting the Gestapo*, 24.
17. *Outwitting the Gestapo*, 26-27.
18. Jacques Renard's *Blanche et Marie* is one of the few films to present a scene depicting this racist exhibition. See Raymond Bach, "Identifying Jews: The Legacy of the 1941 Exhibition, "Le Juif et la France" *Studies in Twentieth Century Literature* 23, no. 1 (Winter 1999), 65–92.
19. *Outwitting the Gestapo*, 133.
20. *Outwitting the Gestapo*, 98.
21. Aubrac, *Cette Exigeante Liberté*, 19.
22. I think it important to note that using feminine stereotypes as a form of life-affirming resistance is a common theme—and practice—of Occupation history. We noted in Chapter 2 that Melville's character, Mathilde, in *Army of Shadows*, effectively used feminine disguises for her work, and that she continually turned to strategies that chose life over death to further the political cause. Similarly, in Sarah Kofman's autobiographical text dealing with the war, *Rue Ordener, rue Labat*, the author stages the heroic death of her father (who tries to save the family by sacrificing himself), in contrast to her mother's feminine guile: the latter, pretending to be pregnant and to have a child under age two, resorts to these deceptions as a way to save her family and herself from the hands of the Gestapo. See Sarah Kofman, *Rue Ordener, rue Labat*, trans. Ann Smock (Lincoln: University of Nebraska Press, 1996).
23. *Outwitting the Gestapo*, 47–48.
24. In the video version, Lucie does not appear on screen at the end.
25. When I first read Lucie Aubrac's memoirs, I immediately took them to be a fictive reconstruction of events, and was thus surprised to see how much faith historians would put in their absolute veracity.
26. I originally accessed this interview of Claude Berri on the Internet Movie Database (December 13, 1997), http://us.imdb.com/M/person-exact ?name=claude+berri. Unfortunately, however, the interview was later dropped from the site. The translation is my own.
27. Frédéric Théobald, "Claude Berri met le feu aux poudres" ("Claude Berri Puts a Match to the Fuse"), *La Vie* 2658 (August 8, 1996), 24.
28. Berri's personal account in *The Two of Us* skirts issues of resistance and collaboration: the war seems far away from the bucolic countryside where the action takes place. The film focuses instead on the daily interactions and developing relationship between the Jewish boy and the Pétainist, anti-Semitic grandfatherly figure (convincingly played by veteran actor Michel Simon), who takes the boy in and grows increasingly fond of him without realizing the child is Jewish. In a delightful scene, the boy cleverly undoes the old man's anti-Semitism. With the two of them gazing into a mirror,

the boy asks what a Jew looks like and, after hearing the old man's description (big nose, ears), the boy exclaims that the old man must then be Jewish because the description is of himself! The passage foreshadows *The Last Metro*'s scene of Lucas Steiner asking what it means to look Jewish as he puts on a fake nose.

29. Aubrac, *Cette Exigeante liberté*, 196.
30. Pierre Péan, *La Diabolique de Caluire* (Paris: Fayard, 1999).
31. One might ask why the Aubracs, with the wide distribution of Berri's film guaranteeing the airing of their version of events before the public, chose to submit themselves to questioning by professional historians. Clearly, the Aubracs wanted both professional as well as public ratification of their story. The encounters between the Aubracs and the historians were taped and published online as "Les Aubracs et les historiens," http://www.liberation.fr/aubrac/ which I accessed November 13, 1997. Unfortunately, the website is no longer available.
32. This issue of "true identity" is one that becomes repeatedly muddled because of the many name changes that Raymond and Lucie effect in order to protect their resistance work. Although Raymond's family name was Samuel, the Resistance historians frequently refer to Raymond's true identity as "Aubrac" because this was his key resistance pseudonym. The name confusion is not trivial because the accusations of treachery depend upon who knew Raymond's and Lucie's identities at given points in the war.
33. See "Les Aubrac et les historiens," in the epilogue, "Des zones d'ombre subsistent" ("Shadowy Areas Subsist"), p. 3. http://www.liberation.fr/aubrac/epilogue.html
34. It is impossible in the span of this chapter to go over the incredibly complicated web of issues that are portrayed in the round table, and the debates preceding it. I have named a few of the problems that came up in the discussions.
35. François Bédarida, "Les Aubrac et les historiens," in the section "Préliminaires pour un débat, L'Histoire et ses acteurs," p. 3. http//www.liberation.fr/aubrac/ch1.html (my translation).
36. The preference of plausibility over unlikely truths is a recurring problem in evaluating Occupation events. In Marcel Ophüls's 1986 documentary film, *Hôtel Terminus*, which deals with the capture and trial of Klaus Barbie, one finds similar arguments: for example, the prosecutor in Barbie's trial does not use the testimony of various witnesses (Michel Thomas, Julien Favet) for reasons of plausibility and credibility, even when he knows that they are telling the truth. The lawyer's argument is that the testimonies must be plausible and uncontestable.
37. Raymond Aubrac, *Où la mémoire s'attarde* ("Where Memory Tarries," Paris: Editions Odile Jacob, 1996), 91.

38. Jean-Pierre Azéma, on the other hand, is interested in comparing its version of things to what the Aubracs remember.

39. Rousso is particularly critical of the inclusion of an appendix in which two other resisters confirm Lucie's account on points that even Raymond contests (namely, that the Gestapo did not know Raymond was "Aubrac"). For those of us with the popular Seuil paperback edition, this criticism does not obtain, because this edition does not contain these additional accounts.

40. Rousso, 122–39.

41. One may wonder how significant it is that Rousso does not mention Bédarida at all in his discussion, since the latter had proffered, so sanguinely, proclamations of faith in the power of the historian.

42. Berri's mysterious woman in red serves as a symbol of these unresolved enigmas.

43. Christian de Chalonge's 1989 film, *Docteur Petiot*, also could be described as postmodern. It is loosely based on the series of twenty-seven horrific murders committed during the Occupation by Dr. Marcel Petiot, who tricked Jewish victims (among others) into thinking he would help them flee the Nazis, and then proceeded to steal their belongings, after which he poisoned, dismembered, and incinerated them.

44. Like his New Wave precursors (especially Resnais, Truffaut, and Chabrol), Audiard shows a constant awareness of the medium he is using. *A Self-Made Hero* is a film about filmmaking and its impact on our understanding of what it stands in for (usurps): an absent past that is both distinct in time and place from what is seen on the screen.

45. Ryan Bishop, "Postmodernism," in *Encyclopedia of Cultural Anthropology*, ed. David Levinson and Melvin Ember (New York: Henry Holt and Company, 1996), 993.

46. I would like to thank Alexandre Dauge-Roth for pointing out this word play (mari-Marianne) in Audiard's film.

47. Truffaut's series of films featuring the character Antoine Doinel plays upon the possibility that the films are either his own autobiography or that of his actor, Jean-Pierre Léaud.

48. Julien Duvivier's 1959 *Marie Octobre*, about a resistance network, also portrays a group with dark secrets.

49. C. Darke, "Monsieur Memory," *Sight and Sound* 7, no. 4 (April 1997), 24. Critic Jill Forbes effectively finds the parallels between Mitterrand's biography *Une Jeunesse française* by Pierre Péan and Dehousse's life construction. The parallels are particularly striking in the way they finesse the parts of their pasts unsuitable to the image of the resistance hero. See Jill Forbes, "Politicians and Performers: *Un Héros très discret*," *Australian Journal of French Studies* 36, no. 1 (January–April, 1999), 125–35.

50. Socialist Mitterrand was elected in 1981 and reelected in 1988.

51. Marey's "chronophotographies" show, for example, a series of photos of a nude man walking in front of a black backdrop.

52. Jill Forbes aptly described Dehousse's "revisionism" as "based less on the discovery of new facts or the reinterpretation of old ones than on problematization of narrative itself" (129–30).

53. M. Temple, review of *Un Héros très discret/A Self-Made Hero*, *Sight and Sound*, 7, no. 4 (April 1997), 47.

54. This colorful scoundrel is no doubt modeled after the real life trafficker Joseph Joanovici, an East European Jew of obscure origins who circulated with ease in German and resistance circles alike, trafficking in sheet metal.

55. Maurice Papon, after serving as a Vichy police official implicated in deporting Jews during the war, was later responsible for the deaths of approximately two hundred Algerians. On October 17, 1961, Papon, as head of Paris police, had his officers storm a peaceful demonstration of Algerians protesting France's fight against Algerian independence. No arrests for the deaths of these civilians were ever made. Papon was eventually convicted of crimes against humanity in 1998 for his role in deporting Jews under Vichy.

56. Henry Rousso's *Vichy Syndrome* is full of instances when contemporary postwar politics are articulated through memory of the Occupation.

57. Review of *The Last Mitterrand*, by R. B. in *New Yorker*, "Talk of the Town" section, 81, no. 10 (April 25, 2005).

58. See Panivong Norindr, "*La Plus Grande France*: French Cultural Identity and Nation Building under Mitterrand," in *Identity Papers*, ed. Steven Ungar and Tom Conley (Minneapolis, MN: University of Minnesota Press, 1996), 234.

59. François Mitterrand, *Agence France Presse*, September 21, 1993 (my translation).

60. See Marguerite Duras and François Mitterrand, "Le Bureau de poste de la rue Dupin," *L'Autre Journal* 1 (February 26–March 4, 1986): 32–40.

61. Pierre Nora, *Realms of Memory: Rethinking the French Past*, vol. 1, trans. Arthur Goldhammer (New York: Columbia University Press, 1996), 3.

NOTES TO CHAPTER 7

1. Andrew Higson, "The Concept of National Cinema," *Screen* 30, no. 4 (1989), 37.

2. The use of tea as the comical identifier for the British is also used more recently in Tavernier's *Safe Passage*, when British intelligence officers continually offer tea to the French filmmaker Jean Devaivre, who does not care for it.

3. Samuel Blumenfeld, "Portrait de Français trop tranquilles sous l'Occupation" ("Portraits of Too Tranquil Frenchmen under the Occupation"), *Le Monde* (March 6, 2002).
4. Similarly, Henry Rousso's *Vichy: L'événement, la mémoire, l'histoire* (Paris: Gallimard, 2001) points to the recent internationalization of the Vichy era, with its juridical issues and questions of reparations crossing national borders.

BIBLIOGRAPHY

Added, Serge. *Le Théâtre dans les années Vichy, 1940–1944*. Paris: Editions Ramsay, 1992.

Adler, Laure. *Les Femmes politiques*. Paris: Seuil, 1993.

Affron, Mirella Jona, and E. Rubenstein, eds. *The Last Metro, François Truffaut, Director*. New Brunswick, NJ: Rutgers University Press, 1985.

Agulhon, Maurice. *Marianne into Battle: Republican Imagery and Symbolism in France, 1989–1880*. Trans. Janet Lloyd. New York: Cambridge University Press, 1981.

———. *Les Métamorphoses de Marianne: L'Imagerie et la symbolique républicaines de 1914 à nos jours*. Paris: Flammarion, 2001.

Allen, Don. *Finally Truffaut*. New York: Beaufort Books, 1985.

Andrieu, René, and Louis Malle. "*Lacombe Lucien* et l'Occupation: Louis Malle s'explique, René Andrieu conteste." *Humanité dimanche* 156 (April 3, 1974): 19–22.

Anderson, Benedict. *Imagined Communities: Reflections on the Origin and Spread of Nationalism*. London: Verso Editions, 1983.

Arendt, Hannah. *The Human Condition*. Chicago: University of Chicago Press, 1958.

Armes, Roy. *French Cinema*. New York: Oxford University Press, 1985.

Asselain, Jean-Charles et al. *Etudes sur la France de 1939 à nos jours*. Paris: Seuil, 1985.

Astruc, Alexandre. "The Birth of a New Avant-Garde: Le Caméra-Stylo." In *The New Wave*. Edited by Peter Graham, 17–23. Garden City, NY: Doubleday, 1968.

Atack, Margaret. *Literature and the French Resistance—Cultural Politics and Narrative Forms, 1940–1950*. Manchester: Manchester University Press, 1989.

Aubrac, Lucie. *Outwitting the Gestapo*. Trans. Konrad Bieber. Intro. Margaret Collins Weitz. Lincoln: University of Nebraska Press, 1993.

———. *Cette Exigeante Liberté: Entretiens avec Corinne Bouchoux*. Paris: L'Archipel, 1997.

———. *La Résistance expliquée à mes petits-enfants*. Paris: Editions du Seuil, 2000.

Aubrac, Raymond. *Où La Mémoire s'attarde*. Paris: Editions Odile Jacob, 1996.

"Les Aubrac et les historiens." http://www.liberation.fr/aubrac. Accessed November 13, 1997.

Austin, Guy. *Contemporary French Cinema: An Introduction*. New York: Manchester University Press, 1996.

Aycock, Wendall, and Michael Schoenecke, eds. *Film and Literature: A Comparative Approach to the Adaptation*. Lubbock: Texas Tech University Press, 1988.

Azéma, Jean-Pierre, and François Bédarida, with the collaboration of Denis Peschanski and Henry Rousso. *Le Régime de Vichy et les Français*. Paris: Fayard, 1992.

Azéma, Jean-Pierre. *1940 L'Année terrible*. Paris: Seuil, 1990.

Bach, Raymond. "Identifying Jews: The Legacy of the 1941 Exhibition, 'Le Juif et la France.'" *Studies in Twentieth Century Literature* 23, no. 1 (Winter 1999): 65–92.

Balen, Noël. *Django Reinhardt: Le Génie vagabond*. Monaco: Rocher, 2003.

Bazin, André. *French Cinema of the Occupation and Resistance: The Birth of a Critical Esthetic*. Intro. François Truffaut. Trans. Stanley Hochman. New York: Frederick Ungar Publishing, 1981.

Beck, Béatrix, and Valérie Marin La Meslée. *Confidences de gargouille*. Paris: Grasset, 1998.

Benamou, Georges-Marc. *Le Dernier Mitterrand*. Paris: Plon, 1996.

Berberova, Nina. *L'Accompagnatrice*. Arles: Actes Sud, 1992.

Bertin, Célia. *Femmes sous l'Occupation*. Paris: Stock, 1993.

Bertin-Maghit, Jean-Pierre. *Le Cinéma sous l'Occupation: Le Monde du cinéma français de 1940 à 1946*. Paris: Olivier Orban, 1989.

Bevan, David, ed. *Literature and War*. Atlanta: Rodopoi, 1990.

Bhaba, Homi K. *Nation and Narration*. New York: Routledge, 1990.

Billard, Pierre. *Louis Malle: Le Rebelle solitaire*. Paris: Plon, 2003.

Bishop, Ryan. "Postmodernism." In *Encyclopedia of Cultural Anthropology*, eds. David Levinson and Melvin Ember, 993. New York: Henry Holt and Company, 1996.

Blanchet, Claude. *Claude Chabrol*. Paris: Rivages, 1989.

Bonitzer, Pascal, and Serge Toubiana. "Anti-Rétro: Entretien avec Michel Foucault." *Cahiers du cinéma* 251–52 (July–August, 1974): 5–15.

Bracher, Nathan. "Timely Predications: The Use and Abuse of History in Contemporary France" *Soundings* Vol. 81: 1–2 (Spring–Summer, 1998): 235–56.

Brasillach, Robert. *Domrémy*. In *Oeuvres completes*, vol. 4. Paris: Club de l'Honnête Homme, 1963.

———. *Histoire du cinéma*. Paris: Les Sept couleurs, 1964.

Burch, Noël, and Geneviève Sellier. *La Drôle de Guerre des sexes du cinéma français: 1930–1956*. Paris: Nathan, 1996.

Braudy, Leo. *The World in a Frame: What We See in Films.* Garden City, NY: Anchor/Doubleday, 1977.

Brooks, Peter. *Troubling Confessions: Speaking Guilt in Law and Literature.* Chicago: Chicago University Press, 2000.

Brossat, Alain. *Les Tondues: Un Carnaval moche.* Paris: Manya, 1992.

Burrin, Philippe. *France Under The Germans: Collaboration and Compromise.* Trans. Janet Lloyd. New York: New Press, 1996.

Buss, Robin. *The French Through Their Films.* New York: Ungar Publishing, 1988.

Byatt, A. S. "What Is a European." *New York Times,* October 13, 2002, 50.

Carey-Webb, Allen. *Making Subject(s): Literature and the Emergence of National Identity.* New York: Garland, 1998.

Chabrol, Claude. *Et pourtant je tourne.* Paris: Robert Laffont, 1976.

———. *Un Jardin bien à moi: Conversations avec François Guérif.* Paris: Denoel, 1999.

Chambers, Iain. "Citizenship, Language, and Modernity." *PMLA* 117, no. 1 (January 2002): 24–31.

Chateau, René. *Le Cinéma français sous l'Occupation 1940–1944.* Paris: Editions René Chateau et la mémoire du cinéma, 1995.

Clavières, Guillaume. "La Fille de la guillotinée." *Paris-Match* 2054 (October 6, 1988).

Collard, Gilbert. "Vérité d'hier, erreur d'aujourd'hui." *Historia* 602 (February 1997): 18–22.

Collet, Jean. *François Truffaut.* Paris: Lherminier, 1985.

Colombat, André Pierre. *The Holocaust in French Film.* Metuchen, NJ: Scarecrow, 1993.

Conan, Eric. "D'Ici Londres à ici Vichy." *L'Express* 2175 (March 18, 1993): 52–54.

Conan, Eric, and Henry Rousso. *Vichy: An Ever-Present Past.* Trans. Nathan Bracher. Hanover, NH: University Press of New England, 1998.

Cook, David A. *A History of Narrative Film.* New York: W. W. Norton & Company, 1981.

Crofts, Stephen. "Reconceptualising National Cinema/s." *Quarterly Review of Film and Video* 14, no. 3 (1993): 49–67.

Dambre, Marc. "The Politics of Provocation in the Hussars." *South Central Review* 17, no. 4 (Winter 2000): 61–71.

Daniel, Joseph. *Guerre et cinéma: Grandes Illusions et petits soldats, 1895–1971.* Paris: A. Colin, Cahiers FNSP, 1972.

Darke, C. "Monsieur Memory." Review of *A Self-Made Hero. Sight and Sound* 7, no. 4 (April 1997): 24–25.

De Baecque, Antoine. *La Cinéphilie: Invention d'un regard, histoire d'une culture 1944–1968.* Paris: Fayard, 2003.

De Baecque, Antoine, and Charles Tesson, eds. "Nouvelle Vague: Une Légende en question." Paris: *Cahiers du Cinéma,* 1998.

De Baecque, Antoine, and Serge Toubiana. *François Truffaut*. Paris: Gallimard, 1996.

De Baroncelli, Jean. "'Lacombe Lucien,' un adolescent dans la Gestapo." *Le Monde* (January 31, 1974): 1.

De Gaulle, Charles. *The Complete Memoirs of Charles de Gaulle 1940–1946*. Vol. 1, *The Call to Honour*. Trans. Jonathan Griffin. New York: Da Capo, 1984.

Debray, Régis. *La République expliquée à ma fille*. Paris: Seuil, 1998.

Delaunay, Charles. *Django mon frère*. Paris: Le Terrain Vague, 1968.

Deleuze, Gilles. *Cinema 1: The Movement Image*. Trans. Hugh Tomlinson and Barbara Habberjam. Minneapolis: University Minnesota Press, 1986.

———. *Cinema 2: The Time-Image*. Trans. Hugh Tomlinson and Robert Galeta. Minneapolis: University of Minnesota Press, 1989.

Deniau, Jean-François. *Un Héros très discret*. Paris: France Loisirs, 1990.

Desjardins, Aline. *Aline Desjardins s'entretient avec François Truffaut*. Paris: Ramsey, 1992.

Diamant, David. *Les Juifs dans la Résistance 1940–1944*. Paris: Le Pavillon, 1971.

Doane, Mary Ann. "The Close-Up: Scale and Detail in the Cinema." *Differences: A Journal of Feminist Cultural Studies* 14, no. 3 (Fall, 2003): 93–94.

Douchet, Jean, and Cédric Anger. *French New Wave*. Trans. Robert Bonnono. New York: Distributed Art Publishers and Editions Hazan/Cinématique Française., 1999.

Dregni, Michael. *Django: The Life and Music of a Gypsy Legend*. New York: Oxford University Press, 2004.

Du Roy, Albert, and Nicole. *Citoyennes! Il y a cinquante ans, le vote des femmes*. Paris: Flammarion, 1994.

Durand, Yves. *La Captivité des prisonniers de guerre français 1939–1945*. Paris: Fédération Nationale des Combattants Prisonniers de Guerre— Combattants d'Algérie, Tunisie, Maroc, 1980.

Duras, Marguerite. *Hiroshima mon amour: Scénario et dialogues*. Paris: Gallimard, 1960.

Duras, Marguerite, and François Mitterrand. "Le Bureau de poste de la rue Dupin." *L'Autre Journal* 1 (February 26–March 4, 1986): 32–40.

Ehrlich, Evelyn. "French Film during the Occupation: The Case of *Le Corbeau*." *Wide Angle* 4, no. 4 (1980): 12–17.

Elster, Jon, ed. *Retribution and Reparation in the Transition to Democracy*. New York: Cambridge University Press, 2006.

Evans, Martin, and Ken Lunn, eds. *War and Memory in the Twentieth Century*. New York: Berg, 1997.

Evleth, Donna. *France under the Occupation 1940–1944: An Annotated Bibliography*. New York: Greenwood, 1991.

Ezra, Elizabeth, and Sue Harris, eds. *France in Focus: Film and National Identity*. New York: Berg, 2000.

Faligot, Roger, and Kauffer, Rémi. *Les Résistants: De La Guerre de l'ombre aux allées du pouvoir, 1944–1989*. Paris: Fayard, 1989.

"Faut-il voir 'Lacombe Lucien'?" *Le Monde* (February 14, 1974): 13.

Ferro, Marc. *The Use and Abuse of History or How the Past is Taught*. Boston: Routledge & Kegan Paul, 1981.

———. *Cinema and History*. Trans. Naomi Greene. Detroit: Wayne State University Press, 1988.

Finley, Moses I. *The Use and Abuse of History*. London: Chatto and Windus, 1975.

Finkielkraut, Alain. *Le Juif Imaginaire*. Paris: Seuil, 1980.

———. *La Mémoire vaine*. Paris: Gallimard, 1989.

Fishman, Sarah. *We Will Wait: Wives of French Prisoners of War*. New Haven: Yale University Press, 1991.

Fishman, Sarah, Laura Lee Downs, Ioannis Sinanoglou, Leonard V. Smith, and Robert Zaretsky, eds. *France at War: Vichy and the Historians*. Trans. David Lake. New York: Berg, 2000.

Forbes, Jill. *The Cinema in France after the New Wave*. London: MacMillan, 1992.

———. "Politicians and Performers: *Un Héros très discret*." *Australian Journal of French Studies* 36, no. 1 (January–April 1999): 125–135.

Foucault, Michel. *Discipline and Punish*. Trans. Alan Sheridan. New York: Vintage Books, 1979.

Frodon, Jean-Michel. *L'Age moderne du cinéma français: De La Nouvelle Vague à nos jours*. Paris: Flammarion, 1995.

———. *La Projection nationale: Cinéma et nation*. Paris: Editions Odile Jacob, 1998.

Gallo, Max. *L'Amour de la France expliqué à mon fils*. Paris: Seuil, 1998.

Garçon, François. "Le Retour d'une inquiétante imposture: *Lili Marleen* et *Le Dernier Métro*." *Les Temps modernes* 422 (1981): 539–48.

Gildea, Robert. *The Past in French History*. New Haven: Yale University Press, 1994.

Gillain, Anne. *François Truffaut: Le Secret perdu*. Paris: Hatier, 1991.

Golsan, Richard J. *Fascism's Return: Scandal, Revision, and Ideology since 1980*. Lincoln, NE: University of Nebraska Press, 1998.

———. *The Papon Affair: Memory and Justice on Trial*. New York: Routledge, 2000.

———. *French Writers and the Politics of Complicity: Crises of Democracy in the 1940s and 1990s*. Baltimore: Johns Hopkins University Press, 2006.

Golsan, Richard J., and Jean-François Fourny, eds. "The Occupation in French Literature and Film: 1940–1992." Special issue, *L'Esprit Créateur* 33, no. 1 (Spring 1993).

Gordon, Bertram. *Collaborationism in France during the Second World War*. Ithaca: Cornell University Press, 1980.

Gorrara, Claire. *Women's Representations of the Occupation in Post-'68 France*. New York: St. Martin's Press, 1998.

Graham, Peter. *The New Wave*. Garden City, NY: Doubleday, 1968.

Greene, Naomi. *Landscapes of Loss: The National Past in Postwar French Cinema*. Princeton: Princeton University Press, 2000.

Guérif, François. *Conversations avec Claude Chabrol: Un Jardin bien à moi*. Paris: Denoël, 1999.

Guichard, Jean-Pierre. *De Gaulle et les mass média*. Paris: France-Empire, 1985.

Halbwachs, Maurice. *La Mémoire collective*. Paris: Presses Universitaires, 1950.

Handourtzel, Rémy, and Cyril Buffet. *La Collaboration . . . à gauche aussi*. Paris: Perrin, 1989.

Harris, Frederick J. *Encounters with Darkness: French and German Writers on World War II*. New York: Oxford University Press, 1983.

Hawthorne, Melanie, and Richard J. Golsan, eds. *Gender and Fascism in Modern France*. Hanover, NH: University Press of New England, 1997.

Hayward, Susan. *French National Cinema*. New York: Routledge, 1993.

Hayward, Susan, and Ginette Vincendeau, eds. *French Film: Texts and Contexts*. New York: Routledge, 2000.

Hewitt, Leah D. "Identity Wars in 'L'Affaire (Lucie) Aubrac': History, Fiction, Film," in "Film in the 1990s," ed. Florianne Wild, special issue, *Contemporary French Civilization* 22, no. 2 (Summer/Fall 1999): 264–84.

———. "Salubrious Scandals/Effective Provocations: Identity Politics Surrounding *Lacombe Lucien*," in "*Cinéma Engagé*: Activist Filmmaking in French and Francophone Contexts," eds. Van Kelly and Rosemarie Scullion, special issue, *South Central Review* 17, no. 3 (Fall, 2000): 71–88.

———. "From War Films to Films on War: Gendered Scenarios of National Identity, The Case of *The Last Metro*," in "Perspectives in French Studies at the Turn of the Millenium," special issue, *Studies in Twentieth Century Literature*, eds. Martine Antle and Dominique Fisher. 26, no.1 (Winter 2002): 74–85.

Higgins, Lynn A. *New Novel, New Wave, New Politics: Fiction and the Representation of History in Postwar France*. Lincoln: University of Nebraska Press, 1996.

———. "Two Women Filmmakers Remember the Dark Years." *Modern and Contemporary France 7*, no. 1 (1999): 59–79.

Higonnet, Margaret Randolph, J. Jenson, S. Michel, and M. C. Weitz, eds. *Behind the Lines: Gender and the Two World Wars*. New Haven: Yale University Press, 1987.

Higson, Andrew. "The Concept of National Identity." *Screen* 30, no. 4 (Autumn 1989): 36–46.

Hill, John, and Pamela Church Gibson. *World Cinema: Critical Approaches.* Oxford: Oxford University Press, 2000.

Hoffmann, Stanley. "Collaborationism in France during World War II," *Journal of Modern History* 40 (September 1968): 375–95.

———. *Decline or Renewal? France since the 1930s.* New York: Viking, 1974.

———. "Regards d'outre-Hexagone." *Vingtième siècle, revue d'histoire* 5 (January–March, 1985), 133–46. "Neither Hope nor Glory." Review of *Au Revoir les enfants. New York Review of Books* (May 12, 1988): 19–21.

———. "Cinquante Ans après, quelques conclusions essentielles," in "Que faire de Vichy?" special issue, *Esprit* 181 (May, 1992): 38–42.

Insdorf, Annette. *Indelible Shadows: Film and the Holocaust.* Rev. ed. New York, Cambridge University Press, 1989.

Jankowski, Paul. "In Defence of Fiction: Resistance, Collaboration, and *Lacombe, Lucien.*" *Journal of Modern History* 63 (September; 1991): 457–82.

Judt, Tony. *Postwar: A History of Europe Since 1945.* New York: Penguin Books, 2005.

Kedward, H. R. *Occupied France: Collaboration and Resistance, 1940–1944.* New York: Blackwell, 1985.

———. *Resistance in Vichy France: A Study of Ideas and Motivation in the Southern Zone 1940–1942.* London: Oxford University Press, 1978.

Kedward, Roderick, and Roger Austin, eds. *Vichy France and the Resistance: Culture & Ideology.* Totowa, NJ: Barnes & Noble, 1985.

Kedward, H. R., and Nancy Wood, eds. *The Liberation of France: Image and Event.* Washington, DC: Berg Publishers, 1995.

Kelly, Michael. "The Historical Emergence of Everyday Life." *Sites: The Journal of Twentieth Century/Contemporary French Studies* 1, no. 1 (Spring 1997): 77–91.

Kessel, Joseph. *L'Armée des ombres: Chronique de la Résistance.* New York: Pantheon, 1944.

Kissen, Eva H. Review of *Une Affaire de femmes. Films in Review* 41 (March, 1990): 172–73.

Klarsfeld, Serge. *Vichy-Auschwitz: Le Rôle de Vichy dans la solution finale de la question juive en France-1942.* Paris: Fayard, 1983.

Kline, T. Jefferson. *Screening the Text: Intertextuality in New Wave French Cinema.* Baltimore: Johns Hopkins University Press, 1992.

Kofman, Sarah. *Rue Ordener, rue Labat.* Trans. Ann Smock. Lincoln: University of Nebraska Press, 1996.

Kritzman, Lawrence. *Auschwitz and After: Race, Culture and the "Jewish Question" in France.* New York: Routledge, 1995.

Laborie, Pierre. *L'Opinion française sous Vichy.* Paris: Seuil, 1990.

LaCapra, Dominick. *Representing the Holocaust: History, Theory Trauma.* Ithaca: Cornell University Press, 1994.

LaCapra, Dominick. *Writing History, Writing Trauma.* Baltimore: Johns Hopkins University Press, 2000.

Lacouture, Jean. "Lucie-la-lumière." *Le Nouvel Observateur* 1685 (February 1997): 57.

Langlois, Suzanne. *La Résistance dans le cinéma français 1944–1994: De La Libération de Paris à Libera me.* Paris: L'Harmattan, 2001.

Lanzoni, Rémi Fournier. *French Cinema: From Its Beginnings to the Present.* New York: Continuum International Publishing, 2002.

Lavabre, Marie-Claire. "Du Poids et du choix du passé." *Cahiers de l'IHTP* 18 (June 1991): 177–185.

Lebow, Richard Ned, Wulf Kansteiner, and Claudio Focu, eds. *The Politics of Memory in Postwar Europe.* Durham, NC: Duke University Press, 2006.

Lefebvre, Henri. *Everyday Life in the Modern World.* Trans. Sacha Rabinovitch. New York: Harper and Row, 1971.

Le Goff, Jacques, and Pierre Nora, eds. *Constructing the Past: Essays in Historical Methodology.* Intro. Colin Lucas. New York: Cambridge University Press, 1985.

Le Roy Ladurie, Emmanuel. *Paris-Montpellier: P.C.-P.S.U. 1945–1963.* Paris: Gallimard, 1982.

Lévy, Bernard-Henri. *L'Idéologie française.* Paris: Grasset, 1981.

Lévy, Jean-Benoit. *Les Grandes Missions du cinéma.* Montreal: Lucien Parizeau & Compagnie, 1994.

Lindeperg, Sylvie. *Les Ecrans de l'ombre: La Seconde Guerre Mondiale dans le cinéma français (1944–1969).* Paris: Centre Nationale de la Recherche Scientifique, 1997.

Linville, Susan E. "Agnieska Holland's *Europa, Europa*: Deconstructive Humor in a Holocaust Film." *Film Criticism* 19, no. 3 (Spring 1995): 44–53.

Malle, Louis, and Philip French. *Malle on Malle.* London: Faber and Faber, 1993.

MacCabe, Colin. *Godard: Images, Sounds, Politics.* Bloomington: Indiana University Press, 1980.

Mallecot, Jacques. *Louis Malle par Louis Malle.* Paris: Ed. de l'Althanor, 1978.

Marsh, Patrick. "Le Théâtre à Paris sous l'occupation allemande." Special issue, *La Revue de la société d'histoire du théâtre* 33, no. 3 (July–September 1981): 197–369.

Miller, Judith. *One, by One, by One: Facing the Holocaust.* New York: Simon and Schuster, 1990.

Metz, Christian. *The Imaginary Signifier: Psychoanalysis and the Cinema.* Trans. Celia Britton, Annwyl Williams, Ben Brewster, and Alfred Guzzetti. Bloomington, IN: Indiana University Press, 1982.

Modiano, Patrick. *Les Boulevards de Ceinture.* Paris: Gallimard, 1972.

————. *Livret de famille.* Paris: Gallimard, 1977.

Mohrt, Michel. Review of *Lacombe Lucien* in *La Nouvelle Revue Française* 257 (May 1974): 116.

Monaco, James. *Alain Resnais.* New York: Oxford University Press, 1979.

Montreynaud, Florence. *Le Vingtième Siècle des femmes.* Paris: Nathan, 1992.

Morris, Alan. *Collaboration And Resistance Reviewed: Writers And The Mode Rétro In Post-Gaullist France.* New York: Berg, 1992.

Mulvey, Laura. "Visual Pleasure and Narrative Cinema." *Screen* 16, no. 3 (Autumn 1975): 6–18.

Murray, Timothy. *PMLA* 3 (March 1999): 280.

Nettelbeck, Colin. "Getting the Story Right: Narratives of World War II in Post-1968 France." *Journal of European Studies* 15 (1985): 77–116.

Nettelbeck, Colin W., and Penelope A. Hueston. *Patrick Modiano: Pièces d'identité.* Paris: Lettres Modernes, 1986.

Neupert, Richard. *A History of the French New Wave Cinema.* Madison, WI: University Wisconsin Press, 2002.

Nichols, Bill, ed. *Movies and Methods,* vol. 1. Berkeley: University of California Press, 1985.

Nogueira, Rui, ed. *Melville on Melville.* New York: Viking, 1971.

Nora, Pierre. *Realms of Memory: Rethinking the French Past,* vol. 1. Trans. Arthur Goldhammer. New York: Columbia University Press, 1996.

Nowell-Smith, Geoffrey, and Steven Ricci, eds. *Hollywood and Europe: Economics, Culture, National Identity: 1945–95.* London: BFI Publishing, 1998.

Ory, Pascal. *L'Anarchisme de droite.* Paris: Grasset, 1985.

————. *Les Collaborateurs 1940–1945.* Paris: Seuil, 1986.

Ory, Pascal, and Jean-François Sirinelli. *Les Intellectuels en France, de l'Affaire Dreyfus à nos jours.* Paris: Armand Colin, 1986.

Ozouf, Mona. "Sans chagrin et sans pitié." *Le Nouvel Observateur* 489 (March 1974): 54–56.

Paxton, Robert. *Vichy France: Old Guard and New Order, 1940–1944.* New York: Knopf, 1972.

Paxton, Robert, and Robert Marrus. *Vichy France and the Jews.* New York: Schocken, 1983.

Péan, Pierre. *La Diabolique de Caluire.* Paris: Fayard, 1999.

Petrie, Duncan, ed. *Screening Europe: Image and Identity in Contemporary European Cinema.* London: British Film Institute, 1992.

Perrault, Gilles. *Paris sous l'Occupation.* Paris: Belfond, 1987.

Peitsch, Helmut, Charles Burdett, and Claire Gorrara, eds. *European Memories of the Second World War.* New York: Berghahn Books, 1999.

Pollard, Miranda. *Reign of Virtue: Mobilizing Gender in Vichy France.* Chicago: Chicago University Press, 1998.

Polly, Marcia. "Women's Business." *Film Comment* 25, no. 5 (1989): 16.

Powrie, Phil. *French Cinema in the 1990s: Continuity and Difference.* New York: Oxford University Press, 1999.

Ravar, Raymond, ed. *Tu n'a rien vu à Hiroshima!* Brussels: Editions de l'Institut de Sociologie, 1962.

Renan, Ernest. "Qu'est-ce qu'une Nation?" In *Oeuvres complètes,* vol. I. Paris: Calman-Lévy, 1947–1961.

Revel, Jacques. "Histoire vs Mémoire en France aujourd'hui." *French Politics, Culture & Society* 18, no. 1 (Spring 2000): 1–11.

Rioux, Jean-Pierre, ed. *La Vie culturelle sous Vichy.* Bruxelles: Complexe, 1990.

Rosen, Philip, ed. *Narrative, Apparatus, Ideology.* New York: Columbia University Press, 1986.

Rossiter, Margaret. *Women in the Resistance.* Westport, CT: Greenwood, 1985.

Rousso, Henry. *Le Syndrome de Vichy de 1944 à nos jours.* Paris: Seuil, 1987.

———. *The Vichy Syndrome: History and Memory in France since 1944.* Trans. Arthur Goldhammer. Cambridge, MA: Harvard University Press, 1991.

———. *La Hantise du passé: Entretien avec Philippe Petit.* Paris: Textuel, 1998.

———. *Vichy: L'Evénement, la mémoire, l'histoire.* Paris: Gallimard, 2001.

———.The Haunting Past: History, Memory and Justice in Contemporary France. Trans. *Ralph Schoolcraft. Philadelphia: University of Pennsylvania Press, 2002.*

Rousso, Henry, and Eric Conan. *Vichy: An Ever-Present Past.* Trans. Nathan Bracher. Hanover, NH: University Press of New England, 1998.

Rosen, Philip, ed. *Narrative, Apparatus, Ideology: A Film Theory Reader.* New York: Columbia University Press, 1986.

Ryan, Marianne, ed. *La France: Images of Woman and Ideas of Nation 1789–1989.* London: South Bank Centre, 1989.

Sarde, Michèle. *Regard sur les Françaises.* Paris: Stock, 1983.

Sartre, Jean-Paul. "Qu'est-ce qu'un collaborateur?" *Situations III.* Paris: Gallimard, 1949, 43–61.

———. *The Words.* Trans. Bernard Frechtman. New York: George Braziller, 1964.

Schor, Naomi. *Reading in Detail: Aesthetics and the Feminine.* New York: Methuen, 1987.

Schwartz, Paula. "*Partisanes* and Gender Politics in Vichy France." *French Historical Studies* 16, no. 1 (1989): 126–51.

Scriven, Michael, and Peter Wagstaff, eds. *War and Society in Twentieth Century France.* Providence, RI: Berg, 1991.

Scullion, Rosemarie. "Family Fictions and Reproductive Realities in Vichy France: Claude Chabrol's *Une Affaire de femmes.*" *Esprit Créateur* 33, no. 1 (Spring 1993): 85–103.

———, ed. "Demythologizing the Occupation." Special issue, *SubStance* 27, no. 3 (1998).

Sellier, Geneviève. "Masculinity and Politics in New Wave Cinema." *Sites: The Journal of Twentieth Century/Contemporary French Studies* 4, no. 2 (Fall 2000): 471–87.

———. *La Nouvelle Vague: Un Cinéma au masculin* singulier. Paris: Centre National de la Rercherche Scientifique, 2005.

Siclier, Jacques. *La Femme dans le cinéma français.* Paris: Cerf, 1957.

Sieglohr, Ulrike, ed. *Heroines without Heroes: Reconstructing Female and National Identities in European cinema, 1945–51.* New York: Cassell, 2000.

Simonin, Anne. *Les Editions de Minuit 1942–1955: Le Devoir d'insoumission.* Paris: Institut Mémoires de l'Edition Contemporaine, 1994.

Simons, John D., ed. *Literature and Film in the Historical Dimension.* Gainesville: University Press of Florida, 1994.

Sineux, Michel. "Le Hasard, le chagrin, la nécessité, la pitié." *Positif* (March1974): 157.

Sirinelli, Jean-François, ed. *Histoire des droites en France.* 3 vols. Paris: Gallimard, 1992.

Sluga, Glenda. "Identity, Gender, and the History of European Nations and Nationalisms." *Nations and Nationalism* 4, no. 1 (1998): 87–111.

Snyder, Paula. *The European Women's Almanac.* New York: Columbia University Press, 1992.

Sorlin, Pierre. *European Cinemas, European Societies, 1939–1990.* New York: Rutledge, 1991.

Stora, Benjamin. *La Gangrène et l'oubli: La Mémoire de la guerre d'Algérie.* Paris: La Découverte, 1992.

Suleiman, Susan Rubin. *Crises of Memory and the Second World War.* Cambridge, MA: Harvard University Press, 2006.

Szpiner, Francis. *Une Affaire de femmes: Paris 1943, exécution d'une avorteuse.* Paris: Balland, 1986.

Sweets, John F. *Choice in Vichy France: The French under Nazi Occupation.* New York: Oxford University Press, 1986.

Temple, M. Review of *Un Héros très discret/A Self-Made Hero. Sight and Sound* 7, no. 4 (April 1997): 46–48.

Théobald, Frédéric. "Claude Berri met le feu aux poudres." *La Vie* 2658 (August 8, 1996): 24–27.

Truffaut, François. *Le Cinéma et moi: Sacha Guitry.* Ed. André Bernard and Claude Gauteur. Paris: Ramsay, 1977.

———. *The Films in My Life*. Trans. Leonard Mayhew. New York: Simon and Schuster, 1978.

———. "A Certain Tendency in French Cinema." In *Movies and Methods: An Anthology*, vol. 1. Edited by Bill Nichols, 224–237. Berkeley: University of California Press, 1985.

———. *Le Cinéma selon François Truffaut*. E. Anne Gillain. Paris: Flammarion, 1988.

Ungar, Steven, and Tom Conley, eds. *Identity Papers*. Minneapolis, MN: University of Minnesota Press, 1996.

Veillon, Dominique. *Vivre et Survivre en France 1939–1947*. Paris: Payot, 1995.

Warner, Marina. *Joan of Arc: The Image of Female Heroism*. New York: Knopf, 1981.

Watts, Philip. *Allegories of the Purge: How Literature Responded to the Postwar Trials of Writers and Intellectuals in France*. Stanford: Stanford University Press, 1998.

Weitz, Margaret Collins. *Sisters in the Resistance: How Women Fought to Free France, 1940–45*. New York: J. Wiley, 1995.

Williams, Alan. *Republic of Images: A History of French Filmmaking*. Cambridge: Harvard University Press, 1992.

———, ed. *Film and Nationalism*. New Brunswick, NJ: Rutgers University Press, 2002.

Wilson, Emma. *French Cinema since 1950: Personal Histories*. New York: Rowman & Littlefield Publishers, 1999.

Young, James E. *Writing and Rewriting the Holocaust: Narrative and the Consequences of Interpretation*. Bloomington, IN: Indiana University Press, 1988.

———. *The Texture of Memory: Holocaust Memorials and Meaning*. New Haven: Yale University Press, 1993.

Zimmer, Christian. "La Paille dans le discours de l'ordre." *Les Temps Modernes* 336 (July 1974): 2492–2505.

Zimmer, Jacques, and Chantal de Béchade. *Jean-Pierre Melville*. Paris: Edilig 1983.

Zuccotti, Susan. *The Holocaust, the French and the Jews*. New York: Basic Books, HarperCollins Publishers, 1993.

INDEX